The Development of International Law After the World War

BY

OTFRIED NIPPOLD

TRANSLATED FROM THE GERMAN BY

AMOS S. HERSHEY, Ph.D.
Professor of Political Science and International Law in Indiana University

THE LAWBOOK EXCHANGE, LTD.
Clark, New Jersey
2004

ISBN 1-58477-270-0

Second printing 2004

Printed in the United States of America on acid-free paper

THE LAWBOOK EXCHANGE, LTD.
33 Terminal Avenue
Clark, New Jersey 07066-1321

Please see our website for a selection of our other publications and fine facsimile reprints of classic works of legal history:
www.lawbookexchange.com

Library of Congress Cataloging-in-Publication Data

Nippold, Otfried, b. 1864.
[Gestaltung des Völkerrechts nach dem Weltkriege. English]
The development of international law after the World War / by Otfried Nippold; translated from the German by Amos S. Hershey.
p. cm.
Originally published: Oxford: Clarendon Press, 1923.
Includes bibliographical references.
ISBN 1-58477-270-0 (cloth: alk. paper)
1. International law—History. 2. War (International law)—History. I. Title.

KZ3390.N57 A343 2002
341'.09—dc21 2002025965

The Development of International Law After the World War

BY

OTFRIED NIPPOLD

TRANSLATED FROM THE GERMAN BY

AMOS S. HERSHEY, Ph.D.
Professor of Political Science and International Law in Indiana University

OXFORD: AT THE CLARENDON PRESS
London, Edinburgh, New York, Toronto, Melbourne, Bombay
HUMPHREY MILFORD
1923

PRINTED IN ENGLAND
AT THE OXFORD UNIVERSITY PRESS

INTRODUCTORY NOTE

For the past twenty years nobody has been more interested than the author of this little book in the creation of an international law which shall meet the needs of the world and be developed in accordance with the principles of justice which either are or should be universally accepted. Nobody has been more interested in analysing new institutions and endeavouring to make them effective. His work on the development of procedure in international disputes (*Die Fortbildung des Verfahrens in völkerrechtlichen Streitigkeiten*), which appeared in 1907, advocated a development of arbitral procedure, and it is not too much to say that the book was worthy of the great subject. Nobody has been more interested in international conferences, especially in the Hague Conferences, or has shown greater skill in describing their proceedings, analysing their results, and criticizing them in the light of a rational development. A German by birth, he has preferred to be a citizen of Switzerland, and his aim has been to bring German conceptions of international law into an approximate relation with the conceptions obtaining in his adopted country and in countries where the development of international law is less closely connected with patriotic ambitions and political projects.

In these circumstances it was to be expected that Professor Nippold would be profoundly moved by the outbreak of the war in 1914; that he would follow its conduct, especially on the part of the Germans, with intense interest and relentless criticism, inasmuch as he had foreseen in Prussian militarism danger of a catastrophe, and in the success of Prussian militarism the blasting of hopes for a rational system of international relations in the future, of which he had made himself in a way the protector and the prophet. Germany's conduct in the war is the subject of a series of monographs from his facile pen which is in course of publication.

To the larger field of international relations, and especially to the institutions which he felt should or would come into being after the war, he has devoted the greatest attention. During the course of the war, and indeed before its outcome was assured, he published *Die Gestaltung des Völkerrechts nach dem Weltkriege*, which appears here for the first time in English under the title, *The Development of International Law after the World War*. This work speaks for itself, but there are certain matters to which attention should be called. Professor Nippold believes in the solidarity of nations to such a degree that he advocates the development of international law under their direction and control, and through an agency of the nations in which all are to be represented, but in which no one nation should have a predominant part ; and an international organization to be created after the war which should be guaranteed not by any one Power but by all of the Powers. He is firmly of the opinion that the violation of the international system thus created should be considered a violation affecting every member of the international organization, and that therefore pressure or force should be used in order to repress the violation and to bring the violator to terms, even to the outlawry of the nation committing the breach, and that nations not members of the organization are to be dealt with by the organization acting as a mandatory of the community of states.

This was indeed to be a new order of things. It was nothing more or less than the League of Nations in all its essentials, which as elaborated by the Peace Conference at Paris appears as Part I in the Treaty with Germany and in all other treaties concluding the war. Professor Nippold is himself aware of his paternity in the premisses, and in a note furnished for this translation, to be found on p. 44, he remarks that ‘ the problem of the League of Nations was pushed into the foreground only after the publication of the German edition of this book ’. We only need turn to pp. 99–101, in which he sums up the results of his examination of the New Postulates, to see to what extent Professor Nippold is justified in his assertions. To the reader who bears in mind that the date of publication of the original volume was the spring of 1917, this would be plain without a note. Professor

Nippold was, however, unwilling to trust to the untutored intelligence. In a foot-note in brackets, which he prepared for the English version to the first clause of the summary of his views, he specifically says: 'I believe that the programme outlined in these 14 points contains, even to-day, everything essential for the League of Nations, in spite of the fact that since then many more extensive proposals have been made.' And in an addition to the original text of the paragraph immediately following the summary he states, on p. 102: 'This conception is, I believe, in complete agreement with the principles which have been expressed by President Wilson, Lloyd George, Lord Grey, Clemenceau, and other statesmen.' And curiously enough, before President Wilson's conditions of peace emerged in his 'Fourteen Points', of which the fourteenth demanded 'a general association of nations', Professor Nippold had formulated his conclusions on a league of nations in fourteen numbered points and had referred to them as such.

This little book is therefore to all practical intents and purposes a commentary on the League of Nations before its birth.

The undersigned is an advocate of the orderly process of development which has unconsciously come into being since the appearance of the immortal three books of Grotius on the *Law of War and Peace*, published in 1625, and of the succession of conferences moulding older conceptions to new uses which began with the Congress of Westphalia in 1648. He believes that the present is the creature of the past, and that the future is merely the prolongation of the two, in the light of new conditions; that history as well as nature *in suis operationibus non facit saltum*, and that sooner or later the current of history, like a great and mighty current of a river, will resume its ancient course, from which it has been diverted momentarily by some convulsion of nature. It is true that the vast expanse of ocean shows no progress to the unaided eye. Orderly processes are slow, but they last.

The undersigned is as eager as is Professor Nippold and those for whom he speaks to press forward to the goal which all advocates of peaceable settlement keep steadily before their eyes. He believes, however, that international order, which is synonymous with peace, can only be brought about by the co-operation of free and independent nations, not by their subordination, and that the present expedients of an organic nature, which every great war of the past few centuries has produced, will pass away, leaving the world to the infinite series of little steps which make up a continuous and a durable progress.

In these days when it is heresy to speak of The Hague, he sees in a return to the Hague Conferences the hope of the future. However, he recognizes that his views have not in the immediate past met with the approval of the statesmen and of the publicists to whom Professor Nippold refers in the present volume, and that apparently much time must yet elapse before the mighty stream of human progress will return to the channel which it forsook in the storm and stress and ferment of the world.

Notwithstanding these personal views, he is nevertheless of the opinion that the publication of Professor Nippold's little book in an English translation will render a service, and not a small one, in that it calls attention to the genesis of the present system of international organization.

JAMES BROWN SCOTT,
Director of the Division of International Law.

WASHINGTON, D.C.
December 25, 1922.

FOREWORD

THE following presentation was originally intended to form the closing chapter of a larger work on international law in this[1] war. The latter is not to appear before the conclusion of peace. The thought that the subject might perhaps be of special interest during the war itself has led me to publish the following material separately. But the larger work will present in greater detail the explanations leading to many of the conclusions drawn in the course of the following pages.

In accordance with its original character, this book offers only a *survey* of the future problems of international law. In this work I have given merely some directing outlines. I have been obliged to forgo entering upon the individual problems here, since this would have claimed materially more space and also more time. But I also believe that in the present hour it is above all necessary to call to mind once more the *fundamental tendencies* in the development of international law.

The problems to be solved for international law in the future are neither simple nor small in number. We may rejoice if, upon the conclusion of peace, we succeed in obtaining an agreement on the basic principles. The future work will, however, take decades.

Of course, I do not presume to be able to contribute much to the solution of these problems in this small work. However, I do not wish to leave unspoken the thoughts which have moved me in the present fateful hour of international law. I hope that some attention will gladly be given one who for a quarter of a century has laboured among the champions of the advancement of international law, and who in his presentations is guided by no other purpose than to win recognition and victory for *law*.

Whether the postulates here considered shall ever be fulfilled, and, if so, when, I do not presume to judge. I for my part am not enough of an optimist to believe that we shall attain everything,

[1] [The first two parts of my work, *Deutschland und das Völkerrecht*, have now appeared: *Part I, Die Grundsätze der deutschen Kriegführung*, 1920, and *Part II, Die Verletzung der Neutralität Luxemburgs und Belgiens*, 1920.]

nor do I believe that it can be done all at once. But even if this should not be the case, it can nevertheless do no harm to trace out anew from time to time the tendencies, so that we may not lose sight of the goal.

If one takes into consideration how great is the labour that needs to be accomplished for international law, and that it depends upon the result as to whether this law shall again be honoured in the civilized world and become a really powerful factor in the life of nations, or whether it shall for all time remain condemned to impotency, then one can only express the wish that many may turn to working upon the problems here considered. It is to be hoped that, after the experiences of this war, the whole civilized world will aid to-day in making secure the dominance of right over might.

OTFRIED NIPPOLD.

THUN,
Spring, 1917.

CONTENTS

INTRODUCTION

	PAGE
The prospects of international law	3
The problem of the science of international law	4
Advancement, not retrogression of international law	5
Old and new points of view	6
Universal international law	7
The relation between international law and the law of war	7
The distinction between these two provinces	9

PART I. INTERNATIONAL LAW

I. OLD POSTULATES

The normal condition for international law	13
The importance of the law of procedure in international law	13
The chief problem of international law	14
The Hague Peace Conferences	14
International procedure in the existing law	14
Mediation	15
Commissions of inquiry	15
The arbitral decision	15
The degree of obligation	16
Particular international law	16
Endeavours toward the advancement of international procedure	16
Guarantees for its application: The obligation	16
The problem	17
The duties of states in general	17
Duties of the disputants. Party initiative	18
Duties of the third powers. The initiative of neutrals	19
The creation of a system of international procedure	20
The development and limitation of jurisdiction in arbitration	21
The development of mediation	23
The development of the commissions of inquiry	23
The American treaties	24
The Hague Court of Arbitration	25
The permanent tribunal	26

II. NEW POSTULATES

	PAGE
Lessons of the war. A further addition	27
Two new points of view	28
The development of international law regardless of resisting parties	28
The eventual formation of a league of states	31
Policy of alliance in general	31
League of states and Hague Conferences	33
The enforcement of international law	33
The moral guarantees of international law	33
Lack of faith	35
The call for real guarantees	35
Legal, not military, real guarantees	36
The basis of international law: international solidarity	39
The community of states in general	41
The Hague community of states	41
The future peace congress	42
The league of states	42
Organic coercive protection	43
The organization of states	43
The world league of states	43
Old and new projects	44
The league of neutrals	45
The position of neutrals and the league of peace	46
Neutrality or solidarity	50
Isolation or co-operation	51
The basis for the creation of real guarantees	51
The collective guarantee	51
The guaranteeing of territorial possessions	52
The guaranteeing of colonies	54
The guaranteeing of conventions	54
The system of coercive measures in international law	56
Coercive procedure or execution	57
Voices in favour of such a system	58
Dumas	58
Nys	60
Weiss	61
Milhaud	62
Alvarez	63
Dickinson	63
Unwin	64
Cabral	64
Holt	65
Houston	66
Otlet	68

PAGE
Tchéou-Weï 68
Leading statesmen 70
Character of coercive measures in international law 72
Economic and military coercive measures 72
Survey of the economic coercive measures 73
Security 73
Boycott 74
Seizure and forcible control 75
Indemnity 75
Fines 75
Non-warlike means of self-help 76
Self-help and coercion in international law 76
Retorsion 77
Reprisals 78
Embargo 79
Pacific blockade 80
The Dutch commission on the boycott 80
A Chinaman on boycott 86
Coercive execution in international law 88
Military coercive measures 89
Police power or military force 90
The results of such a system of coercive measures 92
The goal: the elimination of self-help 92
The opposing system: militarism 93
Agreement on armament 94
The removal of the military system 94
The disappearance of the militaristic mentality 94
The proper moment 94
The *conditio sine qua non* 95
The development of the international system 98
Recapitulation of the new postulates 99
The relation to the states outside 102
The prospects for realization 103
The democratic idea 104
The liberal mind 105

PART II. THE LAW OF WAR

Lessons of the war 109
Postulates before the war 109
Old and new tenets 111
The limits of regulation 112
Divergences of the systems of international law 113
The military war and its vanquishers 114

PAGE
Modern trade . . . 114
Modern technical science . . . 115
Johann von Bloch . . . 115
The *débâcle* of the military system . . . 119
The growing recognition . . . 119
The economic war . . . 121
The claim for the equal rights of both kinds of war in principle . . . 122
Consequences from the lessons of the war . . . 124
The future war is the commercial war . . . 125
The objective point of view . . . 125
The final goal: international law instead of war and law of war . . . 127
The parallelism between international law and the law of war . . . 128
The character of coercive means in international law and in the law of war . . . 129
Practical application for the development of international law . . . 130
Progress, not retrogression in the future development . . . 131
War on land . . . 132
The development of the law of war on land . . . 133
Naval war . . . 136
The development of the law of naval warfare . . . 137
Blockade . . . 137
The law of contraband . . . 139
The right of capture at sea . . . 140
Sea mines . . . 141
Submarines . . . 142
Aerial warfare . . . 144
Reprisals . . . 144
The interests of neutrals . . . 145
Co-operation or league of neutrals . . . 148
The German postulate of the freedom of the seas . . . 149
Voices concerning this postulate . . . 150
The content in international law of the postulate . . . 183
The other postulate: The development and enforcement of international law and of peace . . . 186
The compromise: agreement on armament . . . 186
The combating of the militaristic mentality . . . 187
The way to the goal: the gradual absorption of the law of warfare through international law . . . 187
The goal: The dominance of law . . . 187
Democracy and international law . . . 188
The solidaric interest in the progress of law . . . 188

APPENDIX

I. Other proposals. The postulates: PAGE
(a) of the American Institute of International Law 193
(b) of the American League to Enforce Peace 194
(c) of the Central Organization for a Permanent Peace at The Hague 202
II. My public correspondence with Philipp Zorn on 'Germany and the Hague Peace Conferences' 228

INTRODUCTION

INTRODUCTION

One is accustomed to say of those who have erroneously been reported dead that they enjoy unusually long lives. Perhaps one may, therefore, also say of international law, which during this war has more than once been prematurely laid aside as dead, that there is still a fine future in store for it. It is not alone the fact that one extreme usually calls forth another, and that, therefore, the derision that has been heaped upon international law during these years may perhaps of itself bring about a reaction after the war, which attests to this. But there is still another thing that to-day more than ever might strengthen the belief in the future of international law, and that is the fact that this whole great war has really been nothing less than *one* great lesson for mankind, namely, that those have erred who believed they might trust solely in force, and have scorned the legal and moral factors in international life.[1] The war has shown that nothing can be achieved by force, that in the end it has only a destructive effect. The symptoms bearing witness to the increasing recognition of the fact that the future of mankind must be built upon something higher—if its course is to be upward, not downward—are on the increase. This higher element can be nothing else than law. The *international legal order* must be the guiding star toward which humanity must turn in these dark days and to which are attached its hopes for the future. The recognition of this fact is gaining ground more and more, and the hope that this knowledge will also bring about practical results is all the more justified when one

[1] Max Huber in 'Der Wert des Völkerrechts' (*Neue Zürcher Zeitung* of November 20, 1916) correctly observes: 'It were simpler to speak of a bankruptcy of the policy of might founded upon the ruthless egotism of states, of a policy directed toward the present catastrophe and which for more than two years has been consuming the physical and economic powers of Europe without any visible success, of a policy whose mental war preparedness has turned out so well that, with the present mental condition of nations, peace has become extraordinarily more difficult than the continuation of the war.' Cf. especially Zitelmann, *Haben wir noch ein Völkerrecht?* 1914. Triepel, *Die Zukunft des Völkerrechts*, 1916, p. 7, also points out that at the most only a part of international law could be destroyed and not even the most important, since the international law of peace is not considered at all.

takes note of the fact that leading statesmen of widely different countries have already expressed the view that after this war one of the most essential tasks of nations will be the future development of international law. The war has taught them that it would be foolhardy to recognize in the formation of national frontiers alone the security of the future, and to look upon the aim of this war as more or less a problem of geography. They have come to recognize that they will never be able to reach a state of real security in this way alone, and that one must therefore dig more deeply if one really wishes to lay the foundations of the state structure securely.[1]

Consequently, I believe that an examination of the future possibilities for the reconstruction of international law is to-day no longer such an idle beginning as the belittlers of international law in the press and elsewhere would perhaps imagine. To determine what form it should actually take after the war will of course be a matter for the *statesmen.* It is to be assumed that upon the conclusion of peace they will consider it one of their first and most important tasks to give form and content to future international law, and that to this end they will call together one or several conferences, whose task it will be to draw new conclusions from the lessons of the war and to call into life the new form of international law. In the solution of this problem, the statesmen will have to depend upon the material they possess concerning the experiences this war has produced for international law. It is, however, the business of *science* to make available this material for the statesmen. The science of international law is therefore not allowed to fold its hands idly, as it only too often has done. Instead of wearying itself with the Sisyphean labour of cleansing its own country of all guilt for violations of international law that may have occurred or instead of criticizing violations of international law on the part of enemies of its country even in instances where the facts have not as yet been objectively proved,[2] and by so doing only assisting constantly in the incitement of nations against each other, it will above all have to find its task in the deduction of useful applications from the lessons of this war for

[1] Cf. with this Zoller, *Das Völkerrecht und der Krieg, 1914–1915,* 1915, pp. 141 ff.

[2] I wish in no wise to say thereby that the breaches of international law which have actually taken place should not be ascertained. I shall myself consider this subject in greater detail in my book which is to appear at the end of the war, as I deem it of the greatest importance.

the future shaping of international law and in pointing out the way to nations for the future policy of international law. It would be more than regrettable if the representatives of the science of international law, not recognizing their task, should this time too appear *post festum*. It is the duty of this science to prepare the field for the future work,[1] and, as much as in it lies, to labour toward the end that this work may not again get into the old rut, but that it may this time on the contrary be turned in a direction from which real achievement may be expected.

This latter point is by no means unimportant. The future work in international law must be in the sense of a *development* of the same. There are, however, certain tendencies recognizable to-day which, if allowed to prevail, would directly counteract the development of international law. I need only to mention here Eltzbacher's pamphlet, *Totes und lebendes Völkerrecht*,[2] in order to show that the danger of a *retrogression* of international law is imminent to-day. But so much the more must it be the duty of science to discover in time such dangers in the reconstruction of international law and to point out above all things the directions which a healthy and successful development of international law will have to take.

Nor must this preliminary work begin *too late*, because it is a matter of dealing with most important problems that mankind has ever had to solve, and because upon the nature of the solution of these problems the weal and woe of generations of men may depend. Consequently, these questions must be carefully considered and the conclusions to be drawn must be in no wise hurried. The conviction that preliminary labours would therefore have to be performed in time for the future conferences of statesmen induced me soon after the beginning of the war to sound the call for the study of the pertinent problems and, in order to insure as large a field as possible for such study, I sought, by the establishment of the 'Swiss Association for the Study of the Foundations of a Permanent Peace Treaty', to awaken the interest of larger circles for the discussion of these problems. But in so doing it was my intention that active interest be

[1] Cf. with this my treatise on 'Vorfragen des Völkerrechts', in the *Jahrbuch des öffentlichen Rechts*, 1913, pp. 24 ff.

[2] I published a criticism of this pamphlet in the *Schweizerische Juristenzeitung* for October 15, 1916.

restricted to a scientific treatment of the pertinent questions and that every kind of peace propaganda during the war should be avoided. I have been convinced, however, that a work established upon this serious basis was possible only if undertaken exclusively by specialists who, both in theory and in practice, were thoroughly acquainted with the questions concerned.

If by pointing out the possible forms for future international law in the following short sketch I have attempted to contribute my mite to the necessary preliminary work, I have done so mainly to give expression therein to the *new lessons* which this war has taught me. For if the latter were not the case and I had nothing new to say after the events of this war, I might have spared myself the following examination, inasmuch as I have already, in my book entitled *Die Fortbildung des Verfahrens in völkerrechtlichen Streitigkeiten* (The Development of Procedure in International Disputes), minutely discussed the future development of international law, more minutely, I dare say, than any one else has done. What I shall present in the following pages will therefore virtually be *new* points of view. At the same time I may be allowed to emphasize the fact that the direction of the development of international law, which I indicated in the above-mentioned work, have in all instances been confirmed by subsequent development, and that the present war also seems to confirm the views expressed at that time. If I shall recommend here some new points of view for consideration, they must on the whole be regarded as a *complement* rather than as modifications of the views which I have hitherto expressed upon the subject. In my opinion, one will have to do all that which I earlier proposed. However, after the experiences of this war, we shall not be able to restrict ourselves to that which was proposed then ; on the contrary, we shall have to go several steps *further* ; for to the lessons of this war we may add the following : that the development of international law will have to be along more *radical* lines than were ever thought possible or necessary and useful *before* this war.[1] This is the main lesson of this war, as I have already pointed out, that the foundations of the structure of international

[1] Fried, *Europäische Wiederherstellung*, 1915, p. 4, is right when he says that it must be reconstructed from the very foundations, that the mere covering up of the torn roof, the restoration and retouching of the façade, will not suffice ; the foundation is unstable, and that has been the cause of the catastrophe.

law must be laid deeply and firmly, but according to a different plan, so that they can bid defiance to all future storms without suffering injury.

To what extent *universal law* will be achieved in this new structure of international law, or to what extent perhaps only a smaller group of states will interest itself in the development of international law seriously, remains an open question even to-day.

The following work is of course in the first place to serve *practical* purposes. It is therefore expedient to omit all theoretical discussions. I believe it will be necessary for me to consider only *one* theoretical question, that in reality is in the field of the systematization of law; but I cannot neglect it if I wish to present clearly and minutely my conception of the matters to be discussed. It is the question of the relation between the *law of war* and *international law.*

The science of international law has hitherto apparently gone rather too far in the treatment of the war problem. In the endeavour to interpret war also from a legal standpoint as far as possible, the doctrine has deemed it necessary to invest war with the character of a legal institution, and the doctrinal discussions about war have often strayed far from reality. These theorists overlooked the fact that law will never entirely encompass war and can never regulate it in all its relations; and this for the simple reason that war itself is already a negation of law, and because in the waging of war it is not legal considerations but the necessities of warfare that are the impelling motives. It would have been far better if the doctrine had in general simply adhered to facts. It is a fact that war is not a legal institution but simply the application of force. War is struggle, employment of force, and in so far as it is to serve the enforcement of claims it is self-help. This is the definition military science gives of war,[1] and with this the science of international law should have contented itself; for from this definition of war it already appears that war, considered as a whole, is outside the sphere of law.[2] Nor is this truth

[1] Cf. e. g. v. Hartmann's *Militärische Notwendigkeit und Humanität*, 1878, p. 19.

[2] Consequently, the question of guilt * in a war is not an international question, but a question of morality. International law cannot distinguish between just and unjust wars, since war from the viewpoint of international law *always*

* Note by the translator: Obviously the author here means guilt in causing or beginning the war. He cannot mean guilt in connexion with methods of warfare.

altered by the fact that attempts have been made to regulate war in various ways, or that a modern law of war has been codified. For this code applies only in so far as it sets up rules for warfare. At the same time, however, the necessity of war does apply if one leaves out of account the customs of warfare and the unwritten laws of humanity. This line of demarcation the science of international law must respect. One must render unto war the things that belong to war, and unto international law the things that belong to international law. Just as one may and must demand of the military courts that they respect the law of warfare, so also the military leaders may and must demand that where there are no legal norms of war there military necessities must be allowed to prevail. Each must equally guard against trespassing upon the territory of the other.

From this fact, that war as such is not subject to legal regulation,[1] that it is simply combat or self-help, there follows the self-evident conclusion that war as a whole, *per se*, does not really fit into the system of international law. In a consideration of international law the normal state is, quite naturally, the state of peace.[2] Only this normal state can be considered in forming a legal norm. Consequently, only in this state is an actual authority of law in the relation of the states with each other at all imaginable. Therefore, it alone can be considered as the foundation for a system of international law. The international legal order can accordingly

signifies a negation of law. *Guilt in a war is, however, not decreased through the fact that it is a moral guilt.* Cf. e. g. Lawrence's *Handbook of International Law*, 1913: 'Modern international law does not attempt to decide upon the justice or injustice of war in general, or any war in particular. It leaves such questions to international morality.'

[1] In the *Neue Zürcher Zeitung* for December 29, 1916, E. Hurwicz observes that law is so incompatible with the nature of war that international law which regulates the relations of states in time of war could only have an 'anarchical nature'. The international law of war is, and remains, according to its very nature, only an attempt at adjustment.

[2] This is also emphasized by Max Huber in *Der Wert des Völkerrechts*: 'The standard is the law of peace conditions which from the standpoint of modern history represents the normal state of nations. . . . The tasks with which the international legal order is confronted in times of peace are so significant that this order, and with it the science of international law, could afford wholly to fall back upon this position and treat war as a passing reversion to the natural (or primitive) state of war of all against all, as beyond all legal order and examination. Moreover, even before the war, the conception became more and more established in science that war was something primitive, and that the unusually strong development of the law of war implies an aberration, because it deceives us about the nature of war and obscures the politically fundamental problem: the preservation of a peaceful state of law or a relapse into the lawless state of force.'

only be a regulation of relations between nations in a state of peace.[1] This legal order naturally also seeks to assert itself in disputes between states. In cases where it does not succeed, where self-help and conflict take the place of law, legal regulation of course ceases to exist. When force prevails, law does not prevail. War is not law. This fact the system of international law must take into account. Just as war is not law, so the law of warfare is just as little international law, and just as little does it, *per se*, belong to the system of international law.

It would, therefore, be well to differentiate between the law of war and international law. Not only for the reason that war is only in part under legal regulation but also because the norms of the law of warfare are to a far greater degree exposed to contradictions than the norms of international law, since they can easily come into collision with professed or supposed war necessities. A systematic placing together of the law of war and normal international law can, therefore, only have the result that the discredit which attaches to the law of warfare will also be carried over to normal international law. There is only *one* means of avoiding such discrediting, to which the present war bears all too eloquent testimony, and that is the *cleanest possible distinction between international law and the law of war*. For the system of international law there arises here the possibility of regarding the law of warfare in a manner such as the system of civil law regards self-help. In the latter, self-help appears as an appendix to the system of law, as a remnant of the period of deficient normalization of civil law, which must be registered for

[1] From what has been said, it may be seen to what extent the *science of international law* and *pacifism* agree and differ. International law desires law. Pacifism wishes peace. For international law, *law* is the supreme thing. Peace is, however, the necessary condition for this. To this extent, then, must the science of international law stand up for the maintenance of peace. But the essential difference is that the unconditional pacifists place *peace* above law, and they accordingly stand for peace at any price, whereas the science of international law must in the first place favour the enforcement of the law, the idea of righteousness, and cannot, therefore, at any moment recognize in a peace treaty the best solution. In *theory*, of course, the pacifists deny that they wish peace at any price, but many of them have in this war shown clearly enough that in *practice* they nevertheless stand for peace at any price. Cf. with this question the foreword which I have written for the German edition of Del Vecchio, *Il Fenomeno della guerra e l'idea della pace*, as also my paper on ' Vorfragen des Völkerrechts ' in the *Jahrbuch des öffentlichen Rechts*, 1913, p. 33. Further, Triepel, *Die Zukunft des Völkerrechts*, 1916, p. 15, Strupp in Niemeyer's *Zeitschrift für internationales Recht*, 1916, Parts 4–6, and, in answer to the latter, Fried in the *Friedenswarte*, January 1917.

the sake of completion. Thus the law of war can also be construed systematically. One can enter it as an appendix to the international legal order, in so far as one does not wish to separate it entirely from international law. Nor is the situation at all changed in principle by the fact that this appendix is comparatively large in compass. It simply indicates that the legal order between peoples has not yet progressed as far as between individuals, and that self-help therefore still occupies a large place in the former. But it also points out clearly where the real future tasks of humanity lie ; for one would think that in this respect no doubt can exist to-day, that the development will be in favour of law and opposed to self-help, and that it is, therefore, more important to develop international law farther than the law of war. The separation of the two fields can in turn only help to simplify the recognition of this fact, where it may still be lacking.[1] For this reason also, I should like to recommend here the separation of the two.

[1] Among those who do not yet acknowledge this is Zorn, as his article (reprinted in the appendix to this book) in the *Neue Zürcher Zeitung* for August 12, 1916, shows. He finds it ' almost amusing ' that I have designated the regulating of the law of war as opposed to the development of international law as a side issue. Bornhak, too, in *Der Wandel des Völkerrechts*, 1916, p. 3, writes : ' Not in a dismissal of war by a compulsory court of arbitration whose sentence no one can execute, nor in general disarmament, for which there is no standard, was there to be found a reasonable development of the law of war, but rather in the ennoblement of the forms of warfare.'

PART I

INTERNATIONAL LAW

INTERNATIONAL LAW

I

OLD POSTULATES

THE condition of peace between states is for international law the normal condition. Since it is only in this condition that a real rule of law seems possible between nations, it must therefore also be to the interest of the international legal order that this condition be maintained. The maintenance of the state of peace, the prophylaxis against war, seems from this point of view then as the chief problem of international law. In this the law of international procedure is of the greatest service.[1] As in all provinces of law, one can also distinguish in the field of international law between the material and the formal or the law of international procedure, the latter of which has to do with the procedure for the settlement of international disputes.[2] It is the purpose of international law not only to set up rules for international intercourse but also to bring to a decision, by way of law, disputes between states. Even in disputes, the field of law is not to be abandoned. This appears as one of the main tasks. Where it does not succeed, there international law also fails; there self-help or war begins. One should keep as long as possible within the province of law. The goal in view is, of course, that it will

[1] In respect to *material* international law, Triepel, loc. cit., pp. 11 ff., thinks no great prophetic vision was needed to predict that the larger part of international law, the law of peace, would, upon the conclusion of the war, move along in exactly the same channel as before. The coming changes would in no way affect the fundamental ideas that have hitherto been the impelling forces in international law. In spite of all the devastations which the war may have brought on in the economy of the states and in the souls of the people taking part in it, the threads which world trade has spun will not have been so torn that they cannot again be tied together; the necessity for mutual restoration of the separated systems of industrial economy will tend to assert itself more strongly than the mutual hatred of peoples. I, too, believe that. This does not, however, detract from the fact that new tendencies will be added which consist mainly in a decided accentuation of the idea of law.

[2] Strupp in his *Neue Probleme des Völkerrechts*, 1916, p. 2, proposes the term *Kriegsverhütungsrecht* [law for the prevention of war].

never be abandoned, but we are to-day still far from that goal. In the meantime it is our business to prevent as far as possible a departure from the province of law,[1] which is identical with a strengthening of the idea of law in international relations, with a strengthening of the rule of law in the life of nations.

From all this it follows that the most essential tasks which confront the development of international law after the war will have to be in the province of international procedure.[2] *The development of procedure in international disputes* appears to be the real problem to be solved after this war in the field of international law. In what manner this development might proceed I have set forth in detail in my work dedicated to that subject.[3] In that work I designated this development as the most important problem in the international law of our day. 'There is no problem in the field of international law that makes so urgent an appeal to the co-operation of science and the states, and whose solution might become of such great and eventful significance for the combined international and cultural life of the present and the future. . . . The chief problem which international law still has to solve and the solution of which has in part at least, so it seems, been reserved for our day, is this normalization of procedure in international disputes, the creation of a system of international judicature.'

That this is the most important task for international law and that our present time is called upon to find a solution for this problem is a fact that has also been recognized at the *Hague Peace Conferences*. The work in international law at these conferences concerned the normalization of the procedure of international law. The most important of the Hague Conventions deals with the peaceful settlement of international disputes.

In the discussion of international procedure and of the possibili-

[1] Contrary to the statements here offered, Triepel, loc. cit., thinks that the development in this field has already reached a limit beyond which, according to the nature of things, it will be unable to go. Herein Triepel is in opposition to a demand which is to-day expressed throughout the whole world, and to which even the German Imperial Chancellor dared not refuse to give heed.

[2] Lammasch, too, in 'Das Mediationsrecht der Neutralen' in the *Oesterreichische Zeitschrift für öffentliches Recht*, 1915, p. 241, stresses the fact that it has been shown that the law to *make war* needs regulation, not indeed in an idealistic sense but in a realistic one corresponding to the hard actualities.

[3] *Die Fortbildung des Verfahrens in völkerrechtlichen Streitigkeiten.* Ein völkerrechtliches Problem der Gegenwart, speziell im Hinblick auf die Haager Friedenskonferenzen, erörtert von Otfried Nippold, Leipzig, 1907.

ties of its further development, we shall have to proceed from the point of view that there are, according to accepted international law, three kinds of procedure in international disputes: mediation, commissions of inquiry, and arbitration. One or the other of these kinds of procedure can be employed according to the character of the controversy.[1]

Since *mediation* is limited to an *endeavour* to adjust the controversy, and is in no wise binding for the parties concerned, this manner of procedure will be of importance and applied in controversies of so serious a nature that the controversial parties would without further ado hardly consent to submit them to a court of arbitration, or where the parties would withdraw from a decision proceeding exclusively from legal viewpoints. Since mediation is only a friendly endeavour, and nothing more, it can as such also be used in *any* important controversy. Whether and how far mediation has been employed, has hitherto depended solely upon practical political considerations.

The same may in general be said of *commissions of inquiry*. They, too, in no way wish to impose an adjustment of the controversy upon the opponents; but confine themselves to an *attempt* at adjustment by seeking to establish objectively the facts in the case. Having done so, the disputants can then draw whatever conclusion they prefer. Ordinarily, they will no doubt employ the same as a basis for the peaceful settlement of the dispute.

Arbitral decision goes one step farther. It does not limit itself to the establishment of the facts in the case, but it also passes judgement, and, indeed, with the intention that the parties shall be bound by this judgement. Here we have to do not only with an endeavour toward adjusting the dispute but with an actual adjustment between the parties, just as in the case of a judicial sentence within a state. It may be said that states have hitherto in every instance adhered to this judicial sentence in spite of the fact that the possibility of an actual enforcement of such sentences has, quite in accordance with the peculiar character of international law, up to this time been lacking.

[1] As a characteristic mark of international procedure I have designated the co-operation of neutrals. This follows as a result of international legal solidarity, through which this procedure stands out in contrast to self-help on the one hand, and to the superior internal justice on the other. Cf. *Fortbildung*, p. 165.

According to the law of the Hague Conventions, it is for the states in dispute to decide when they wish to employ this procedure offered by existing international law, and which of the three kinds of procedure they desire to put to concrete use. The nature of the selection will no doubt be determined by the character of the particular dispute. But the application of international law procedure is also entirely optional, according to the Hague Conventions. These conventions confine themselves to a platonic recommendation or to a purely fundamental obligation of moral significance only. The states in controversy can accordingly refrain entirely from making use of international law procedure, and make use of self-help without any more ado, in order to enforce their real, supposed, or alleged claims.

The respective moral obligations or recommendations of the law of the Hague Conventions apply in general to the disputants, and only exceptionally to the states standing outside the controversy. In this connexion, Article 48 of the first Hague Convention should be recalled, in which it is designated as a duty to remind the contestants of the existence of the Hague Court of Arbitration.

Particular international law, it must be added, goes in various ways far beyond the law of the Hague Conventions. There are political treaties in which the idea of obligation has already been introduced in the most far-reaching measure.

Thus international law procedure is in about the same state of development that it had reached upon the outbreak of the present war. But even earlier earnest efforts had been made to bring about an *advancement* of this legal situation ; the labours of both the Hague Peace Conferences were for the most part dedicated to the solution of the problem of such progress. It was recognized that the first task would be to *guarantee* the application of legal procedure in disputes in such a way as to preclude self-help. *Guarantees* were sought for the employment of international procedure ; these were recognized in the creation of a so-called duty of *obligation*, i.e. an actual legal duty to enter upon ways of arbitration, to submit the dispute to a commission of inquiry, or to ask for (or offer, as the case might be) mediation. Arbitration, commissions of inquiry, and mediation were within certain limits to be made obligatory. That was *in nuce* the problem with which the Hague Conferences occupied themselves and the solution of which has not yet been achieved. At the Second Conference a strong majority was in favour of the adoption of a plan for obligatory arbitration. Nevertheless, the work at The Hague in 1907 also remained a fragment in consequence of the well-known opposition of certain states.

The problem, still the same as in 1899 and 1907, is as follows: In what way can the application of procedure in international disputes *be made secure*? In my book concerning the development of procedure I have amplified upon the manner in which especially guarantees for the use of arbitral procedure might be created: on the one hand, by making the court of arbitration obligatory for the field generally conceded as belonging to it; on the other hand, by also giving in a legal sense an obligatory character to the influence of neutral powers used in the employment of this procedure. But I also proposed that the process of mediation should likewise be placed upon an obligatory basis, and, indeed, in the sense that this duty to mediate must be recognized not alone by the disputants but also by the community of states. I arrived at the same conclusions with regard to the commissions of inquiry. I found that the problem confronting the states, generally speaking, lay in the necessity of increasing the international *duties* of states; and in fact not only in increasing the duties of the disputants but of the neutral powers as well, since the international principle of the solidarity of interest finds its desired expression only in a full recognition of the duties to be assumed by the community of states.

Of this necessity of assuming legal state obligations [1] as an unavoidable hypothesis for all further development of international law, I have written as follows in my work entitled *Die zweite Haager Friedenskonferenz*: [2]

If it was a characteristic of international law of the past that states, boastful of their sovereignty, claimed *rights* for themselves, it is characteristic of modern international law that the states, knowing the solidarity of their interests, recognize *duties*, both toward the other states and toward the community of nations. This surely does not sound as pleasant as the former. One would rather speak of sovereignty than of duties. And yet the latter must be the

[1] Cf. also Zoller, *Das Völkerrecht und der Krieg, 1914–1915*, 1915, p. 136.

[2] Cf. my *Zweite Haager Friedenskonferenz*, vol. i, Prozessrecht, p. 229. I would recall here the fine words of Renault: 'If the community of states could become more and more conscious of its duties no less than of its rights, then the international relations would obtain that security which is necessary for them.'

watchword. That happens to be the trend of modern times, and only therein is revealed the power of the legal community. From the standpoint of the state, it is easy to see that governments will only hesitatingly enter upon the new path. And yet they will all have to go that path of duty, especially all those who are members of the international community. Those who delay longest and only follow reluctantly will in the end only need to blame themselves if, having arrived at their destination later than others, they should not be satisfied with the reception they receive there. All states must fare along this path of duty. From this legal development, which the work at The Hague is to serve above all, no state, however powerful, can withdraw. This work is too great for single individuals to accomplish. The great ideas which are to be realized at The Hague are entertained to-day by the whole civilized world. Certainly collaboration in that which future development seems to be bringing demands a good measure of self-denial on the part of the sovereign state structures. But it is all the more necessary that this word duty should also be applicable to governments, so that future developments and future Hague Conferences be impeded by 'no petty species'.

In the establishment of international law obligations, as already shown, a distinction must be made between the duties to be imposed upon the *parties in controversy* and the duties of *neutral states*.[1] In the first place, the parties should naturally be obliged to make use of international procedure. They are to 'appeal' to an arbitral court, to a commission of inquiry, or to mediation. It is this that I have designated as *party initiative*. This party initiative must be regulated by fixed rules; in fact, the shaping of international law competencies in the several kinds of procedure must be to some extent parallel.[2] The states must pledge themselves in advance to make use, under certain premises, of one or the other mode of procedure, so that definite competencies may arise. I developed the idea that even if an absolutely fixed regulation of competencies in international law were out of the question, yet progress would doubtless be possible in this direction.

If one should once succeed in establishing a duty of party initiative for all kinds of international procedure, an uncommonly great advance in international law would be made. This would be true, even if this duty were not in all kinds of procedure an absolute or equally far-reaching one, confining itself, for example, in an arbitration court to certain kinds of disputes, just as to-day it depends in mediation upon the stipulation of circumstance. *As soon as the principle of obligatory party initiative for procedure were once generally recognized,* these restrictions would do no harm, because where one method of procedure might fail, the other might be able to take its place.

[1] Neutral here in the sense of not having part in the dispute.
[2] Cf. with this my *Fortbildung*, pp. 488 ff.

But with the international obligations of the contending states would have to be associated the obligations of the *neutral* states. With the 'appeal' to mediation will come the 'offering' of mediation; or, as the case may require, reference to the arbitral court or the commission of inquiry. To the aid of party initiative comes the *initiative of the neutrals* or of the international community. Where for some reason or other party initiative fails, the initiative of a neutral can intervene, and in this way bring about an application of international procedure. It can be shown by the present law of the Hague Convention that neutral states already have a legal title to this method. The first Hague Convention recognizes the principle that neutral powers have a right to work to the end that use be made of international procedure. Attention need only be called to Articles 1 and 3, as well as Article 48 of the Convention. In the last article mentioned, this principle has even come to be regarded as a 'moral duty'.[1] It goes without saying that the recognition of this principle is already of the very greatest significance for the future formative possibilities of international law. But at The Hague the tendency went far beyond the mere recognition of the principle, as the discussions about Article 48 (previously 27) clearly show. Even at that time they desired to establish an actual legal duty.

But such legal duty would have to be generally established, not only with respect to the arbitral court, but with regard to the application of international procedure as a whole. I have called the creation of such a general legal duty—the remodelling of Articles 1 and 3 into a real legal obligation— the greatest legal progress that the Hague Convention could bring about in a long time. International solidarity could scarcely better authenticate itself than in such *peace-bringing activity on the part of neutrals*; and in the *more decided accentuation of solidarity*, in international disputes as well, lies *the way that the development of the international legal order has to take.*[2] Also it may be said that thus far there is legally no reason why such a progress should be not attainable, since neutrals by such reference only remind the opposing parties of a duty which already exists. In many a case

[1] Cf. *Fortbildung*, p. 490.

[2] Cf. *Fortbildung*, p. 491 and p. 167, where I have pointed out that a complete attainment of this goal would be synonymous with a realization of the dominance of law in the life of nations. Whether such a goal is ever attainable cannot be answered.

of procedure it might be decidedly necessary to place the centre of gravity on the initiative of neutrals and not on the party initiative; this is especially so in mediation. Many doubts which exist about 'appeal' in international procedure cease in the case of initiative on the part of a third power. Under certain circumstances the *neutrals* can far more unhesitatingly have recourse to the initiative to which they are entitled or obligated.[1] One can therefore say that a *more extensive development of the initiative of neutral states in the peaceful settlement of international disputes* is likewise one of the main problems in the future progress of international law.

It follows, then, that this development everywhere tends toward the creation of actual legal duties, both on the side of the disputants and of the neutrals, and that an obligatory development on the part of the Hague Convention, in the spirit of the above plan, appears in fact as the chief end; this is also true from the standpoint that had to be taken upon this question *before* the outbreak of this war. To-day it has become quite clear that without the creation of new legal duties no further development of the international legal order is thinkable.[2]

In the establishment of these duties it will be necessary, however, to bear in mind constantly 'that the purpose and content of all the legal progress here striven for are in truth only the maintenance of *one* legal obligation, upon which in reality all our postulates on the creation of new legal obligations in the Hague Convention are concentrated, namely: The convention shall and must offer a guarantee that an *endeavour* toward a peaceful solution of the conflicts of states will *always* precede self-help [combat] in international intercourse, no matter whether this endeavour proceeds from the disputants or the neutrals. In order to bring this about, it is simply impossible to avoid the establishment of actual legal duties in the convention.'[3]

From what has been said above, it can be seen that in my opinion one must not merely take up and develop one of these kinds of procedure, e. g. arbitration, but that one must proceed to create an actual *system* for international procedure, developing

[1] It should be remembered that I assume in all this a state of peace.
[2] In this sense v. Ullmann also expresses himself, in his *Völkerrecht*, p. 253.
[3] *Fortbildung*, p. 495. For this reason I also pleaded for the dropping of the various diplomatic clauses.

the several kinds on somewhat parallel lines. It must not be forgotten that they are parts of one system, or are to become so, and that they are to this extent interdependent. Just as little dare one overlook the fact that none of these kinds of procedure can be adequate to *all* needs. This monition is surely not superfluous in view of the tendency, which appears often enough, to emphasize one mode of procedure at the expense of others, and in a certain measure to commend it as a palladium against all dangers to international law.

It is well known that such misuse has been made especially in the case of *arbitral procedure*.[1] I have elsewhere discussed in detail the legal and political limits that stand in the way of an unconditional recourse to arbitration courts.[2] As late as 1914, in treating *The Problem of Obligatory Arbitration* according to the position of theory and practice at that time, I uttered a warning against the overrating of the institution of arbitration.[3]

It was doubtless a delusion when it was hoped in pacifistic circles, especially in earlier years, that a more or less absolute palladium against war was to be found in courts of arbitration. And it is so much less necessary to see in arbitration such a panacea for the reason that there are in international law still other ways and means for the adjustment of disputes; and also for the reason, as will be shown, that the future result of all efforts toward progress in the international law of procedure will by no means have to depend upon the one-sided development of a single one of these legal paths, but, quite to the contrary, on the harmonious construction of *all* existing legal methods into a complete *system* of legal procedure.

The results of my investigation at that time,[4] which I might even to-day recommend as the most rational solution of the problem, were to the effect that the positive way (taken at The Hague in 1907) of setting up a list of unconditionally arbitrable cases in

[1] On the other hand, Triepel, *op. cit.*, p. 14, might also be in error, when he considers it impossible that the idea of an obligatory arbitration court can win for itself an essentially larger place in international life than that which has been hitherto allowed to it. Triepel here judges according to the feeling in Germany, but does not know the sentiment in the other countries.

[2] Cf. *Fortbildung*, pp. 168–230.

[3] Cf. *Jahrbuch des öffentlichen Rechts*, 1914, pp. 1 ff. Among the extensive literature on the problem of arbitration, compare further the works of Lammasch in the *Handbuch des Völkerrechts*, vol. iii; and of Lange, *L'arbitrage obligatoire en 1913*, 1914.

[4] Cf. also Lammasch's recent *Ueber die Begrenzung der internationalen Schiedsgerichtsbarkeit* in the Recueil de rapports sur les différents points du programme-minimum of the *Organisation centrale pour une paix durable*, La Haye, 1916, vol. i, p. 294.

general international law be given up, and in its place be taken the negative way of *setting up a general arbitral obligation, with the reservation of the actual vital interest of the states.* The court of arbitration would then *in dubio* always have to be regarded as competent.[1] Where it would not be competent, other ways of procedure would have to be employed.

I vigorously opposed the continuation of the struggle for the complete elimination of the above reservation clause, since without the same a general arbitral treaty could never be obtained.

Surely more progress would have been made at The Hague in 1907 had it not been taken for granted that this clause must under all circumstances be put aside, at least for isolated categories of disputes. The inner sense of right will not permit the reservation of the highest interests to be contested. Humanity's great struggles for existence cannot be removed from the world by doing away with a clause about arbitration. Conflicts, in which the independence, sovereignty or autonomy of a state are at stake, elude an arbitral decision.[2] But, on the other hand, one may comfort oneself with the thought that these great struggles and problems of existence seldom occur, and that therefore the arbitral decision, unconcerned with these questions that cannot be submitted to it, may function very regularly in spite of this and fulfil all the hopes placed upon it. The great majority of disputes between states will, according to international law, be subject to the duty of arbitration from the moment when, according to the law of the Hague Conventions, nothing but an appeal to the highest interests can liberate states from this duty.[3]

[1] The newer American state practice tends to refer everything that is 'justiciable' to the court of arbitration and everything else to the commissions of inquiry. It is a question whether much is won practically by this conception (of justiciable). *Most* disputes between states also contain legal elements which permit legal decision, being in other words 'justiciable'. The criterion for submission to the court of arbitration does not really lie in the legal but in the political province, and perhaps for this reason the solution above offered by me might be preferable. I cannot go into the matter more deeply here, and therefore refer to the chapters on 'The character of international disputes', 'The legal limits of the employment of arbitration courts', and 'The political limits of the employment of arbitration courts', in *Fortbildung*, pp. 127–230; as also to 'Das Problem der obligatorischen Schiedsgerichtsbarkeit', in the *Jahrbuch des öffentlichen Rechts*, 1913, *op. cit.*, p. 41. Cf. further Rafael Erich: *Probleme der internationalen Organisation*, 1914, pp. 19 ff.

[2] Triepel, p. 16, thinks that if the great powers were really foolish enough to conclude with one another a general arbitration treaty containing a renunciation of the clause relating to interest and honour, the treaty would be scattered like chaff to the winds upon the first severe test of its stability. Still I should be inclined to doubt this. I do not believe in a second Belgium. Those who do not wish to keep a treaty should not sign it. The fearful thing in such a matter is above all the breaking of the word, and that can be avoided by not entering upon such a treaty at all. Moreover, the renunciation of the clause is not at all necessary, since another kind of procedure would doubtless in many cases be more suitable than arbitration.

[3] [Translator's note: Of which, however, the states themselves are the sole judges.]

The question as to whether the premises for such an appeal are given *in concreto*, might be referred for judgement to The Hague.[1]

In those disputes which do not fall under this arbitral duty, the other kinds of procedure would then naturally have to be called into use. It remains for mediation and the commissions of inquiry to fill up the gaps which the arbitral procedure leaves open. Consequently, their further development in the direction of making them obligatory likewise becomes one of the problems to be dealt with here. *Mediation* in itself is no doubt capable of being used in the case of any dispute, even in such as concern the highest interests of the states ; and if made in the form of a *collective mediation*, when it appears as the mediation of a whole group of states or even of the international community, as the expression of the international conscience, then it also has the greater prospect for success. Thus attention has frequently been called with emphasis to the institution of mediation in recent years.[2]

The same applies to the *commission of inquiry*. This institution, together with arbitration, has recently been placed more and more in the foreground, especially in America. In the treaties which Taft proposed in 1911 it was already provided that in case opinions differed as to whether a dispute should be brought before the court of arbitration, a mixed commission of inquiry was to determine this preliminary question ; further, that such a commission should also be instituted for cases that are not arbitrable, if one party should so desire ; under certain circumstances such

[1] Cf. *Jahrbuch, loc. cit.*, p. 51.

[2] In the literature that has appeared *since* the beginning of the war, mention need only be made of Lammasch's 'Das Mediationsrecht der Neutralen' in the *Oesterreichische Zeitschrift für öffentliches Recht.* He gives special attention to collective mediation and tries to put the institution on a basis as nearly as possible independent of the disputants. This basis should be the interest and the wishes of those who are not direct participants in the dispute, but still indirectly endangered by it, or, in other words, the neutrals. At any rate it is indisputable that neutrals have the *right* to offer their mediation. We shall have to agree with Lammasch when he writes : 'The question as to whether the conditions are favourable for offering mediation will, after the experiences of this war, be an essentially different one for neutrals than previously. Their interest in the prevention of any war, which is clearly not of a purely local character, whose spreading and far-reaching effect seems therefore not completely precluded, is, as shown by these experiences, such an immeasurable one that they will always have to answer this question in the affirmative. They will have to say to themselves : the conditions are favourable because they demand it. . . . On the basis of this experience no state will any longer be in the position to look upon a war between world powers as a *res inter alios acta*.'

a commission, even in cases which are beyond a doubt arbitrable, should function before the court of arbitration. A kind of mediator's rôle was at the same time intended for the commissions of inquiry, so that in these treaties a whole system of legal remedies might be employed.[1]

In contrast to the above, emphasis was placed exclusively upon the investigating commissions in the so-called *Bryan treaties*.[2] These treaties mark a decided advance in the field of particular international law. In substance they provide that the parties obligate themselves to submit all disputes between them, of every nature whatsoever, which cannot be adjusted in a diplomatic way, to an international commission for examination and report; that during such investigation and pending the report they are not to declare war or begin hostilities. In these treaties a proviso is generally made for entering upon arbitration in accordance with the treaty. Generally, the report of the previously appointed commission, consisting of five members with the privilege of acting on their own initiative, is to be made within the year. The parties have the right to act freely and independently after the report of the commission has been made. Since August 1913, no less than thirty states have concluded such treaties with the United States 'for the advancement of peace', of which sixteen were ratified in November 1915. To these must be added the so-called A. B. C. Treaty, between Argentine, Brazil, and Chile of May 25, 1915, which likewise provides for a permanent investigating commission.[3]

It must be observed, moreover, that these investigating commissions differ in no small way from those of the Hague Convention, since it is a question here of permanent commissions and since all disputes of whatever nature are to be submitted to them; accordingly, they have a far greater field for application, and to this extent are in a position at the same time to exercise the function of mediation. However, a mediation can be attached to the investigation as well as to a court of arbitration. Lange

[1] A sketch of one of these treaties is reprinted in the *Jahrbuch*, *op. cit.*, p. 26.

[2] In reference to these, cf. especially the work of the meritorious General Secretary of the Interparliamentary Union, Dr. Lange, *Die amerikanischen Friedensverträge*, 1916. Further, see *Jahrbuch*, *op. cit.*, p. 28; *Fortbildung*, pp. 555, 579; Fried, in the *Friedenswarte*, January 1917; and Scott, *Treaties for the Advancement of Peace*, 1920.

[3] Cf. on the same subject Lange, *op. cit.*, p. 19; Alvarez, *La grande guerre européenne et la neutralité du Chili*, 1915, p. 67; and Fried, in the *Friedenswarte*, *loc. cit.*

rightly points out in connexion with the declaration of these new American treaties :

The procedure introduced by the new peace treaties does not exclude arbitration: it can be applied to other questions or it can serve as a kind of rectifying process, whereby the possibility of finding a basis for a final adjustment through arbitration can be tried.

From all this follows what has already been emphasized above, namely, that one should not attach himself narrowly to *one* procedure, to the investigating commissions and to mediation no more than to a court of arbitration. The whole problem reads : the advancement of international procedure in general.

In this sense I have expressed myself in the *Denkschrift über die Grundlagen eines dauerhaften Friedensvertrags.*[1] In it I have especially demanded that Articles 1, 2, 3, 9, 39, and 40 of the first Hague Convention be developed fully in the sense of establishing a legal obligation, with reservation of the clause bearing on actual vital interests in the case of arbitration. These demands may be summed up briefly :

In place of the present system, which leaves the employment of international legal means to the free will of the states, there should be substituted an obligation, a legal duty, within limits attainable at the present time. In place of the individual declarations mentioned above, the Peace Congress might therefore eventually issue a *single* declaration to the effect that the powers at the Congress consider themselves henceforth legally obligated to the use of legal modes of international procedure, and they might express the wish that the Third Hague Conference introduce the obligation in the above-mentioned way. . . . All in all, the various legal means form a system that makes it possible under all conditions to find an appropriate way of settling *every* dispute, no matter of what nature. What is lacking is therefore merely the legal obligation of states to make use of this system, under any circumstances, be it in this or that form. Therefore, it is absolutely the business of the Peace Congress to create this obligation once for all, and to prepare for its further execution. . . . As long as the Hague Conventions do not wish to recognize any actual legal duties, the whole Hague structure stands upon an insecure footing.

Naturally, the development of the *Hague Court of Arbitration* would also have to go hand in hand with the further development of international procedure. It has been much regretted that the latter only consists of a list of arbitrators, having therefore no really permanent character. In spite of this, it has until now functioned well. Its further development would naturally be

[1] *Die Grundlagen eines dauerhaften Friedensvertrags*, Denkschrift herausgegeben vom Schweizerischen Komitee, Olten, 1915.

welcomed. It is well known that the Second Hague Conference also expressed the wish that the conferring powers might adopt its prepared plan for a 'Cour de justice arbitrale'. In so doing, the errors made in 1907 must, however, be guarded against.[1] One must not wish at The Hague to act contrary to a fundamental principle of international law, such as that of *legal equality* between the states, if he does not wish to imperil the entire work of The Hague. There is no reason why the great powers should have larger representation in a permanent international court of arbitration than the small states. On the contrary, the arbitrators from small neutral, disinterested states seem *a priori* far better fitted for impartial judicature than the members of more frequently participating great powers. So much the more is this the case, inasmuch as the *actual* nationals of the states participating in the dispute would in the future have to be altogether rejected as *arbitrators* because of bias. This, too, is one of the progressive steps that should be striven for after this war.

This court functioning side by side with the Court of Arbitration should have the character of a *real court*. Details in regard to this can, however, not be discussed here.[2] All these problems will not only continue to exist, but will have to be examined again with redoubled zeal after this war.

[1] Cf. with this my criticism of that plan in *Die zweite Haager Friedenskonferenz*, vol. i, pp. 221 ff.

[2] In reference to this subject, the publications of James Brown Scott may be recalled. Cf. in particular 'The Proposed Court of Arbitral Justice' in the *American Journal of International Law*, 1908, p. 772, and 'The Evolution of a Permanent International Judiciary', *ibid.*, 1912, p. 316. More recently, Scott, *An International Court of Justice*, 1916; *The Status of the International Court of Justice*, 1916; *Une Cour de Justice Internationale*, 1918; *L'évolution d'une juridiction internationale permanente*, 1919.

II

NEW POSTULATES

SUCH was the legal situation and condition of affairs in respect to the endeavour towards progress of international law *before* the outbreak of this war. Does it continue to be the same ?—or have the points of view, the standards necessary in such efforts toward progress, undergone a change in consequence of the war ? There can be no doubt that the situation has suffered a material change. But hardly in the sense that the objectives striven for before this war have ceased to be of value or significance. Quite to the contrary. All that we have considered above worth striving for as necessary for the development of international law remains worth striving for also to-day. The difference then simply lies in the fact that new viewpoints have been added to the old, and that the previous endeavours, after the experiences of this war, can now *not* be regarded as *sufficient*. The foundation, as we have described it above, remains the same, but it requires *more additions* than were considered necessary before the war. It is surely far less difficult to make such additions to-day than it was before the war. For the whole world to-day demands international guarantees. The time has come when the rebuilding of the structure of international law must be begun *earnestly*. New problems have been added to those which before this war were already recognized as needing solution. In my book on the further development of international procedure I have already anticipated such a situation :[1]

> It shall not be denied that further improvements than are here mentioned lie within the realm of possibility, but such further possibility of development presupposes a material change in political ideas, and can only be expected when such changes have taken place. It is not improbable that such changes may at some time in the future take place. The present form of politics, especially European international politics, might in time have to come to an end ; for in

[1] Cf. *Die Fortbildung des Verfahrens in völkerrechtlichen Streitigkeiten.* Ein völkerrechtliches Problem der Gegenwart, speziell im Hinblick auf die Haager Friedenskonferenzen, erörtert von Otfried Nippold, Leipzig, 1907, p. 606.

case our politicians do not themselves come to the realization of the necessity of more intensive co-operation, the Asiatic and American states might see to it that they come to this realization. As soon, however, as the present pathological condition of mutual distrust shall once have been overcome, the possibility of further progress in this field will not be dismissed.

Out of the experiences of this war there have come new tasks and new viewpoints for the further development of international law. In what do these consist ?

I should like to put in the very forefront and give *practical* expression to two points of view in which, above all others, seem to me to be concentrated what this war teaches us.

1. The further development of international law must continue, under *all circumstances, without regard* for those who may obstruct the progress of international law.

2. It is not sufficient to *guarantee* the preservation of the status of law between states, and particularly the application of an international law of procedure, by the creation of legal obligations which are furnished with a mere moral guarantee, but the attempt must be made *to enforce* the observance of international law by the creation of ' real guarantees '.[1]

These two propositions in all probability contain the most important things that this war teaches from the point of view of international law. To turn now to the first one of these propositions.

In those efforts that were directed toward the creation of an international law of universal application before the war, i. e., at the Hague Peace Conferences, we allowed ourselves to be guided by the principle that unanimity, or at least a quasi-unanimity, would be necessary for all resolutions that were passed. Consequently, the veto, by one great power, or by several second-rate and small powers, was sufficient to cause even such progressive steps to fail as had been favoured by an overwhelming majority of states. I cite as an example the scheme for compulsory arbitration which had been outlined by the Second Hague Peace Conference. This scheme had been adopted by a majority of

[1] Holt, in *Recueil de Rapports*, vol. ii, p. 23, distinguishes four steps in this development: (1) The creation of a machinery for international law. (2) The obligation of having recourse to the same. (3) The obligation of the application of force against those who will not use it. (4) The obligation of the use of force against those who will not abide by the decisions of the court. The first stage had already been reached. At the present time there exists on all sides an inclination toward the second, but the third and the fourth stages would now also have to be attained.

thirty-two votes against nine, and three not voting.[1] Accordingly, an effort was made to save the scheme by proposing to make it a subject of a special convention, or by an additional act to give the powers that favoured it the opportunity to acknowledge their submission to the principle of compulsory arbitration in definite cases ; this additional act would therefore have been binding only upon the signatories or those who had acceded to it. But even this could not be passed. It was insisted upon at The Hague that unanimity must be the first principle of the Conference. In particular, the representative of Germany declared that his government would abide by the practices current at all times in international conferences, it would not accept the principle that the majority should decide and that the minority would have to accept this decision. Such a conception, he claimed, would endanger the future of international conferences. The representatives of England and the United States took the opposite view. After a large majority had accepted the scheme, it would not be possible simply to renounce the results attained and again lay aside the question for further examination. The scheme showed that a definite number of nations existed that had sufficiently studied the question to conclude, at once, a general arbitration treaty. The commission had expressed its will by a crushing majority. It would not be possible for the minority to prevent the majority from acting and to cause them to abandon what had been gained. The conference, however, clung to the principle of unanimity, in spite of this.

I do not believe that this practice will prevail in the future.[2] If individual states are unwilling to adjust themselves to the pace of general development of civilization and law, this is not a reason why the remaining states, on their part, should renounce the progress of law. Otherwise there could never be any further progress in human development ; since there will always be individual obstructing states [3] which in their political development have

1 The two powers, Germany and Austria-Hungary, and seven smaller states voted against it.

2 Cf. my article on 'Die Erzwingung des Friedens' in the *Neue Zürcher Zeitung*, November 18, 1916: 'The question must be raised whether *after* this war the same considerations will obtain, or whether those states that are favourably inclined to the progress of law will not then proceed in a more radical manner. Evidence is not wanting to show that they will.' See also my book, *Durch Wahrheit zum Recht*, 1919, p. 82.

3 Strupp, *Neue Probleme des Völkerrechts*, p. 9, recommends to Germany after

made less progress than the others and where views still obtain that may probably have been justified in earlier times but no longer have a place in modern times. Whoever has his eye turned to the past instead of to the future, who still has the views of the Middle Ages and lives in the period when might makes right, will of course not care to hear much about international law. But can this be a reason why the other states should retard the pace of their development? Never! Those who are *seriously* bent upon progress must henceforth proceed without regard for the fact that a few states do not care to keep pace with this development and are left behind. The disadvantages will not accrue to the progressive but to the non-progressive ones.

At the present time it may seem questionable whether one could get acceptance by a Hague Conference of the principle that it is necessary to proceed with the development of law regardless of those who would always resist its progress. But in my opinion this is by no means decisive. To be sure, it is desirable that a step forward in international law should have as nearly as possible a universal character, and it is also desirable that the Hague Conferences will in the future, as they have done in the past, form the centre of the development of international law.[1] But should such development prove unattainable, this fact ought not to retard further progress. What cannot be achieved at The Hague must then be achieved elsewhere. Those states that really desire serious guarantees for international adjudication must simply *organize among themselves* and undertake to further international law on their own account. For through this war it has no doubt become clear on every hand that the day of false deference is forever past. Whoever desires law must know how to proceed so that law actually attains mastery.

At any rate, the opinion that this will be the mode of procedure

the war reservation in place of isolation. But reservation against the progress of law is as little to be sanctioned as isolation.

[1] In this connexion it is to be remembered that at the present time certain governments do not enjoy the confidence of the others. But in spite of all real guarantees confidence will remain the basis of all legal relations. This confidence must, however, be *won*. It will not return overnight. And not until it has been restored will *universal* progress be possible. The necessary condition precedent for confidence is, however, in the first instance, *trustworthiness*. Only when this is again enthroned, will confidence ripen and thereby make possible once more *universal* progress in law.

in the future has also been expressed by others. Thus, Lange writes :[1]

> The rule hitherto observed by Hague Conferences, that unanimity or quasi-unanimity is necessary in order to make it possible for the Conference to accept a treaty, prevented a continuation of the discussion of the terms under which arbitration should be obligatory. It is to be hoped that when the question comes up for action again, it will be taken for granted that such nations as are ready to bind themselves by a general treaty shall be free to come to such an agreement, even though a minority of states should still happen to be opposed to the proposition. To permit a *liberum veto* to gain the upper hand in diplomatic conferences is putting too many and too serious obstacles in the way of international progress. To be sure, certain questions may arise, especially such as pertain to the laws of war, on which quasi-unanimity will be necessary ; the question of the jurisdiction of a court of arbitration and of peaceful procedure in general is surely not one of them. The tragic world conflict which we witness to-day challenges us all to make the most serious endeavours to find a ' better way ' of settling international differences than war with all its horrors.

In the event that, in future Hague Conferences, or in other Congresses that may take the place of these, no agreement can be reached on the subject here under consideration, we may possibly look forward to the formation of a special *League of States* for the purpose of carrying out a progressive programme of international law.[2] As strenuously as I have personally been opposed to treaties of alliance in general, since I regard this latter-day policy of making alliances as one of the prime *general* causes of this war—carefully to be distinguished from the specific *origin* of the same—with just as little hesitation would I welcome the formation of such a league. Political alliances which aro a relic of mediaeval offensive and defensive alliances may, in an age of Hague agreements, of treaties for the safeguarding of commerce and law, be regarded as unnecessary in principle. Whenever they take on the form of special alliances they bear within themselves the seeds of future conflicts, since other states will always be of the opinion that such alliances are aimed at them and that they must therefore prepare themselves against the same. Accordingly, they tend in reality

[1] Lange, *Die amerikanischen Friedensverträge*, 1916, p. 84.

[2] See further discussion below. In *Recueil de Rapports*, vol. i, pp. 192 ff., Schücking expresses the hope that the Hague Conferences may retain the rôle of leadership, holding that there is not the slightest reason for abandoning this incompleted structure, in order, as it were, to erect a new edifice elsewhere. Schücking fails to observe that lack of confidence in those that have broken international covenants might furnish such a reason.

not to preserve peace but to endanger it. If, therefore, this system of alliances could be done away with, and if there could be set up in its stead a juridical organization, the Hague Union of States, a League of States, or something of that type, it would beyond a doubt be a blessing to mankind. To be sure, it would probably prove very difficult in the immediate future to put an end to the political era of separate alliances, with its political systems based on these alliances. Nevertheless, no harm can be done by at least pointing out, even under present conditions, the fundamental superfluousness of this system.[1] Moreover, in spite of all objections, it may be asserted that a transition to a different system of national policy would surely at no time be easier than immediately after a war by which the whole world has been more or less changed. Besides, if success should attend the efforts to reorganize international jurisprudence in the desirable form as mentioned above and give it a position of authority, then it would be by no means improbable that in the course of time special alliances would be relegated to the background.

Be that as it may, no matter what arguments one may advance against the system of separate alliances and the whole policy of the last few decades of forming alliances, these arguments in no wise apply as against a league of states which puts forward as its programme the development and safeguarding of international jurisprudence, and which would, therefore, simply be a legal organization. Any scruples that one might have would be all the less valid, since it would doubtless tend by its very

[1] In his message to the Senate of January 22, 1917, President Wilson has said: 'I am proposing that all nations henceforth avoid entangling alliances which would draw them into competitions of power, catch them in a net of intrigue and selfish rivalry, and disturb their own affairs with influences intruded from without. There is no entangling alliance in a concert of power. When all unite to act in the same sense and with the same purpose, all act in the common interest and are free to live their own lives under a common protection.' Ed. Bernstein demands 'unceasing labour at the task of solidifying the nations by a setting aside of all special alliances and all exclusively politico-commercial coalitions, as well as educating the people to a complete understanding of the fact that just as in the inner life of states, so also in the relations of nations one to another, the removal of everything that savours of the doctrine that might is right and the setting up of a unified system of justice for all, not only guarantees the highest moral civilization but also the greatest material welfare.' Cf. *Denkschrift über die Grundlagen eines dauerhaften Friedensvertrags*, p. 10, as well as my article 'Keine Bündnisverträge mehr!' in the *Blätter für zwischenstaatliche Organisation*, March 1915. Of a different opinion is Strupp, *Neue Probleme des Völkerrechts*, p. 7.

nature to erect a confederacy of states, as nearly *universal* as possible and with admission free to all those that seriously desired to advance the cause of legal progress. In fact, this latter would have to be made the unconditional prerequisite for admission. Moreover, the conditions necessary for participating in such a league would have to be of such a character that, as a matter of fact, *only* such states would and could become members as were bitterly in earnest about having juridical thinking practically applied in the life of a people, no less than between the states.

It must not be forgotten, as above intimated, that such a league may prove the only means whereby our first postulate can be realized and thus the way paved for further progress. Moreover, this seemingly circuitous method must alarm us the less, inasmuch as such an alliance would obviously be so attractive that it would not only in its practical significance be in no wise inferior to the Hague Conferences, but would in the end perhaps lead back to the same again. Whether the method of realizing our postulate be the one or the other, whether the one or the other seem the more nearly perfect, the main thing is that we seek to realize this postulate.

Our second postulate demands that after this war we be no longer content with *ensuring* the observance of international law, but that real guarantees be created; in other words, that the observance of the same be *enforced*. That is, instead of mere safety regulations, some form of *coercive measures* must be devised.

I confess that the conviction of the necessity of such coercive measures was virtually wrung from me, so opposed is it to my whole former conception of international law. I would still prefer that there were in fact no need of such coercive measures in international jurisprudence. But this war has been a severe lesson, and accordingly many views have had to go absolutely by the board. Why should it then be different in the case of international law alone?

Before this war, i.e. in a normal state of law, or in times of peace, we recognized a sufficient guarantee in the setting up of legal norms. Often we have contented ourselves with mere recommendations or with the recognition of definite moral obligations; whenever we succeeded in establishing a real legal duty or a judicial obligation then we believed that we had done and obtained everything that was necessary. To establish *legal obligations* seemed the very acme of development. To demand further guarantees or sanctions over and above this seemed to most people, both in doctrine and practice, more or less superfluous. The fact that the guarantees with which such a judicial obligation in international law are invested were simply of a moral nature made no difference. We assumed that the modern civilized state deserved confidence; that it would observe its treaty obligations.[1]

This also was my attitude before this war. Whenever the question was raised whether the execution of an arbitral decision had to be guaranteed by special sanctions, I have explained that in international law the execution of a decision against a state could be left to that state; that the state had to be trusted, as a subject of international law, loyally and faithfully to perform its obligations as such.

Whoever is not willing to impose this confidence in a state cannot believe in such a thing as international law. Whenever I hear complaints about the lack of executive power in international law, I cannot help feeling that those who utter these complaints must really at heart have a very low opinion of the moral power and the moral value of law in general, and this is a regrettable circumstance. Whoever can picture to himself law with only a straight jacket ready at hand has a very poor appreciation of the inner power of law. For him it would be difficult indeed to enter into the spirit of international law. On the other hand, it may be asserted that if any field of law offers one the opportunity of convincing himself of the actual moral power of law, it is unquestionably international law, and therein especially the chapter on the execution of the arbitral sentence. Better than in any other phase of international law may one here be convinced of the power that *law as such*, the plighted word, can operate without coercion and without any special judicial agency.[2] This observation, which is justified by abundant historical evidence, raises international law to a lofty position, in my opinion far above any other field of law, in spite of the organic coercive sanctions peculiar to them. For what is the moral significance of obeying a legal obligation that results merely from the pressure of a coercive agency? The history of international law, and particularly that of cases settled by arbitration, offers us, indeed, a most encouraging

[1] Lammasch, 'Vertragstreue im Völkerrecht?' in the *Oesterreichische Zeitschrift für öffentliches Recht*, rightly emphasizes that in international law the sacred name of justice must not be blasphemed, that the right under certain circumstances to break a treaty must not be recognized. Recognition of such a right would tempt nations to toy with fidelity to treaty obligations.

[2] Cf. especially the article by Egger, 'Die Macht der Rechtsidee', in *Wissen und Leben*, August 1, 1916. Egger points out that the power of the idea is revealed to us most vividly by war itself.

chapter. It teaches us that never yet has a state unlawfully refused to accept the arbitral award. This is probably the best proof that the present organization of international law in this direction is a sufficient one, but it is also an additional reason why the development of international law need *not* be replaced *along this line* unless one should wish to set up a system of international law on an entirely different basis than that on which the present structure rests. In view of the fact that those who are the subjects of international law submit without hesitation to the power of international law recognized by them, it often seems quite frivolous that the possibility of non-observance of an arbitral decision is discussed again and again quite unnecessarily in the literature of international law. Just as if one wished to put this to the conscience of the states instead of simply reckoning with the loyal and faithful execution of the decision as with a given fact, in accordance with theory and practice. By so doing one makes civilized states and governments worse than they really are. No civilized state, no member of the community of international law, will to-day refuse to accept so notorious a legal obligation as is obedience to an arbitral decision that has been pronounced. Why will one not be content with this fact ? [1]

That was written *before* this war! The experiences we have had since then have of necessity shaken this faith to a certain extent.[2] The war has brought us face to face with the relentless fact that international treaties have been broken. On the occasion of the violation of the neutrality of Belgium, such a treaty was even described as a 'scrap of paper'. This occurrence is fortunately without precedent in the history of international law and it is to be hoped that it will remain the only one of its kind. But faith in the moral power of international law has thereby suffered a shock from which the civilized world will not very quickly recover. This enables us to understand why, to-day, the call for more real sanctions for the international legal order has been heard on every hand.

I do not believe that this call dare be ignored. It is the expression of a conviction universally shared at the present time by the whole civilized world, and the science of international law must not presume to set itself up against it. To be sure, I am of the opinion, as I have already explained above, that by way of reaction against the contempt for international law which has come to light in this war, and for which the press is largely to blame, after this war there will presumably come a great increase of appreciation of international law.[3] But this

[1] Cf. *Fortbildung*, pp. 375 ff.
[2] Cf., for example, Klein, *Die Kulturgemeinschaft der Völker nach dem Kriege*, 1915, pp. 50, 74.
[3] Cf. also my article in the *Neue Zürcher Zeitung* of November 25, 1916.

prospect cannot relieve us of the necessity of raising the question, in what way international law can be invested with still *further guarantees* which are not merely of a moral nature but which also partake of the character of *real sanctions.* For the basis of international law has hitherto been *confidence,* and unfortunately there can be no doubt that at the present time this confidence is lacking. But where confidence is lacking, international law can only be founded on *compulsion.* This is the sad result of this war !

But of what would such ' real guarantees ' have to consist ? In what way can one hope to *enforce* observance of international law ? In this connexion it will have to be emphasized that these new guarantees naturally must rest upon the basis of *law.* This emphasis is necessary because there are, unfortunately, in some countries, even at the present day, a number of people whose mode of thought is so one-sided and so dominated by military suggestions that they believe that securities, guarantees for the preservation of peace conditions and a legal status, can be derived from military conquests. Among the ' aims of war ', the idea which on closer analysis cannot be called other than foolish still plays among many people a very important rôle, namely, that one can contribute to the maintenance and securing of peace by a change in the geographical boundaries between the states. In view of present-day technique, is not such a mode of thought truly childish ? Are there any boundaries at all, or fortified places, that are able to hold out unconditionally against modern artillery and other modern technical contrivances ? This whole mentality, which even to-day believes that guarantees can be secured by the extension of boundaries or the acquisition of strategic places, can under present conditions be described only as pathological, as an anachronism. As above stated, it is the result of suggestions emanating from military circles or an unthinking press and utterly out of date.[1] If one were to follow

[1] As an example of this militaristic mentality I cite here from the speech which the Supreme Court Councillor, Peters, delivered before the Juristic Society in Leipzig on October 28, 1914, the words in which he expresses the view that no dependence can be placed on treaties made solely under the sanctions of international law : ' Therefore when that time shall come, in the event of final victory, to fix those conditions for the conclusion of a peace that we regard as indispensable for safeguarding the German Fatherland against a surprise attack, such as the present one, we shall not dare to be content with paper promises, with mere promises and guarantees even in the most solemn treaties. In so far as we need

the idea of a guarantee by the protection of the boundary to its logical conclusion, one would be obliged constantly to push these

any security we shall rather have to depend *on the strong occupation* on all sides of the territories we now have and shall always keep in our possession. Only strong, firmly built ramparts that defy all efforts to take them can protect us against a return of the floods with which those who envied and hated us thought to destroy the German Empire. But how these ramparts are to be erected should be determined neither by so-called general principles nor by any other considerations except those based solely upon our own interest in a happy future for our Fatherland, upon its stability, its growth, and prosperity.' This is only *one* example of the mentality of whole circles of people. In such language the spirit of law does not speak, but rather what must be designated the spirit of militarism. In similar vein are countless pronunciamentos, especially in Germany. Thus the central committee of the *National Liberal Party* expresses its conviction 'that only an extension of the boundaries by land and sea of the German dominions in the east and in the west and overseas can secure for the German people the necessary real guarantees for its military, political, and economic salvation.' I pass over in this connexion the pronouncements of the 'Independent Committee for a German Peace', of the 'Memorial of the Six Economic Unions' which represent German steel and allied industries, of the declarations of the 'Pan-Germanic Union', of the 'German Colonial Society', &c., since they all agree in this one-sided conception. The German historians Brandenburg, Schäfer, Meinecke, Marcks, &c., all take exactly the same position. Thus the Leipzig historian Brandenburg has expressed himself against the so-called international securities from which many expect the prevention of the recurrence of war. The best measure of security was and will continue to be the extension of the territorial domain in the west and in the east. Similarly Meinecke expressed himself in *Das grössere Deutschland*. In the *Magdeburgische Zeitung* of April 2, 1915, the guarantee is spoken of as follows: 'A people in the highest state of development, ever prepared for war, which also promises the richest rewards in peace, "a people in arms" is the best, indeed the only, assurance of peace in the world; any other assurance of a long enduring peace is theoretically not possible; 'peace can only be assured by an overwhelming might that is guided by an equally strong consciousness of its responsibility to the cause of justice and civilization on the earth. This might can only exist and continually reside in a people which in all its parts is filled with the strictest consciousness of its obligation toward itself and mankind, which knows its great mission and stakes everything on being constantly worthy of and equal to it. This lofty task is now incumbent upon the German people. They will be equal to it if they keep themselves in prime physical, intellectual, and moral condition for defence in this war.' The *Hamburger Nachrichten* of February 15 discusses 'Bismarck und das Wesen der realen Garantien': 'Paper agreements between two peoples have hitherto in the world's history been valid only so long as they did not prove a hindrance to anything that was vital to either one of the interested parties, and obligations were imposed as much as possible on the other party. For the impelling force of treaties is egoism and not altruism; loyalty and fidelity in the intercourse of nations have always constituted a more or less uncertain ground.' Bismarck had given definite expression to this thought, that treaties never could be real securities, never 'real guarantees', that these would have to be territorial in their nature. Abundant material on this subject is to be found in the work by Grumbach, entitled *Das annexionistische Deutschland*, 1917. It is probably not saying too much to characterize such a mentality as one-sided militarism. It is well known that the conception here described has in Germany made inroads even in social democratic circles, and it is therefore not going too far to designate it as the *prevailing* one in Germany to-day. In contrast with this it is interesting to note that the *Bayerische Staatszeitung* of July 18, 1916, names 'greed, the boundaries farther and farther without, in fact, ever finding a place to stop. Extensions of domain are, in reality, not in the interests of peace and law but solely in the interests of the imperialistic desires for power.[1] And at the same time these peculiar logicians who prate about protecting the boundary never once think what feelings must be aroused on the other side by every territorial conquest; that instead of guarantees for the preserva-

desire for the possession of more land, even if it belongs to another, the demand for riches, power, and prestige in the world' as the chief cause of wars, and excludes Germany alone from this 'mania for more territory'. On this point cf. also the article 'Politische und militärische Grenzen' by Gädke in the *Bochumer Volksblatt* of December 17, 1915. Gädke calls those boundaries which correspond most nearly to the needs of protection of a state against the assaults of hostile neighbours military or natural boundaries: 'One would suppose that throughout the history of the world the efforts of the nations had been directed primarily to the gaining of natural boundaries behind whose shelter they could further their own development in peace and realize their national ideas. As a matter of fact history shows us that exactly the opposite has been the case. With a certain frivolity, or let us rather say with conscious intent, nations throw away the armour that nature has placed about them and seek to advance beyond it into the domain of their neighbours as far as their political or military superiority allows, and they are indifferent as to whether in this way better or worse boundaries be found.' Natural boundaries have never been able to check the needs for expansion of political states. 'It will always be found that the warlike clash of the states of the earth has never been for boundaries, but in reality for the acquisition of territory. Ever since there have been bloody wars, their cause has never been a desire to find in the geographical configuration of the boundaries a better protection for a people, but rather the desire for the extension of power, the impulse to gain lands and people, to extend the domain of the state. The "natural" boundary was never more than a pretext, a diplomatic feint to call greed by a fairer name in order to conceal it by alleging a cause that could be supported by moral considerations.' In the *Neue Zürcher Zeitung* of January 31, 1917, R. Said-Ruete very properly warns of the danger of such greedy imperialists. We are dealing here, in fact, *not with the creation of* '*real guarantees*' in the interests of peace but, and this is not known by many people, *with imperialism*, which means the *very opposite of such a guarantee.* But those critics that are biased by the militaristic mode of thought, and besides are tainted with war psychosis, unfortunately do not admit this.

[1] In *Wissen und Leben* of January 1, 1917, the author of *J'accuse* remarks: 'The idea of the buffer state, of the military security of the boundary, is an old game of the oldest style. The idea of a judicial organization of the nations is a new game of the newest style. A union of the two modes of thought is logically impossible. A simultaneous attainment of the desires of both is practically impossible. The idea of the judicial organization of the states of Europe will make all the buffer states superfluous. That is the only object and purpose of such an organization. Law is to be the buffer which is to prevent a coming to blows and make all material buffetings unnecessary.' Elsner also justly emphasizes, in *Jedem das Seine*, 1915, p. 10, that *imperialism*, which partly for industrial, partly for national reasons, and in part also for the mere sake of power, includes the subjugation and violent annexation of foreign territories in its programme, is the very opposite of the community of interest idea which the legal organization demands. Commercial points of vantage for gaining world markets could also be obtained by treaty. The prosperity and welfare of a state does not depend upon its position as a world power.

tion of peace being created on the contrary peace is directly endangered.[1]

By 'real guarantees', therefore, must be meant something other than that which the military castes in their short-sightedness have been wont to understand by that phrase from time immemorial, and which they would now like to transfer automatically to present conditions. The 'real guarantees' must, and on this point there can be no doubt, be *juridical* in their nature.

Now if we mean to create guarantees on a foundation of law, we must of necessity start from the thought, from the fact of the *solidarity* of international law. The solidarity which is founded on the community of the interests of the states is the basis of modern international law.[2] Because this international law serves common interests, it is also able, in spite of all obstacles, to develop into real law in the full meaning of the term and to perform new tasks in the life of the nations that will ultimately make possible the reign of law. I have shown above that the solidarity of international law will in the future have to document itself above all on the activity of third, nonparticipating states, on an activity tending to serve justice and establish peace. The whole procedure of international law is founded upon the idea of this solidarity. The co-operation of third states not only enters into the case in every action in international law procedure; but over and above this, as we have seen, third states can act efficaciously in getting contesting parties to apply the legal remedies of international law. That which makes them competent to do this, which on principle gives them authority and imposes the duty upon them, is nothing else than the fact of the solidarity of interests.

One will, therefore, have to start out from this fact if it is a question of winning further guarantees for the use of international law procedure. This is true of the new 'real' guarantees to be created no less than of the moral and legal guarantees to which recourse was had before the outbreak of this war. The starting-point for all future progress in international law will always be the thought of this solidarity. It is this thought,

[1] Cf. the *Denkschrift über die Grundlagen eines dauerhaften Friedensvertrags*, pp. 25 ff.

[2] For a more detailed discussion, see *Fortbildung*, pp. 35 ff. Cf. also Alvarez, *loc. cit.*, p. 113.

therefore, for which, above all other things, there must be provided a comprehensible expression and a comprehensible form in the coming legal institutions.[1] All legal institutes that may be called into existence in order to secure guarantees for international jurisprudence will always derive their inner justification from the community of interests of the participating states.[2]

> The solidarity of the international community . . . must in the course of time express itself unconditionally on this point, that this community recognizes legal duties as against all quarrelling and wrong doing among the nations and executes these obligations in a practical way.

Thus I wrote as long as ten years ago,[3] but what I said then is as valid to-day as ever and even far more so than at that time. The juridical duties which the community is to recognize and practice must no longer consist merely as to-day in reminding the contending parties of their obligations, but of *compelling* them to fulfil the same. Only then shall we be able to speak of the presence of ‘ real ’ juridical sanctions when the community of states shall have recognized that it is morally bound to intervene in all cases where contending states endeavour to avoid the procedure laid down by international law, by making war or opening hostilities without first having had recourse to such procedure.

[1] Under this point of view the motives which our Swiss Federal Council gave for declining, as was comprehensible for material reasons, a petition to issue a protest against deportations from Belgium go perhaps a little too far. It is claimed in this connexion that the Hague Conventions had indeed created mutual obligations among the states, but they had not established a solidarity between all contracting parties in the sense that the violation of one state obligated other states to oppose this violation, or, at least, to protest against it. From the standpoint of the law as it now is, and from previous practice, the decision of the Federal Council can be approved ; and yet the question may be raised whether it was called upon to lay down such a far-reaching fundamental reason for its action. For if this motivation *de lege lata* be ever so correct, yet it is opposed to what the coming development of international law obviously will bring with it, and it was in my opinion in no wise called upon, under the circumstances, to emphasize the failure of the solidarity in such a fundamental way. If this solidarity does not yet make itself practically felt to-day, it may do so to-morrow ; and it would therefore have been more prudent not to express oneself so apodictically on this point, all the more so since, as will presently be shown, there is also *a strengthened protection of neutrality* in the recognition of the solidarity. Cf. my article ‘ Der grundsätzliche Standpunkt für die völkerrechtliche Betrachtung ’, in *Wissen und Leben*, July 1, 1916, as well as pp. 47 and 50, below.

[2] In the *Deutsche Revue* of October 1916, Prince Wrede writes : ‘ International law agreements are to serve the needs of all. It is obvious that no great finality can be attained so long as each one of the contracting parties enters the council chamber with the fixed intention of gobbling up some special advantage for himself.’

[3] Cf. *Fortbildung*, p. 499.

Two things then have been gained by the discussion thus far. First, *the basic principle* out of which the 'real guarantees' for the application of the international law procedure must develop, that is, the *solidarity* of international law; and, secondly, the *instance* from which the practical application of the guarantees to be created will have to proceed; this instance is what I have briefly designated '*community of states*'.[1] Such a community may be understood in a narrower or a broader sense. In the case in hand we would naturally prefer to apply it in the broader sense. The real guarantees should then apply, in an ideal case, to *all* the states that were united in the community of international law. This community of states has found its external expression primarily in the Hague Peace Conferences. One could then refer to *the Hague Community of States*, that is, to all those states that dwell together in a legal community under the authority of the Hague Conventions, as that instance which not only would have to incorporate the fact of the solidarity of international law but also lend it visible expression by guarding against infraction of the norms of international law and bringing the offender to account.

But however fortunate it would be if one were to see such a progressive step taken at The Hague, the attainment of such a goal still seems remote to-day.[2] It will perhaps be as much as can be expected if the actual legal obligations for the application of international law procedure, as mentioned above, can be codified at The Hague within a reasonable time. To expect beyond this that the Hague Conference powers will succeed to such an extent as to compel, in case of necessity, the performance of these obligations would perhaps be giving oneself over to a certain extent to Utopian hopes; for it would no doubt become evident that the resistance which would become unmistakably noticeable within so large a community of states, in the face of so far reaching a postulate, had been greatly under-estimated. The prospect that these hoped-for 'real guarantees' will find their prime support in the Hague Community of States appears

[1] See also pp. 31 ff., above.

[2] Cf., for example, the scruples in Hooper, *The Wider Outlook Beyond the World War*, p. 26, 1915. Cf. further, Unwin, 'A League of States', in the *Recueil de Rapports*, vol. i, p. 212; Williams, 'A League of Nations', *ibid.*, p. 229; and Woolf, 'The International Authority and the Prevention of War', in *The New Statesman*, London, July 10 and 17, 1915

therefore not very strong, even though this hope ought not to be rejected without further consideration.

Besides the Hague Community of States, *the congress of the states concluding the peace* might itself ultimately constitute that instance which has to undertake the practical application of the coercive measures of international law. Perhaps this possibility is also the greatest probability, provided that there be a real peace conference—something which can naturally not be foreseen.[1]

In case, however, there should be neither a peace congress nor the community of all the Hague States, then a narrower meaning will probably have to be assigned to the phrase, 'community of States'. I have explained above that we will possibly have to get used to the thought of the formation of a special *league of states* in which all those states that accept as their task the achievement of a progressive programme of international law would be united. In fact, I believe that especially the postulate regarding the enforcement of the norms of international law will only be able to be realized, at least for the present, through such a league. Unseeing provincials would seek to make such a radical step as illusory as possible. Such a revolutionary change can obviously only be introduced between such states as are firmly decided to sacrifice all in order to realize this idea. But there is no doubt that there are states to-day that have this will and the decision to make it efficacious. It is this fact that divests the thought of its Utopian character and gives promise of the prospect of realizing it.[2]

Thus one may in all seriousness reckon on the probability that

[1] Cf. the *Denkschrift über die Grundlagen eines dauerhaften Friedensvertrags*, pp. 9, 50.

[2] Cf. also Dickinson, *After the War*, 1915, p. 25, who points to the utterances of Asquith, Grey, &c., and remarks: 'An idea thus endorsed not only by pacifists and thinkers but by practical statesmen is worth serious consideration.' In favour of such a league, see also Hooper, *The Wider Outlook Beyond the World War*, 1915, p. 25, who emphasizes the democratic character of such a league: 'If an influential group of states should voluntarily resign the supposed right to making war on one another, and at the same time agree that no one of them would carry on military operations outside its own territory without the consent of the others, and that the defence of their respective territories should be a common duty, this would probably secure the peace of the world in the end.' Further, Unwin, *loc. cit.*, p. 227: 'A treaty shall be made as soon as possible whereby as many states as are willing to combine for the purpose shall form a league binding themselves to use peaceful methods for dealing with all disputes arising among them.'

the desired real guarantees on a basis of law will be actually found after this war. However, one must be content with the probability that this step will at first be possible of realization only within a smaller group. But this naturally does not at all exclude a gradual extension to a larger group of states. We have already discussed above the conditions under which such an alliance would have to be formed.

That the creation of real 'sanctions' for international law might presumably have as a necessary condition precedent the formation of a special league of states is by no means a new thought. On the other hand, it has before this been pointed out.[1] To be sure, former schemes had in view, for the most part, not so much the securing or enforcing of the *application* of international law procedure as the *execution* of it, and especially of the arbitral decision. The proposals of former years aim for the most part at the creation of an international court whose judgements could be forcibly executed. But it was also realized that such a compulsory execution of sentence could only be carried into effect within the bounds of some confederation of states.

And so it is in fact. As soon as one arrives at the point where an *organic coercive protection* of any sort is to be introduced into international law, there is at once the *need of a special organization*. This can only be in some sort of federation of states, an alliance, league, or whatever name you may wish to give it. The postulate of force in international law necessarily points to an organization of states.[2]

It must be admitted that the idea of such an organization of states has been very much abused. This circumstance constrains me to linger over the theme. The kernel of countless schemes for an organization of states is the idea of a more or less *universal federation of states*. Many people have, indeed, before this war dreamed of a world league of states or even of a world federation. This idea has been rejected, even on the part of pacifists, as being all too extensive.[3] I cannot at this point review

[1] Cf. the literature in *Fortbildung*, p. 378.

[2] Fried recommends above all other organizations a '*co-operative Europe*'. Cf. especially his article entitled 'Die internationale Kooperation als Grundlage einer internationalen Rechtspflege' in the *Recueil de Rapports*, vol. i, p. 167. See further *Denkschrift über die Grundlagen eines dauerhaften Friedensvertrags*, p. 23.

[3] Cf. on this point Fried, *Handbuch der Friedensbewegung*, 2nd Edition, vol. i, p. 114; *Die Forderung des Pazifismus*, p. 14. Cf. further my *Vorfragen des*

the countless schemes for a universal league of states that have appeared *before* this war.[1]

Since the outbreak of the present war schemes for an organization of states have come forward as numerous as the sands of the sea. However, in spite of this, it cannot be said that the problem is much nearer solution by reason of them. The older schemes before the war were distinguished, in part, by much greater thoroughness than many creations of the war-literature, which often bear closely the earmarks of dilettantism.[2] Some

Völkerrechts, p. 41, as well as my essay in the *Politisches Jahrbuch der schweizerischen Eidgenossenschaft*, 1914, p. 370.

[1] Out of the pertinent literature let here be recalled the striking treatises of Count Kamarowsky, of Pasquale Fiore, Revon, Mérignhac, Dreyfus, Descamps, Leone Levi, Dudley-Field, Laveleye, Darby, Dumas, Schlieff, Schücking, &c.

[2] [The above naturally only applies to the first years of the war. The problem of the League of Nations was pushed into the foreground only after the publication of the German edition of this book.] Some citations on the war literature of that time, covering the problem of a federation of states, can be found in the *Denkschrift über die Grundlagen eines dauerhaften Friedensvertrags*, p. 19. Cf. also Van Houten, 'Staatengemeinschaft', in *Wissen und Leben* of October 1, 1916. See further Alvarez, *La grande guerre européenne et la neutralité du Chili*, 1915, pp. 82 ff.; and especially Paul Otlet, who, in *La fin de la guerre, traité de paix générale basé sur une charte mondiale déclarant les droits de l'humanité et organisant la Confédération des États*, 1915, sets up a scheme for a league of the states of the world, or rather a world confederation. See also his other work, *Les problèmes internationaux et la guerre*, in which he gives a birdseye view of the status of the international problems in general. There may also be found numerous but not exhaustive references. On pages 340 ff. Otlet takes up the new international law. He would like to see international law reconstructed *ab ovo* on the basis of a world law to be enacted by a congress and a parliament which is to meet periodically. In regard to the sanctions he remarks, 'The new law will organize the sanctions. It will realize the coexistence and union of force and law.' 'Justice without force', Pascal has already said, 'is powerless; force without justice tyrannical; justice without force is a contradiction because there will always be wrongdoers; force without justice is a culprit. It is necessary, therefore, to bring together justice and force, and to this end make what is just, strong, and what is strong, just.' 'A collective force of sanction will be put at the service of peace and justice. The sanction will no longer be something theoretical, vague, purely moral. Its ultimate form will be the threat of armed intervention, then of war, but of war conducted by all against the recalcitrants. After the disaster of this war, this threat will be only of such a nature as to act as a restraining force, for no longer will any one be disposed to consider it as a merry, happy, or desirable thing.' Otlet demands further 'A criminal international law, declaring certain grievous offences against this law a crime against the society of nations. . . . Hereafter, there will have to be a public and solemn trial of the guilty before a European tribunal followed by their capital execution.' Besides Otlet, the work of the Chinese Tchéou-Weï deserves special attention, *Essai sur l'organisation juridique de la Société internationale*, 1917. This essay not only contains a striking review of the problem up to date, but he also presents a peculiar scheme of his own for the realization of which he looks to the Third Hague Peace Conference. In it he demands an international organization and, what is more, an 'international legislative power' (International Parliament), an 'international judicial power' (International Tribunal), and 'international executive power' (adminis-

of the newest proposals which seem to deserve special consideration will be mentioned later. If I here refer to the subject at all, it is, in part, in order to emphasize the fact that the thought of an alliance of states which should seek to compel the application of an international law procedure (and are, therefore, simply striving for a juridical organization) has, in itself, nothing in common with the grandiose schemes for a political world confederation. But it is to be observed that every step in the direction of interstate organization can, and presumably will, lead to further steps in the same direction.

I should here also like to mention the scheme for the formation of an *alliance between the neutral states.*[1] The war has made many a project realizable to-day to which we would otherwise only have come after long years. Thus it is to-day already a fact that neutrals co-operate with one another; indeed, there is in many places a serious tendency toward an actual union between them. But in this movement two quite different objects are kept in view, according as one is bent on universal interests or specifically neutral interests. Whether a league of neutral states in one or the other sense will come into existence within a reasonable time I shall not venture to judge. I do not care to attempt prophecy. But if a league of states should be organized for enforcing the observance of international law, and especially the application of the procedure of the same, then presumably the present neutrals would join such a league. Such a league would therefore in form and purpose be nothing other than a veritable league of neutrals in the broader sense of this term. It would serve the true interests of *all neutrals* in the narrower and in the broader sense, and to that extent perhaps make a special league of specific neutrals superfluous. Since it would simply serve the ends of *law* and would derive its strength from the basic principle of international law, namely, the *solidarity* of the interests of the participating states, such

tration and international public forces). Be it noticed also that in Holland a special committee called 'The European Federation of States' has been formed.

[1] On the problem of an alliance of neutrals, Bornhak thus expresses himself in *Der Wandel des Völkerrechts*, 1916, p. 101: 'A league of neutrals against the overthrow of international law would even yet be within the realms of possibility. To be sure, it is made more difficult of realization because all the great powers of Europe are involved in the war.' The question of such a league would naturally not come up until *after* the war.

a league of states would therefore in fact, in the world of states, be naught else than 'a league of neutral states'.

Whether, in addition to such a universal league, there would also be formed a league of specifically neutral states for the preservation of *specifically neutral interests* can, as stated, not as yet be foreseen.[1] The solidarity of the interests of neutrals is certainly much more obvious than ever before.

In any case, to-day more than ever before, the words of Barclay may be recalled :

> Neutrality is no longer a passive situation. The interests of neutrals are to-day the interests of the majority, consequently of the more powerful. The time will come, and perhaps soon, when neutrals will combine against belligerents and invest them with a sanitary cordon just as one checks plagues and fires.[2]

But it should not be forgotten to-day that Christian Wolff, in his *Jus Gentium*, 1749, took the view that every state was bound to render assistance to every other that conducted a *just* war, whereas no state dare support a state whose war was *unjust*. The right to remain neutral was, therefore, according to this view limited to those cases where the justness of a war was doubtful. Lammasch is right when he says that this is the most nearly perfect ethical conception of the rights and obligations of neutrals.[3] Even though neutrality were not absolutely abandoned, yet there would be a very careful distinction between the obligations of a neutral as against one who wages a just war on the one hand and one who wages an unjust one on the other.

Lammasch is of the opinion that neutrals will more and more refuse to conceive of their rôle as a purely passive one and to permit themselves to be doomed to inactivity ; that they will rather claim to exert an influence, not only on the form of law in war, but even on the exercise of the *right to make war*. The more firmly and fundamentally a state were determined in future wars to remain neutral, so much the more important would a clearer definition of the *right to neutrality* become for it. Doubtless also in the future many states would decide to abstain from

[1] The Spanish Government has recently manifested a disposition in favour of such an undertaking. In Scandinavia there is also said to have been a movement in this direction.

[2] Barclay, in the *Annuaire de l'Institut de droit international*, 1904, p. 35.

[3] Lammasch, 'Das Mediationsrecht der Neutralen', in the *Oesterreichische Zeitschrift für öffentliches Recht*, 1915, p. 222, and Lammasch, 'Der Beruf der Neutralen', in the *Internationale Rundschau* of June 1915.

the wars of others, not merely by deciding as each case presented itself, but rather they would, once for all, make it an abiding rule or programme of their governments. Out of such a 'self-neutralization', however, obligations would rest upon other powers only if they recognized such duties of neutrality.[1] But even in spite of this the one-sided published decision of a state to remain perpetually neutral would be significant. Lammasch thinks that the efforts of neutral countries like Switzerland, Holland, and the Scandinavian countries to carry out a peace policy would, as each case arises, gain new adherents in states that wished in the given case to remain neutral. Likewise many of those powers now engaged in war would not remain aloof from such a league of neutrals.

Lammasch comes in this way to a league of neutrals that corresponds approximately to the one I have outlined above, and which the league of peace to be founded would have to realize. But he thinks that those states that are committed to perpetual neutrality would form the kernel of such a league. It can certainly be said that these states ought to form the base of such a league of peace. At any rate, I proceed from the assumption that *all* members of the league of peace, not merely the perpetual neutrals, would wish a lasting peace and would also endeavour to keep it. Therewith the element of a perpetual neutrality within such a league would lose its practical significance.[2]

[1] Lammasch thinks that this recognition will in the future meet with still greater obstacles than hitherto, for political reasons. To the extent that a league of peace for the enforcement of international law be formed, to that extent doubtless such new neutralizations as are not historical growths would lose in practical force. Compare on this question my treatise on 'Das Völkerrecht und der jetzige Krieg', in the *Politisches Jahrbuch*, 1914, pp. 374 ff., as well as the essay printed in the Appendix of the German edition of this work, pp. 250 ff.

[2] In the *Internationale Rundschau, loc. cit.*, Lammasch writes: 'If the states that are seriously bent on remaining neutral in future wars unite into a permanent league, if they in common offer their mediation and likewise unitedly threaten the consequences attendant upon a refusal of their offer, this league would represent a power so great that even the mightiest would hardly care to provoke its opposition.' Lammasch is not wrong in remarking that in such a league of neutrality, unarmed but capable of arming under certain conditions, *would perhaps be found also a more effective security for the preservation of the neutrality of its members than in the former treaties of guarantee.* Such a league might form the cornerstone for the juridically ordered structure of a society of states. The members of the league might conclude far-reaching arbitration treaties with one another and in many other ways grant each other mutual advantages, and in this way strengthen the bonds that united them. The main objective of the league would be the forestalling of wars between the powers by the means described.

What Lammasch says of his league of neutrals might also be applied at least in part to a league of peace. He is of the opinion that the league would be powerful and consist of many members, and if it should come forward united and resolved, even the mightiest could not deny it the privilege of making its desires known. To be sure, Lammasch has here in view merely *collective mediation*, whereas the aims of a league of peace would naturally have to be more far reaching. But for this right to mediate Lammasch proposes a further development that might likewise be accepted by the league of peace in the case of collective mediation; it might, in fact, without further question be appropriately made part of its programme. He thinks that the party refusing to listen to an offer to mediate thereby violates its duty to the powers that have a right to mediate. It could accept or reject the advice; but to give it a hearing is its duty.

If a party violates this duty, then those having a right to offer to mediate would have the right to consider the war that resulted from said party's premature and irregular entrance into it as *bellum nec justum nec pium*, and to treat this party less favourably than the opposing party, and, even after the conclusion of the war, to demand compensation for all the harm that had accrued to it by reason of the war. The powers that are concerned about keeping the peace, that wish in their own interests and in the interests of humanity in general to avoid its sufferings, are justified in declaring to both parties desiring war, simultaneously with their offer of mediation, that they will grant their nationals the right to support that party which is ready within a suitable time to listen to their offer of mediation; and that they will, on the other hand, forbid their subjects on pain of punishment to support the party that declines such mediation or prematurely breaks it off.... The mediators may see to it that both parties will accept mediation under these conditions by making as effective an announcement as possible of the differentiated treatment to be accorded to the warring parties in the event of one or the other parties not accepting mediation.

The advantages of preparation and of an immediate entrance upon war would in this case be overbalanced by the disadvantage of the support that would in this way be offered the opponent. As to *which* party the neutrals should permit their subjects to support, the criterion would in this matter be perfectly clear in contrast to the proposal of Christian Wolff. Lammasch thinks that perhaps the objection will be raised that the proposal, instead of guarding neutrals against the indirect losses of war, will expose them to the danger of becoming involved in the war. But this objection fails, if the offer of mediation under the proposed sanction issue from a league of neutrals which is numerous, powerful, mighty, and united. The total power of the states interested in the preservation of peace would always be greater than that of one of the two powers ready to wage a war.

Nobody, be he ever so powerful, will wish to engage so many accessory enemies in addition to the power against whom he is eager to wage war.

As a further means of strengthening the force of the offer to mediate, Lammasch recommends the declaration that neutrals shall hold the party declining mediation or prematurely breaking off negotiations accountable for all direct and indirect injuries that may accrue to them and their subjects in the course of the *bellum iniustum impiumque* through the operations of both parties to the war.

Naturally this threat would also presuppose the firm resolve and the power of the league to secure such satisfaction.

It would have to consist of a sufficiently large number of sufficiently powerful states.

It will be easily seen that the line of argument which Lammasch here pursues is in the direction of the postulates I have laid down for the development of international law. If one merely substitutes the league of peace or community of states for the league of neutrals and international law procedure or international law in general for mere mediation, contact with the postulate of Lammasch is at once established. And Lammasch himself [1] agrees with me entirely that the building up of arbitral jurisdiction and of its necessary corollary, the Institute for Mediation, must be fostered :

Those powers that have a determined will to keep peace, that are resolved in future entanglements to keep neutral, must unite to form a league in peace times in order to establish a corresponding emphasis of their desire that others may keep the peace and settle whatever conflicts may arise between them by courts of arbitration, commissions of inquiry, and the acceptance of mediation. Such a solemn resolve would not be unwarranted interference with the affairs of others, since it follows as a result of an attempt to guard one's own just interests. The time must come when, in the words of Louter : 'The law of neutrality will dominate the law of war.'

It remains, now, to discuss the sanctions. Desirable as are the proposals of Lammasch in respect to these, they can hardly be

[1] Lammasch, in *Recueil de Rapports*, 1916, vol. i, p. 303. Cf. further, Lammasch, 'Unjustifiable War and the Means to Avoid it', in the *American Journal of International Law*, October 1916.

called sufficient. Corresponding to the higher goal and the greater power at the disposal of the parties striving to attain the purpose described, there must be substantially more far-reaching means to serve the achievement of said purpose. These means will, therefore, have to be specially discussed here.

I should like to remark that what I have said about a league of neutrals leads to still another conclusion, to which I have, indeed, referred above, but which deserves to be re-emphasized here, since the experiences of this war have unfortunately fully confirmed it. The league of peace, whether one care to designate it a 'league of neutrals' or not, will have to be built up, as we have seen, upon an increasing recognition of the solidarity of the interests of neutrals. This recognition has doubtless been especially strengthened by the fact that in this war we have perforce had to experience that *neutrality, and what is more, guaranteed neutrality has in itself been by no means a sufficient protection*. High, then, as in a neutralized country like Switzerland the value of neutrality must be rated, and it cannot be valued too highly;[1] nevertheless, by reason of the experience of the present war, the question must be raised whether there is not perhaps something that in actual practice affords a *higher degree of protection*, something that must therefore be rated still higher than mere neutrality, inasmuch as it is the true guarantee of the latter. This other higher thing can be naught else than just this recognition of the *solidarity of interests*, provided of course that one does not stop at lauding it as a fine principle, but sees to it that it be made correspondingly efficacious in practice. As soon as this is achieved—and the 'real guarantees' which we shall presently discuss are to serve this very end—then in the relations between states, not merely neutrality, but solidarity as well, must be inscribed on the banners. This will and must be *the guiding motive* of all future progress in international law. Without knowledge and recognition of solidarity, no serious progress can ever be made in international law; not even by the observance of neutrality, no matter how universally it be practised. But for this very reason also, I do not favour efforts in the direction of a 'league of neutrals', but rather a league of peace; for by this means the thought of the solidarity of international law is much more emphatically expressed, whereas a 'league of neutrals'

[1] Cf. on this point my paper, *Neutrale Pflichten und nationale Aufgaben*, 1916

merely seems to symbolize neutrality. Neutrality, however, primarily signifies isolation, while the very thought of solidarity seems to point to *co-operation.* But the future must stand under the emblem of co-operation; of this there can be no doubt. Only when the states with a will to peace shall actually co-operate, only when they not only regard, but also treat, the observance of international law and the preservation of a state of peace as *a matter of universal interest,* only then will serious progress be possible. *Solidarity* and *co-operation* will, accordingly, have to be unreservedly the watchword of nations after this war.

After having discussed the fundamental principles from which the creation of real guarantees of international law would have to issue, and after having treated the instances which might possibly create these guarantees and watch over their execution,[1] we must turn to a consideration of these 'real guarantees'. Of what might these 'real guarantees', these coercive measures in international law, conceivably consist?

Before I take up the real coercive measures in detail, I wish to place in the very forefront a guarantee which I have proposed earlier, although in its character it belongs in the same category as the mere 'moral guarantees' of the *ante bellum* international law. It might at least serve as a formal basis on which the real guarantees that are to be created could be built up. In discussing the question whether the Hague Conventions might not possibly set up still further guarantees, so that their provisions and principles would really be observed in practical life, I touched on the possibility that the Hague treaty powers might expressly guarantee the observance of the provisions of the Hague Conventions.[2] In other words, it would be a question, whether

[1] In passing be it noted that there have also been proposed a league of Central European States (v. Liszt) and a League of Arbitration of Central Europe and Hither Asia (Mehrmann in the *Grenzboten* of January 1916). See also my *Denkschrift*, p. 24.

[2] Cf. *Fortbildung*, pp. 501 ff. Cf. also my book on *Der völkerrechtliche Vertrag*, 1894, pp. 213 ff., 218 ff. The proposal of a collective guarantee has, up to now, been seldom made. In the year 1873 the former Belgian Minister of Justice, Bara, proposed a united guarantee of treaties between states on the part of all civilized governments, whereby a breach of treaty would be made difficult, indeed impossible, and thus an actual solidarity in international relations and in international law be brought about. Pasquale Fiore, 'L'Organisation juridique de la société internationale', in the *Revue de droit international*, vol. xxxi, p. 240, also emphasizes this: 'It must be admitted that it is the duty of all the states formed into a union to ensure respect for the common law determined by them, and to establish the authority of the same by means of legal measures that are drawn up

a *collective guarantee* could not be created of such a nature that the signatory powers would jointly and separately guarantee an exact observance of the obligations assumed in the agreement, and to the same degree regard every act contrary to the same as a question of universal interest. In such a collective guarantee through which the application of international law procedure would be rendered certain, the basic principle of international law solidarity as against a violation of international law would receive notable expression. Should the states—be they members of a league of states or signatories of a peace conference or of the Hague Final Acts—expressly declare that they regard such questions as of universal interest, they would not only sanction the principle of international law here emphasized, but they would also pave the way on which, in case of need, they could proceed even by force against the transgressor of the organization based on international law. And so I believe that such a collective guarantee could and should, in fact, form the *basis* upon which one could best found the system of real international law guarantees that is to be set up. The procedure would not be without historical precedents,[1] and the guarantees might naturally be adjusted to the nature of the instance from which the guarantees would issue.

I have come back to this proposal in the memorial on the principles of a lasting peace treaty (*Denkschrift über die Grundlagen eines dauerhaften Friedensvertrags*), and have there shown[2] in what way the strengthening of international jurisprudence might be taken up by future peace congresses. If such a congress wishes to strive to make more secure the foundation of the international legal order, it should, on the one hand, on the conclusion of peace, put the *territorial possessions of a state*, including its *colonies*, under the guarantee of the powers at the congress; and also, on the other hand, place under its express guarantee the basic *international conventions* to which all the

in accordance with international law. . . . For the protection of a common law a more efficacious form of protection than the collective guarantee of the associated states could not be found.' Cf. on the same point *Fortbildung*, p. 515. See further Rafael Erich, *Probleme der internationalen Organisation*, 1914, pp. 72 ff.

[1] We only need to recall the Paris Peace Treaty of March 30, 1856, and April 15, 1856.

[2] Cf. *ibid.*, pp. 39 ff. Zoller, *loc. cit.*, expresses it as his opinion, and rightly, that one would unfortunately have to agree that treaties of guarantee and neutralization are not sufficient as a protection of the international order, and that the guaranteeing of these treaties depends to a certain extent on the question of international coercive execution.

powers of the congress are a party, especially the first Hague Convention concerning the peaceful settlement of international disputes. With reference to the former, I have shown that if it were desired really to put the international legal order on a firm basis, the first requisite would be that the states to the congress mutually guarantee to each other their territories as fixed in the peace treaties.

The territory of the state, the boundaries within which a state exercises its imperium, must, once for all, be fixed and take on the form of something unchangeable. From the legal point of view this may seem obvious; but since, in spite of this, portions of a foreign territory have frequently appeared as objects of political aspiration and have thereby become the occasion of wars, it is by no means superfluous to protect, with a special guarantee, the system of states territorially by the peace treaty. We are well aware that the institution of the international law guarantee has been by no means strengthened in this war. But this is no reason why it should not be brought into an honourable position again. One must not without further consideration lose faith in the future of law because of acts committed in contravention of the same; and there is no doubt that just this institution of guarantees is capable of a much further development.[1] A collective guarantee by all the signatory powers of the treaty of peace in favour of the territorial boundaries fixed in that treaty would not only be by no means superfluous, but might also be of the greatest practical significance and contribute to the prevention of future conflicts between the powers or nip them in the bud. Prophylaxis is by no means to be despised, even in the life of nations. The stronger the judicial protection of the given situation or of a legal relation appear to be, the less likely will there be any attempt to shake it. In fact, the guaranteeing of the same may be regarded as a confirmation of the solemn will of all the participants to recognize that condition or legal relation, and, in case of necessity, to defend and protect it. Conversely, it may be said that if this will to protect the law is actually present—and let us hope that when peace is made it will really be present in all the contracting parties—then there is no reason why the states should not document this will with all clearness. On the contrary, they must wish to give the clearest expression possible to the seriousness of their will to have the law observed. This cannot be done in a more effective way than by an act of collective guarantee. It is the surest safeguard possible from the standpoint of present-day international law, and as long as the introduction of coercive measures in international law and the creation of an international executive are not contemplated, it is the only guarantee conceivable in the realm of this legal order. The situation would naturally be different if a league of states were to be created, since other means then would exist.[2]

[1] It should be recalled that the Interparliamentary Conference at Geneva, 1912, likewise took up the question of the guaranteeing of territorial integrity. In America the 'Anti-Conquest Resolution' has already many adherents.

[2] On the question of guaranteeing the territorial integrity of a state, cf. also Elsner, *Jedem das Seine, eine völkerrechtliche Studie*, 1915. Elsner justly writes:

In addition to the territorial possessions in Europe, I have especially recommended that the *colonies* be included in the guaranteed protection, since colonial aspirations are the very things that, in the last decades especially, have endangered peace. What all states had recognized and guaranteed to protect would then probably, without further question, be withdrawn from the desires of colony-grabbing politicians.[1]

With reference to the *international conventions*, I have explained that the guarantee probably could be extended to them also, or that they could be taken under the protection of a special guaranteeing clause. On the conscientious observance of the first Hague Convention would depend, in every conflict, the question of peace or war. It is a basis of international peace, and enough could not be done to assure complete observance of it, in every single case. Why, therefore, should a collective guaranteeing act of the powers at the congress not be extended to them or be made to apply to them ?

Why should the signatory powers of the peace congress not take all Hague Conventions and eventually also other general agreements based on international law under their express protection ? In our opinion, this would be a further means of supporting, in an effectual way, the now apparently tottering structure of international law. . . . Moreover, a collective guarantee should in this case be all the more easily attainable, since it is in this case a question of the foundation of the entire structure of international law, in which all the states are equally interested, in favour of which therefore all states would doubtless have equal cause to come forward.[2] If the solidarity of interests of the states of the world finds expression anywhere, it is in the case where it is a question for each one of

' If the relations of the states to one another are to be founded on a legal order, then above all else it must be declared the right of a state, as the very foundation of these relations, to have its territorial sovereignty clearly fixed by express wording, and to have the same put under the mutual guarantee of the states.' The material rights of the states in their relation one to another, the *juridical* fixing of the ' mine ' and ' thine ' of states, have not yet been recognized in the international law of to-day. It is to be hoped that the world war may become the starting-point of an international legal order under the guiding principle *suum cuique*. Two things would have to be fixed : the mutual recognition of a definite territorial possession as a recognized legal possession, and the mutual obligation of all the parties to the treaty to protect the recognized territorial possession against violent separation, to guarantee the territorial integrity.

[1] In the article, ' Die Neutralisierung Afrikas ', in the *Deutsche Revue* of April 1914, I have expressed myself *against* a real neutralization, but in favour of a mutual recognition by treaty and a mutual guaranteeing of the colonial territorial possessions. Dernburg recommends further in the *Neue Freie Presse* of May 11, 1915, a neutralization of all seas and straits by a universal agreement, guaranteed by all the powers. Cf. also Elsner, *loc. cit.*, p. 10.

[2] With the exception of those who rate might higher than right, and who would therefore be unwilling to resign any of the prerogatives of might.

the security of its own territory, and besides this, where for all of them it is a question of safeguards for the preservation of peace.

Elsner too has raised the question [1] whether the states will be inclined to guarantee to each other the territorial domain which they will recognize in the coming peace treaty, or—in reference to states that have remained neutral—which they have recognized in former treaties; and whether they will be able or will care to abide honestly by the guarantees undertaken.

The assumption of the guarantee binds the guaranteeing state to exert all its power, even by force of arms if necessary, in behalf of the pledge given. The strong nations that come victorious out of the world war will not hesitate to be accountable for the maintenance of the territorial domain that will be fixed by the coming treaty of peace; the weaker states will have learned that they shall not, within any conceivable period of time, be able to realize their desire to enlarge and to destroy, and that by joining in the universal guaranteeing treaty they will derive the advantage of having their own territorial integrity guaranteed; those states, finally, that were not even moved to give up their neutrality, by the world war, will not hold themselves aloof from the necessity imposed by the interests of all, and will help to put the relations of the states upon a legal basis . . . . It will be for neutrals especially to decide whether the guaranteeing treaty shall be realized. The power of the neutrals must not be underestimated. . . . The guaranteeing treaty transforms neutrals from spectators condemned to silence into a mighty phalanx of defenders of the *status quo*, who need not flourish the sword in order to make individual disturbers of the peace realize the hopelessness of their undertaking. Agreement will certainly be possible in respect to the executive side of the programme. A form of force ordained by representatives of the states is not war but police force.

The relations between the states would have to be put on a firm judicial basis, on that of the regulation of the 'mine' and 'thine'. The attempts to arrive at a lasting peace without restoring a judicial basis would constantly prove of no avail. Elsner further emphasizes the fact that if the territorial integrity of the states is protected by a guaranteeing treaty against attacks from without, and the most vital interest of the state thereby put on a clear and sure judicial basis, then the chief obstacle in the way of obligatory arbitration would be removed, and it would be possible to settle differences in bloodless ways. Once the foundation of a judicial procedure were laid by guaranteeing treaties, there would surely be further development along legal lines. With the disappearance of the policy of conquest, a baiting, backbiting press would be deprived of its *raison d'être* and pass

[1] Elsner, *loc. cit.*, p. 12.

out of existence, and the shattered confidence of the nations would gradually be built up again. No state could refuse to become a participant without wishing to be openly branded as a rapacious disturber of the peace. In case a league of peace should actually come into existence after the war, then it will obviously be in the most favourable position to frame such a collective guaranteeing act, not only in reference to the territories, but also in respect to the conventions and the procedure of international law. It would also be in a position to see to it that the guarantee *be executed.*

As to the possibility of executing it, Elsner writes :

Treaties by which several large powers guarantee the independence and integrity of a smaller state and the mutual treaty of guarantee between all civilized states are of an essentially different nature. The former partake of the nature of a treaty of confederation, the latter of an act of international legislation.

Although in general the number of the contracting parties would be a matter of indifference, here the number of the states thus uniting would be a warranty that the special desires of individual states would founder on the sense of law and the power of the great majority. From the fact that in international anarchy held in check merely by force not all treaties are observed, the conclusion must not be drawn that an overwhelming majority of states would not maintain a legal order unified by the totality of states. This will naturally be the case in a still higher degree, if this legal order is provided with sanctions.

Starting out with the view that the states—whether all or merely a number of them—will, after this war, especially regard the application of international law procedure as a legal obligation to which they possibly will give a special sanction in the form of a collective guarantee act, I assume that these states will wish to invest the observance of these and other norms with external guarantees, with actual coercive measures. The creation of such coercive measures will, therefore, according to this view, constitute one of the chief tasks in the development of international law after this war.[1] The task of creating a system of coercive measures

[1] Zitelmann, *Haben wir noch ein Völkerrecht?* 1914, p. 9, writes : 'To be sure, such means of enforcing its decrees is lacking in international law, *must* needs be lacking, for every genuine state is sovereign. . . . Were it subject to a higher organization of states equipped with a judicial coercive force, it would no longer be a sovereign state, but a member of a new state. . . .' From the point of view of the international law of *ante bellum* days, it is true that coercive apparatus is

for international law will have to engage our attention. Just as the task accomplished in the period *before* this war consisted in the main of the creation of a *system of international law procedure*, so now the *new* task to be faced by reason of this war consists in *devising a system of coercive measures based on international law for the application of this procedure*, and especially for the observance of treaty stipulations—coercive measures in which the 'real guarantees' for the maintenance of peace demanded by the world to-day will find their external expression. There are *two systems*, one of them representing the old *ante bellum* international law, the other representing the new international law born of this war.

Even before this war there has been theoretical discussion of the coercive measures that international law might offer, even though these proposals had won scant esteem, since they not only seemed to contradict the very nature of international law, but also because there did not appear to be any prospect of realizing them. Since the case is different to-day, these proposals naturally now merit closer examination. It will be the task of practical statesmen to make suitable selection from among the various coercive means at their disposal and to fit them together into a proper system. Science must be content with apprising statesmen of the presence of these means.

It must not be forgotten that already at the time of the Second Hague Conference, the proposal was made

> that every power waging war without attempting to avoid the appeal to arms, in conformity with the recommendations of peaceful adjudication, will be considered an enemy of the human race, which should no longer count on the trade, nor on the moral or the financial assistance of the signatory powers.[1]

As I have already indicated, the sanctions in international law unfortunately have hitherto been sought primarily with a view to the execution of international law procedure; or, what amounts to the same thing, the execution of the arbitral decision, since this represents the sole procedure where the question of execution in general can arise. It was not recognized that the forcible execution of international law could be, under

lacking, but that is not saying that it must ever be so; and still less is it true that with its creation, sovereignty would have to cease and that a new state necessarily would come into existence. See on this point my discussion in *Fortbildung*, p. 44.

[1] Cf. the *Courrier de la Conférence* of October 3, 1907, and Wehberg, *Kommentar zur Haager Konvention I*, p. 52.

all circumstances, only of minor significance, as compared with the postulate of a subordination to international law procedure in general. This error rested on an overdrawn analogy with civil law. In the latter the individual citizen is without further question naturally subject to the jurisdiction of the state. There is consequently merely need of a coercive *execution.* Conversely, however, in international law it is necessary first of all to create a subjection to a jurisdiction ; the execution will then for the most part seem assured, as the experience of courts of arbitration has sufficiently demonstrated.

Several voices from the literature of international law may show us how people have conceived of these coercive measures in the past.

The Frenchman Dumas, in particular, has dealt exhaustively with this subject,[1] and, among the coercive means that he cites, a few may be of interest with reference to the *application* of international law procedure.

Dumas recognized the importance of the moral guarantees throughout,[2] but is of the opinion that

> optimism does not however exclude prudence ; and with due respect to the loyalty of states . . ., it is wise to try to invest the arbitral institution with every guarantee.

Among the 'material sanctions', Dumas treats of *retorsion, reprisals,* and *blockade.* To these subjects I shall return later. According to Dumas, *intervention* also belongs to this category. I have at another place taken sides against Dumas, because in his systems of international law sanctions, he has, in my opinion, ascribed an unjustified position to intervention, and I have pointed in turn to the international law institute of mediation. This naturally referred to the *ante bellum* international law.[3] From the moment, however, when a league of states is formed for the purpose of enforcing the application of international law pro-

[1] Jacques Dumas, *Les sanctions de l'arbitrage international,* with a Foreword by d'Estournelles de Constant, 1905. In addition to this must be recalled especially the excellent work of Count Kamarowsky, *L'arbitrage international.* Cf. *Fortbildung,* pp. 393 ff.

[2] Among the 'moral sanctions' Dumas attributes the greatest significance to public opinion and the force of the plighted word. Kebedgy, in the *Revue de droit international,* 1897, pp. 113 ff., designates as sanctions of international law primarily natural interest, rank in the international community, solidarity of interests, and public opinion.

[3] Cf. on this point *Fortbildung,* pp. 396–405.

cedure, intervention on the part of this league will no longer be a right but a duty. Intervention will then appear as the outward expression of international solidarity and will obviously lose the character of unjustified meddling.[1] It can then no longer be cited simply as a *special* coercive measure, since the thought of intervention now necessarily lies at the very base of the *whole* system of the coercive measures of international law. But it must always be limited to the objectives which the league of states has in view, it must simply serve for the enforcing of international law and must not be misused for political purposes.

However, Dumas seems to be willing to attribute to intervention such universal significance. He says at the end of his book:[2]

> A single one of these sanctions, if intelligently applied, would dispense with all the others. We wish to speak of the exercise of the right of intervention.

The idea of collective intervention seems especially to hover over his mind. I previously proposed that instead of intervention, the expression 'co-operation of third parties' be employed as the one upon which the entire international law procedure is based. A co-operation of third parties for the purpose of establishing peace would in fact, as Dumas proposes, have to be collective and restricted to the concrete questions at issue. In only one respect has the situation changed since then: the co-operation can no longer now be purely one of diplomatic force; external force would also have to be applied now.

To the 'material sanctions' belong, further, the *civil sanctions*, according to Dumas. About them he writes:[3]

> It would be useful to establish certain civil sanctions of arbitration with a view to international agreement. While moral sanctions concern themselves only with public opinion and penal sanctions punish merely individual crimes,

[1] To this I have already called attention in my *Völkerrechtlicher Vertrag*, 1894, p. 233. Through treaty agreement 'a collective proceeding and interference by third states against treaty violations as well as against violations of international law in general and the endangering of the universal interests of the international community is made possible, without this 'meddling' necessarily assuming the character of intervention. To be sure, in the supposed cases a 'meddling by third parties' is often in the highest degree desirable from the international standpoint. But at the same time, as a matter of principle, it is in the interest of international law that a violation of a state's independence should, under no circumstances, obtain judicial sanction. Consequently, the problem is to fix in as general a way as possible, by treaties, the cases which from the international viewpoint justify this common interference.' What, a quarter of a century ago, I designated as the problem seems now about to be realized.

[2] Dumas, *loc. cit.*, p. 417.

[3] Dumas, *loc. cit.*, pp. 426 ff. Cf. *Fortbildung*, p. 408.

committed intentionally, the civil sanctions would be destined to reach the state that refused to execute a judicial sentence in respect to its moveable or immoveable property as also in respect to its domain public or private.

The 'civil' coercive measures especially proposed by Dumas are these :[1]

1. The appointment of a *judicial sequestrator* to administer the territories involved in the quarrel. As such, Dumas names either an international commission or a third party, especially a neutral state, which would peacefully take control of the territory in dispute.

2. The depositing of a *pledge* by the states involved.

3. The administration of certain *public revenues* to confer a right of preference upon the state entitled to the same.

4. *The taking possession* of all public and private *claims* of the state in question, both in their own territory and in every foreign country.

Dumas further discusses '*penal sanctions*' and '*political sanctions*' which, however, offer less interest to us in this connexion. The former are to be directed against guilty persons, especially Cabinet Ministers ; the latter proceed from the idea of a federation of states. Of these we shall speak later. Dumas then takes up the question of the creation of a 'coercive power' which is to fall primarily upon the powers signatory to the Hague Conference. The future, he adds, will show whether, in addition to 'legislative power', there will be need also of an 'executive power'.

The well-known Belgian professor of international law, Nys, has also discussed the question of sanction.[2] He writes :

For certain authors it is sufficient to entrust execution to the good faith and honour of the parties ; for others, collective intervention of a purely diplomatic nature is efficacious ; for still others, measures of execution offer utility.

Nys finds that

there is a measure to which judges might have recourse—the attachment, that is to say, the fixing of damages for delay in the execution of the obligations imposed by the sentence ; from the standpoint of juridical principles, this may be looked upon as a coercive measure or as a reparation for an injury, or better still, as the penalty for refusing to obey the injunction.

[1] These 'civil sanctions' are suggested to Dumas by way of analogy with the civil law. Civil law has special ways of executing obligations in cases that arise from arbitral decisions, such as making a payment or restitution. These sanctions could be transferred to the mutual obligations that an arbitral decision creates between states.

[2] Cf. Nys, in the *Revue de droit international*, 1906, p. 22.

Since the outbreak of the war, general interest in the question of sanctions has, as we have seen, measurably increased. The great French professor of law, André Weiss, takes about the same position that I do.[1] He rightly says :

International law will survive the tragic events which we have the horror and the pride of passing through ; it will even be able to imbibe a new youth. The international law of to-morrow will profit by the experiences so dearly bought. It will appreciate better than the international law of to-day what has made them possible. Other tasks will await it. Every effort will have to be made to prevent a return of the bloody hecatombs, to establish peace, when finally gained, on less precarious foundations ; to substitute victorious realities for the brutally disappointing illusions of the past. It will be necessary to organize peace, to defend it against the efforts of those who would wish to disturb it. . . This terrible war brings with it a lesson, the tragic eloquence of which can no longer be challenged. It demonstrates the actual imperfection of international law, but it also opens up before it new horizons.

Weiss does not wish to anticipate the conclusion of the statesmen of the future peace congress.

Nevertheless it is permitted to make a survey of the character and extent of the problems that will confront it. The goal to be attained . . . will be to organize peace, a definitive peace, a lasting peace, the peace of law to assure to our descendants a better existence than we have known.

Weiss stands up for the principle of nationalities and the European balance of power, but adds justly :

However, all this will amount to nothing as long as international treaties reduced to the value of ' scraps of paper ' are transgressed with impunity by those who made them. The essential task of the next congress of diplomats who will make the international law of to-morrow will be to fortify the *sanctions* strongly enough to discourage those who would be tempted to break their word.

Weiss mentions especially the problems of obligatory arbitration, of the creation of a permanent court of arbitration, and of the development of the international commission.

But all these procedures on which the Hague Conferences had based such great hopes will be powerless if the arbitral awards, if the opinions of the commissions of inquiry remain at the mercy of the bad faith and the ill humour of the states that will have feigned to accept them at first ; we will always reach the same conclusion. All progress will be vain ; all reforms fruitless, if the prescriptions of international law do not ultimately get the compelling force and effective sanctions that have been wanting hitherto. Where shall these necessary sanctions be sought for ? What are they ? Will there be a *pecuniary forfeit* analogous

[1] André Weiss : ' Le droit international d'hier et de demain ' in *Scientia*, vol. xix, fasc. i, as also in *La Paix par le Droit*, 1916, pp. 65 ff.

to that which Article 3 of the Hague Convention relative to the laws and customs of war has attached . . . for failure to observe the rule in question ? A *personal punishment* inflicted on the officer or agent responsible for the infraction ? A *boycott* of the state offending against the other members of the society of nations ? A suspension of the economic advantages for this state resulting *from commercial treaties* of earlier date ? Or even a military *execution* to which all the signatory states which have guaranteed the broken agreements would be asked to unite ? It is proper to hesitate before selection is made from among the solutions I have just indicated, and I have no right to express my preferences. But it is indispensable that some solution be devised. *The international law of to-morrow, the law of peace cannot exist without sanction.* This is the urgent lesson that the events, taking place before our eyes, teach.

In a vein very similar to Weiss, the Frenchman Milhaud expresses himself.[1] He starts out from the viewpoint that 'if it is imperiously necessary to be invested with guarantees against certain units, it is possible to find them close at hand in the union of the others'. These guarantees

will be established by the existence of sanctions, and of sanctions so efficacious and decisive that their very existence will suffice to prevent the violation of the treaties; and in any case will impose sure and large damages upon the violator. A quite natural and yet quite simple form of like sanction would be to *release all the signatories of like treaties from every obligation* to the violator of a treaty. . . Another sanction of quite a general character against the violation of the law of nations would consist in the *suspension of all relations* between the ensemble of nations and the violating nation. There would be no exchange of goods, no postal communications, a sort of universal blockade, a putting under the ban of the civilized world. The international tribunal at The Hague would impose this penalty for a fixed period.

For making these sanctions effectual Milhaud demands the creation of an international armed force stronger than any national force, and concludes :

Public international law has remained up to now an incomplete law because it was a law without sanctions, and it was a law without sanctions because there did not exist a force superior to individual states capable of guaranteeing the execution of these sanctions. The hour has come—it is too late to argue further—to create sanctions. And with the same hour has arrived the time to create an international force to apply the guarantees. . . Once a system of international sanctions is established, once a strong international force capable of applying

[1] Edgar Milhaud: *Du droit de la force à la force du droit*, 1915, pp. 108 ff. Cf. further the article by Milhaud in *Humanité* of October 17, 28, and November 1, 1916. Milhaud there especially emphasizes that a system of organized international sanctions means the common, collective, and universal action of all the others against the offending state or states. The latter would, therefore, know that in case of attack they would have the whole world against them. This fact would not only be repressive, but also preventive. Cf. also Milhaud, *La Société des Nations*, 1917, and *Plus jamais*, 1919.

the guarantees or of guaranteeing their application is organized, it will no longer be possible for any nation, no matter how powerful, to regard international agreements as scraps of paper. From that time on, the work accomplished up to now by the Hague Conferences will immediately take on a consistency that they do not have. Events have proved this, and it ought to be possible to develop this work further and speed it on to its logical conclusion; the *compulsory* reference to the Hague Tribunal of all differences that the interested parties prefer not to settle freely in the diplomatic way. . . Future conferences will be able and will know how to frame principles of law which will permit the international tribunal, the Supreme Court at The Hague, to settle disputes of every kind that may arise between nations.

Milhaud is right in remarking that the sacrifice of millions in this war would have been in vain 'if it did not end in the abolition of the ancient type of relations between the nations and the advent of an entirely new régime. *The time for petty reforms is past.*'

I mention next the distinguished Chilean student of international law, Alvarez,[1] who likewise declares it necessary

to establish a sanction strong enough to assure the carrying out of the decrees issued. . . . The Hague Conferences have indeed introduced some sanctions of a moral, material, and civil character, but there remains much to be done along this line. The sanction which should be established before every other is that of *pecuniary indemnity*. . . . Another sanction which might also be established, but with a certain amount of caution, would be the *boycott* by the offended state of the commerce of that state which, after having committed the offence, refused to give satisfaction.

The Englishman Dickinson,[2] who comes forward in favour of a league of peace, remarks on this point:

It will be impossible, I believe, to win from public opinion any support for the ideas I am putting forward, unless we are prepared to add a sanction to our treaty. I propose, therefore, that the Powers entering into the arrangement pledge themselves to assist, if necessary by their national forces, any member of the League who should be attacked before the dispute provoking the attack has been submitted to arbitration or conciliation. Military force, however, is not the only weapon the Powers might employ in such a case; economic pressure might sometimes be effective.

Dickinson emphasizes the fact that a non-military power

could nevertheless exercise a very great pressure if she simply instituted a financial and commercial boycott against the offender. Imagine, for instance, that at this moment all the foreign trade of this country were cut off by a general

[1] Alejandro Alvarez: *La grande guerre européenne et la neutralité du Chili*, 1915, p. 22.

[2] G. Lowes Dickinson: *After the War*, 1915, p. 26.

boycott. We should be harder hit than we can be by military force. We simply could not carry on the war . . . such economic pressure . . . would be a potent factor in determining the policy of any country. It is true that no nation could apply such a boycott without injuring itself. But then the object is to prevent that greatest of all injuries, material and moral, which we call war. We can then imagine the states included in our League agreeing that any offender who made war on a member of the league, contrary to the terms of the treaty, would immediately have to face either the economic boycott, or the armed forces, or both, of the other members. And it is not unreasonable to think that in most cases that would secure the observance of the treaty.

The Englishman Unwin also proposes :[1]

The signatory states shall jointly use forthwith both their economic and military forces against any one of their number that goes to war or commits acts of hostility against another of the signatory states before submitting the question at issue to the appropriate Tribunal.

But he further proposes :

The signatory states shall make provision for mutual defence in the event of any of them being attacked by a State not a member of the League which refuses to submit the question at issue to an appropriate Tribunal or Council.

The Brazilian João Cabral makes the following proposals :[2]

I. That there be solicited the acceptance, by the greatest possible number of the Powers—but without the preconcept of unanimity—of the project creating a new and real Court of International Justice, such as was formulated by the Second Peace Conference with the system of electing the judges as presented by the Brazilian Delegation or other which may best satisfy the higher interests of justice.

II. That the signatory states, once there has been constituted a sufficiently strong nucleus to this end, undertake to prepare themselves for complying and forcing compliance by the respective governments and by all other states, whether previous to the breaking out of any armed conflict, or even after hostilities may have broken out between any of them, to all the precepts established in conventions as well as the principles of international law as generally accepted.

III. That there be adopted, as coercitive measures to ensure respect for the decisions of the Court, the following proposed by Komarowsky :

1. The exclusion of the rebel state from the bosom of the said Court.
2. Rupture of diplomatic relations with the rebel state.
3. The annulment of every pact especially favourable to the rebel state.
4. Denial of the faculty of residence of any citizen of such state in territory belonging to the other states.

[1] R. Unwin : ' A League of States,' in *Recueil de Rapports*, vol. i, p. 212. See also Williams, ' A League of Nations,' *ibid.*, p. 229.

[2] João Cabral : ' The Sanction of International Law,' in the *Recueil de Rapports*, vol. ii, p. 6.

5. Prohibition of import and export of produce as between the former and the latter.

6. Blockade of the rebel state. And finally, as a last resort,

7. The employment of armed force.

The American Hamilton Holt enumerates, as means of 'concerted action' in addition to public opinion, 'economic pressure' and 'force'.[1] He questions whether the tying up of intercourse or economic pressure would be sufficient to enforce observance of the principles of a league. There is agreement that if a nation were absolutely cut off from all intercourse with the rest of the world it would be compelled to yield. If all credit, all loans, and all trade were stopped, if even letters and telegrams were held up, no nation could endure such strangling isolation, and would quickly come to its senses. But Holt is of the opinion that although such pressure would doubtless be a powerful force in international life and would doubtless be sufficient in many cases to enforce the rule of law, still there were reasons for believing that it would not always suffice—for one reason because physical pressure would always be stronger than economic, because 'the resistance of the interests effected will be at least as great against an economic boycott as against war, and they will be constantly striving to break it down, whereas war once declared silences opposition'. Also because of practical difficulties, for how are the enforcing Powers to divide the pressure among themselves? This would always be more difficult in the case of economic pressure than of military. Recourse would therefore have to be taken to the application of force as *ultima ratio*. Root has correctly remarked:

> Many states have grown so great that there is no Power capable of imposing punishment upon them except the power of collective civilization outside that state . . . and the only possibility of establishing real restraint by law seems to remain to give effect to the undoubted will of the vast majority of mankind.

Holt asks whether eventually some members of the league might not avail themselves of economic and others of military pressure, but he regards this as of doubtful expediency. There would have to be a distinction made between stages where economic pressure was proper and those that demanded military pressure. Certainly, under certain circumstances, the economic pressure could have no time at all [within which to operate]. But in the course of time not only compulsory use of the international law procedure

[1] Hamilton Holt, 'Concerted Action,' in the *Recueil de Rapports*, vol. ii, p. 14.

could be enforced, but perhaps also the execution of judicial decisions. For the present Holt regards the former as sufficient. As to the question whether the league should also use its concerted powers against such nations as are not in the league but who attack one of its members, Holt would make this dependent upon the relation of the forces within and without the league. The matter would not dare to be pushed so far that leagues opposed to one another would be formed, for that would merely be a return to the old system of two groups of powers.[1] Holt, in conclusion, is of the opinion that the basis of a league of peace and its sanctions might be limited to some few basic principles. The working out of the same, however, would be a great task for statecraft. The question might be raised whether the time is ripe for this, but at any rate people are now thinking of this matter and the idea can never again be killed.

The American Herbert S. Houston likewise discusses *Economic Pressure and World Peace.*[2] He emphasizes the fact that the American chambers of commerce, when they accepted the programme of the *League to Enforce Peace*, thereby placed economic coercive measures in the foreground, and that the Executive Committee of the League has accepted the proposal. The new element in the present proposals is that of force, but through the present war the world has become so convinced of the value of peace that it has been found worth while even to fight for it ; and if it be said that this in turn again would mean war, the answer would have to be given that such a war, waged as a last resource, would be a war to enforce peace, to preserve the integrity and authority of the world court to carry out a programme of international law and righteousness. Moreover, if it were used as a coercive measure, the powerful force of international trade would in most cases suffice to bring a nation to reason even without the application of military force. How would such a coercive force have to be conceived ? To the international

[1] President Wilson has also, in his message to the Senate of January 22, 1917, rightly emphasized : 'It will be absolutely necessary that a force be created as a guarantor of the permanency of the settlement, so much greater than the force of any nation now engaged or any alliance hitherto formed or projected that no nation, no probable combination of nations, could face or withstand it. If the peace presently to be made is to endure, it must be a peace made secure by the organized major force of mankind.'

[2] Herbert S. Houston, in *Recueil de Rapports*, vol. ii, p. 27. Cf. also the same in Publication Number 26 of the *League to Enforce Peace.*

forces that would have to be reckoned with belong, primarily, money which has gold as its common basis. Credit, on the basis of gold, is international. Trade, on the basis of money and credit, is international. Likewise the network of agencies that uses money, credit, and trade is international. Banks, cables, mails, and means of communication are all international forces. They are common to all nations and independent of race, language, religion, culture, government, or other human limitations. This makes them a most efficacious force, if the court were reinforced by economic pressure. Through commerce the nations are united by a thousand bonds and are dependent on each other to such an extent that already there is talk of establishing an international 'clearing house'. This could be made a powerful means of exerting economic pressure. Houston then cites several examples from history to show how already economic pressure, for example, the withholding of loaned moneys, has actually operated to prevent war. If individual powers can exert such a pressure, how much more effectual might be such pressure through the concerted action of the powers. A nation acting contrary to its will would put itself beyond the pale of law. Why should not the other nations at once declare an embargo of non-intercourse against such a lawless nation by refusing to buy from or sell to it or have any relations whatsoever with the same? Such a coercive measure would have the advantage of operating from within and of affecting the war chest. It would be possible to fight with money and credit that back the bullets instead of with bullets. The world would have to use the power of commerce which is at its disposal for the protection of civilization. It would only be necessary to declare an economic embargo against an attacking nation. True it is, of course, that such economic pressure would also work injury to the nations applying it, but this injury would be far less than that of war, and if war could be averted there would be no injury. A war between other nations is also the greater injury from a purely economic standpoint. Why, therefore, should commerce, which has brought the world so close together, not be used to protect the world from the wounds of war? All international forces, art, science, religion, trade, &c., that unite mankind, ought also to contribute to the protection of mankind through the preservation of peace on the basis of justice.

The Belgian pacifist, Paul Otlet, likewise discusses *Concerted Measures to be taken by the States.*[1] He, too, has his eyes fixed on economic as well as military measures. Among the former he demands 'all measures capable of being made to strike at the economic interests of a state'.

The delinquent state would then be put outside the law of nations by a sort of ban isolating it from the world; its frontiers would be absolutely closed against the transit of persons, goods, correspondence or communication, aerial, telegraphic, or radiographic; all foreign goods, whether they belonged to the state or to its nationals, would be sequestered and an embargo proclaimed against all those subject to the jurisdiction of the state which is held to be an enemy of humanity. The embargo would be against vessels, cars, and locomotives; every purchase or sale, every recovery of sums of money, every act of borrowing would be forbidden. Eventually, all the subjects of the state would be conducted to its frontiers or interned in concentration camps. It does not seem that the efficaciousness of such measures, taken simultaneously and compulsorily by all the states, can be doubted.

In reference to military measures Otlet demands that the national armies be required to put certain contingents for the international army at the disposal of the 'Council of the States'. Moreover, these measures would have to 'be able to take on any of the forms that circumstances might require, or that might result from the declaration of a 'state of international war!' Otlet has as appendix to his discussions the 'project for international government' reprinted below,[2] to which the reader is referred.

In a work which has just appeared the Chinese Tchéou-Weï has likewise discussed the sanctions.[3] He writes thus about the 'international rebellion':

Each time, after every appeal and every other resource has been exhausted, a state . . . refuses, expressly or tacitly, to apply or to execute the laws and judgements issuing legally from the league of nations, when this recalcitrant state has been a principal or a third party interfering with international justice, if after being summoned and put in suit, it still persists in its refusal, it will be declared a rebel state by the international tribunal, which has pronounced judgement upon it. This tribunal will, at the same time, pronounce one or several judicial restraints against the rebel. . .

[1] Paul Otlet, in the *Recueil de Rapports*, vol. ii, p. 98.

[2] Translator's note: [For Otlet's Project, see p. 226 *et seq.* of Nippold's *Die Gestaltung des Völkerrechts nach dem Weltkriege.* It is omitted in this translation.]

[3] Tchéou-Weï: *Essai sur l'organisation juridique de la société internationale,* 1917, pp. 74, 141 ff.

Tchéou-Weï demands, before all else, 'that institutions for the application of international justice be established'.

The following restraints could be applied separately, simultaneously, or even all at once, by the international tribunal according to the circumstances, needs, and exigencies of the instance, and the real vital force of the states and nations against which the restraints were to be executed. We will enumerate them in the order of the seriousness of the measures.

1. General cessation by the other states of the commerce and the industry of war with the rebel state.

2. Temporary exclusion of the rebel state from one or all the existing international unions.

3. Stoppage of payment of credits due the rebel state by all other states.

4. Partial economic isolation of the rebel state.[1]

5. Temporary suppression of political, civil, commercial rights, &c., granted to those under the jurisdiction of the rebel state.

6. General breaking of diplomatic relations with the rebel state.

7. Exclusion of legislators, judges, superior officers, and administrative agents, officers of every rank, &c., of the rebel state from the public service of the world league until it submitted to international laws and judgements.

8. Complete economic isolation of the rebel state. A general boycott, the rebel state being held to indemnify the other states for all injuries and damages caused by such act.

9. General pacific blockade of the rebel state by the other states in its terrestrial, maritime, fluvial, and aerial domains.

10. Temporary or perpetual cancellation, by a judgement issuing from an international tribunal, of all the advantages of every sort and kind granted to the rebel state by the other states, in the treaties or conventions concluded between them, no matter what their date or purpose.

11. Attachment, seizure, sequestration, embargo, &c., by the other states, of all goods belonging to the rebel state and those subject to its jurisdictions, with a view to their preservation or as security, indemnity, or for purposes of legal or judicial confiscation.

12. Nullification by law (absolute and radical nullification) of all the advantages of every sort and kind obtained by the rebel state over one or more states in violation of international laws and judgements; treaties and conventions concluded by violence (threats of war, war) shall be void without notice.[2] . . .

[1] This sanction is to consist primarily of the following:

1. Closing of the financial markets by all states.

2. Cancellation or suspension of loans already contracted for abroad by the rebel state.

3. Stoppage of certain categories of trade.

4. Closing of certain measures of communication.

[2] The author remarks: 'We affirm here, by this essentially juridical restraint, the supremacy of law over force; the postulate 'right excels might' is on this occasion at least true and indubitable; arms and armies threaten, kill, seize everything, obtain everything by the desire of the stronger; one thing alone soars over them, rules them, disturbs them . . . it is law . . . this juridical supremacy we make known by this twelfth judicial restraint.'

13. The rebel state will be condemned by a judgement issuing from a competent international tribunal to disband its forces, on land and sea and in the air; its military budgets will be nullified, its internal security will be guaranteed by simple militia or by international armies themselves.

14. Perpetual neutrality may be pronounced by a special judgement issuing from the international Supreme Court against the rebel state whose bad faith, fraud, and premeditated aggression shall have been legally proved and judicially established.

15. Pecuniary restraint may be pronounced by an international tribunal against a debtor state that delays payment on its judicially recognized debts.

16. Other restraints, such as dynastic change or change in the form of government, furnishing of security, prestation of surety for appearance before court, &c., may be pronounced by international law against the state that is a violator of right and law.

All these quotations I have cited, at least in part, to show how strong the desire is at the present time for the creation of international law sanctions. I should like to note emphatically that the number could be increased *ad libitum.* Indeed, the above-mentioned desire is so universally expressed, as I have already noted, that the science of international law dare no longer be deaf to it.[1] That science will not be seeking a Utopia when it endeavours to realize this desire is shown by the fact that *the leading statesmen of almost all countries* have expressed before the whole world this desire for sanctions.[2] This not only *justifies,* but even *obligates* us to seek to realize this desire.

[1] In a broad sense, Triepel, *loc. cit.*, p. 5, is certainly correct when he says that international law is not guarded by a force of the same kind as that which aids state law in its power to pronounce and execute judgement through judicial and executive authorities. But that is not saying that this cannot at some time be changed. In a broad sense, Triepel goes too far when he says: 'In international life, states can only secure their rights by their own might, by means of self help.' Only ?—Bornhak is more correct in writing, in *Der Wandel des Völkerrechts*, 1916, p. 8: 'In international law the legal constraints of the partners at law, for want of a super-state, is the only method of forcible realization, but this legal restraint is national because the parties are states. When China, at the end of the last century, attempted to resist the international law in whose fellowship it had lived, the European powers, the United States, and Japan, by force of arms, compelled it to submit again to the international legal order.' Perhaps Bornhak could find still more recent examples.

[2] Not only the leading statesmen of America, England, and France, but also the German Imperial Chancellor has declared, on November 9, 1916, that he was ready to co-operate for the realization of these plans to form an international organization, that Germany was at all times ready to join a league of nations, even to put itself at the head of a league of nations to hold disturbers of the peace in check. But cf. my article in the *Neue Zürcher Zeitung* of November 18, 1916. In view of this attitude, now universal, it must certainly sound strange when, according to the *Neue Zürcher Zeitung* of January 23, 1917, these proposals were declared Utopian from a Swiss source. According to such reasoning, every

Also, such authors as have not taken up the question of sanctions have at least expressed themselves as sympathizing with the idea of a league of peace.

Von Liszt writes,[1] with respect to the movement in America, that the goal of a legal organization of the anarchic world of states seems about to be attained. The enticing force of the thought has won adherents among the leading statesmen of the warring powers far beyond America. 'The new organization of states will come as soon as the fighting men have returned to their homes.' A lasting peace is 'unthinkable without the legal organization of the states of the world. . . . A state of law that makes a new world conflagration for generations to come, if not impossible, at least improbable, is the demand of all peoples to-day'.

Lammasch, too, as noted above, has repeatedly expressed himself in favour of the 'future league of peace'.[2] Lately he has especially emphasized the importance of the concerted action of neutrals through collective mediation,[3] and demands the firm resolve among those not engaged in the struggle to introduce vigorous action in the interests of the preservation of peace. The objection that by so doing they would expose themselves to a much greater danger seems only to be correct theoretically; in practice there is no reason for such a fear if the offer to mediate proceeds from a large, powerful, united, and resolute league of states. This united power would at any time be greater than one of the warring parties, and would therefore be practically in a position to exert pressure. Notice of the differential treatment to be accorded to the two parties would suffice to induce the party inclined to war to refrain from carrying out its intention. Lammasch should have gone one step further and

forward step would then in the last analysis be a Utopia, that is, as long as it were not yet realized. Then would the saying be really true, that the Utopias of to-day are the realities of to-morrow. Moreover, I myself have never been enthusiastic for Utopias; on the other hand, I have at all times come forward in favour of *progress in law*. There are not wanting those abroad who have expressed the fear that we, in our democratic Switzerland to-day, unfortunately take a much more conservative position in regard to progress in law than most other countries. We must, in our turn, seek to disarm these sceptics by our future actions.

1 Cf. v. Liszt, in *Die Zeit* of November 20, 1916.

2 See pp. 47 ff., above. Cf. further Lammasch, in the *Neue Freie Presse* of November 30, 1916, and in *Die Zeit* of November 12, 1916.

3 Lammasch, 'Unjustifiable War and the Means to Avoid it,' in the *American Journal of International Law*, October 1916.

discussed the sanctions in detail. It is probable that the differential treatment would not in all cases suffice. The attempt must be made to make law applicable by all means.[1]

The opinions I have cited belong in part to the time before this war, and in part to the period of the war, but they nevertheless agree in general tendency and in the choice of means proposed. If those be excepted which simply bear the character of strong executive measures and would therefore not be available for more general application, it may be affirmed that the remaining means deserve on the whole closer examination with a view to their applicability.

Before proceeding to enumerate the individual measures that seem to me especially adapted to the future system of international law coercive measures, I must devote a brief space to a preliminary theoretical remark. It is always a mistake in international law to deal too much with analogies in other fields of law ; for in that way the peculiar character of international law is all too easily lost sight of. This also holds true of the question of sanctions. The proper point of view for passing judgement on the coercive means of international law is lost, if they are straightway divided into 'civil' and 'penal', after the analogy of law within a state. The elements that were decisive in such a classification are at any rate in no wise determinative for the question of the possibility of enforcing the use of the international law procedure. Conclusive rather from our standpoint of international law is the simple fact that the observance of international law must be enforced ; and from this fact it follows naturally that in the creation of a system of coercive measures for international law, it is merely necessary to raise the further question : What applicable means are at the disposal of the community of states in order to make such coercion real ? It is a matter of absolute indifference whether the suitable means applied be, in municipal law, of civil or penal nature.

From the standpoint of international law the character of the coercive measures to be applied may be distinguished on the basis of whether it is a question of measures that are purely *economic* and intended to affect the state to be coerced merely

[1] Bornhak is right when he says, *loc. cit.*, p. 9 : 'Right must be might in order to prevail. It is therefore very easy for the mighty one to make sport of right and override it.' At any rate the war has taught us this much.

in its economic existence, or whether it is a question of the application of real force in the *military* sense. Just as in war distinction is made between economic war and military war, so the coercive measures to be discussed here fall *a priori* into these two categories.

I shall take up first the *economic coercive measures*. In my opinion, especially the following might possibly come up for consideration as such :

1. The giving of *securities* by the states that are parties in the case.
2. The economic *boycott*.
3. *Seizure* of the properties, claims, &c., of the offending state, in foreign countries.
4. Awarding of an *indemnity* to the injured state.
5. Payment of a sum of money to the league of states as a *fine* or *punishment*.
6. The so-called non-warlike measures of self-help: *retorsion, reprisal, embargo, blockade*.

Let us now briefly consider these coercive measures singly. When the league of states is formed, or when the peace congress meets, it might be decided that every participating state would have to deposit a certain *security* for the fulfilment of the obligations assumed by it. This might consist of a sum of gold to be deposited. In this connexion attention might be called to a proposal by O. Busch for the creation of a 'peace trust'.[1] According to this scheme the members of the trust are to deposit a sum of gold apportioned according to the number of their inhabitants. This gold deposit is to be administered by the trust through a special institution of its own in a neutral state. For their deposit the associated states are to receive peace bank-notes as international legal tender. The deposits of those states that are declared originators of or aggressors in a war shall be forfeited to the trust. Instead of this it should be said that those who avoid the use of the international law procedure or otherwise notoriously fail to observe international law shall be subject

[1] Cf. *Neue Zürcher Zeitung*, Nos. 1245 and 1251 of 1915, and Nos. 1765 and 1770 of 1916. See also my article on 'Die Erzwingung des Friedens' in No. 1893 of the *Neue Zürcher Zeitung* of November 25, 1916. Cf. further the proposals on p. 96, below, note, on monopoly of explosives, increase of tariffs, &c.

to forfeiture.[1] Likewise, the notes that have been issued on the security of the gold deposit shall lose their value. This idea of a 'peace trust' might indeed be utilized by the league of states. It might demand a deposit of securities in the form of gold deposits or in some other form. This would doubtless be a suitable means through which, in the contigency, a disposition to observe the principles of the league might be inaugurated. To be sure, whether this means would prove sufficient in all cases may appear questionable, and it therefore seems necessary to create other coercive measures over and above these. The more the league of states surrounds itself with economic coercive measures for the achievement of its purposes, the more can it contribute to the observance of international law and the enforcement of peace.[2]

A more effective means would no doubt be found in a *boycotting* of the state that violates its treaty obligations. If all the other states of the league should suspend intercourse with such a state and regard treaties with it as inoperative, such treatment would doubtless in the end have the desired effect, since it would operate as a *prophylactic*. In such a boycott different degrees or stages would naturally be conceivable. It might be limited to preventing all goods, or at least all goods of a certain kind, from entering the boycotted state, and especially to regarding as suspended all commercial treaties containing the most favoured nation clause, &c. But over and above this, all intercourse with[3] the offending state might be completely stopped, so that a condition of absolute isolation of the boycotted territory analogous to a state of war would be created.[4] It is clear that such a boycott

[1] Kitzinger, 'Bürgschaft im Völkerrecht?' in the *Leipziger Zeitschrift für deutsches Recht* of November 1, 1916, sees in this also the basic idea that the real bail is to be answerable not only for the preservation of peace, but also for the general observance of international law in war and peace; thereby there is to be created a compensation for the enforcement of this law, which is now totally lacking.

[2] Kitzinger, *loc. cit.*, is correct in saying: 'While breaches of international law which easily lead to warlike entanglements would thus weaken the offending state with respect to its wealth and thereby in its preparedness for war, and on the other hand strengthen the injured state, ruthless conduct of war contrary to international law would have exactly the same result . . . and in that way the guarantee for international peace would be increased. But the main thing remains ever the penal coercion for the entire body of international law in peace as well as in war.'

[3] Therefore also including all postal and telegraphic communication.

[4] This postulate is set up, e. g. by Neukamp, in the *Zeitschrift für Völkerrecht*,

would not be without political and moral consequences. No state probably would expose itself to such measures unnecessarily. Also in the course of time it is conceivable that there would be degrees of such a boycott according to the seriousness of the case. Then the boycott might also be accompanied by other coercive measures destined to make the criminal more tractable.

In particular, the property and especially the goods of the offending state and its subjects within the confines of the league of states or of the states of the congress might be *distrained* by these. In like manner claims of offending states or of its subjects might be seized or payment stopped. Likewise, the fulfilment of obligations stipulated by treaty might be declined. To this might be added the *abrogation of the rights* and *privileges* of the state to be coerced. Besides the *seizure* of property there might ultimately be raised the question of *confiscation* of the same. Also one might eventually take *forcible control* of the distrained properties. By such measures the economic isolation aimed at by the boycott might be made more poignant, especially if some of these measures were given not merely a temporary but rather an abiding character, so that the offender would have to count on lasting economic disadvantages.

Since on occasion the opponent will be harmed through evasion of legal measures by the offending state, it might further be agreed that in such cases the offender would have to make payment in *compensation*. The decision whether and under what limitations this should take place might in concrete instances be referred to the Hague Court of Arbitration, in so far as the league cannot or does not wish to decide.

Besides this, it might be agreed that the law-breaking state should have to pay to the community of states of the league a sum of money by way of *fine* or *punishment*.[1] This means would especially be worth considering in the case where the

viii. 567. He is of the opinion that with the present development of commercial and economic life the exclusion of a state from the commercial and economic community would suffice to overcome a state's resistance to an arbitral decision, without the need of applying warlike coercive measures. In extreme cases, it would have to be coerced by the use of the war power of all the remaining states.

[1] If it be desired to apply the ideas of law as they exist in municipal law, then here as well as in the case of other coercive measures their penal character may be emphasized. But one must not go too far in this direction. To be sure, Kitzinger,

league does not demand previous security to be forfeited in case of transgression. But probably the system of giving bail might commend itself in general, for in that event the league would have in its possession from the start something that would give a more effectual form to coercion and make possible coercive execution unnecessary. In respect to decreeing a fine or pecuniary penalty, the same instance would have to decide as in the case of a possible forfeit of bail or a gold deposit. It might be the community of the states united in the league which, however, might delegate this right to decide, for example, to the Hague Court of Arbitration or any other international or neutral court.[1]

I have considered here all the possible coercive measures that must come up for consideration without first raising the question whether, and to what extent, these means are identical with the so-called '*non-warlike means of self-help*' of the international law now in force. For it is clear from the outset that in entering on the path of force in the above described manner we are going beyond the range of international law as it has been recognized hitherto ; and it does not therefore matter whether and to what extent the old and the new means are identical or whether one goes further than the others. But this does not relieve us of the necessity of examining whether the means of the so-called non-warlike means of self-help are not likewise proper to be considered as means of enforcing international law and peace.

This I must preface by a few fundamental words. *Self-help* signifies the opposite of law. There can be no question at all of granting it a perhaps wider sphere of activity in the international law of the future than it has enjoyed in the international law of the past. The exact opposite will have to be the case. The attempt must be made to restrict self-help more and more, and finally to make it impossible. This will take place to the

loc. cit., is not wrong when he speaks of a penal constraint to be created in international law in the form of a practicable penalizing of property. But he goes too far when he wants to create a veritable 'penal code for international law' with regularly graded penalties. The analogy with municipal law must not be carried so far.

[1] On the possibility of affecting the observance of international law by the definitions of *internal penal justice*, Hafter has expressed himself, according to the *Neue Zürcher Zeitung* of January 23, 1917. These possibilities refer, however, exclusively to the law of war. But they can no doubt exert a favourable influence on the form of the international law of war.

same extent that law makes headway. And law can undoubtedly make headway as long as peace prevails between the nations. It is only in war that law loses ground and self-help triumphs. But if in spite of this we now concern ourselves with the 'non-warlike means of self-help', this is naturally not to advocate self-help, but merely to examine whether the means that have been made use of to serve the cause of self-help are not capable of being applied to enforce international law. For these means lose the character of self-help as soon as their application is based, not on mere self-help on the part of a state, but on the collective interposition on the part of a group of states united by treaty agreement or on instances delegated by the group to make this interposition. This is the element that everywhere distinguishes law from self-help. In municipal law the authority of the law of the state takes the place of self-help. In international law it is the authority of the treaty made by states of equal rank that takes the place of self-help. If in the one case it is the law from which the state derives its authority to interfere, so in the other case it is the treaty. In both cases the contrast with self-help is expressed in the 'co-operation of a third party', no matter whether this third party be a state or a league of states. Where once the right has been granted by treaty to a league of states to make use of coercive measures in case of transgression, these coercive measures are from the very outset divested of the character of self-help. And in this sense we can therefore also test whether and to what extent the non-warlike measures, which were used in the case of self-help, can also be considered available for our purposes.[1]

Retorsion will scarce need to be considered in this connexion. Its sphere is absolutely in the realm of international law as now in force, and it does not presuppose any delictual conduct by the one party. For as long as the conduct of a state keeps within the bounds of law, the conditions are lacking under which the demand for an increase of the international law guarantees has arisen. The circumstance that a mere act of injustice justifies a return in kind by the other party could hardly be of any significance to a league of states. To be sure, just as in the case of any single state, the league is permitted even by the international law now in force to make use of retorsion. But mere retorsion

[1] Wagner especially has exhaustively discussed these means, *Zur Lehre von den Streiterledigungsmitteln des Völkerrechts*, 1900.

could never take place in the form of one of the above-cited coercive measures.

The case is different with *reprisals.* These always presuppose conduct of a state delinquent in the sense of international law. Corresponding to this, reprisals themselves consist 'of violent treatment which partakes objectively of the nature of such delinquent conduct, but in respect to the occasion for entering upon them, they are in international law recognized as a legitimate form of coercion of which the wronged state makes use in order to secure satisfaction for wrong undergone and compensation for injury received'.[1] Our system of coercive measures likewise presupposes delictual conduct by a state contrary to a treaty and international law. Our coercive measures are likewise of a violent, or if objectively expressed, delinquent nature in that they violently invade the domain of law of the offender. Because unified, they also seem a legitimate restraint of international law. Their purpose may be satisfaction and compensation for injury; more than this, preservation of the international legal system and the enforcement of peace and law. Thus our system of coercive measures seems to be about on a par with the international law reprisals. In the same way, reprisals with reference to content seem to correspond to our coercive measures. For instance, a reprisal may be the seizure of properties or claims of the state or of its subjects, or the refusal to carry out treaty stipulations, or the abrogation of rights and privileges. Nevertheless, I do not believe that anything would be gained by pushing into the foreground the retaliatory nature of the system of guarantees to be devised for international law. For reprisals take place between two states or groups of states in such a way that *a priori* the position of the two parties could not be called different except for the priority of the wrongful act. Reprisals remain acts of self-help. Our system of coercive measures seems by contrast the expression of international law solidarity that makes for law and safeguards law. It would be lowering the ideal value of the new international law guarantees to be created were they to be put on a par with reprisals.

Reprisals, as such, do not therefore concern us in this connexion.[2] Nevertheless here, where the formation of international

[1] Thus, for example, v. Ullmann, *Völkerrecht*, p. 456.

[2] It is different with war reprisals. These will be discussed under the law of war.

law after this war is being considered, there must be a little further discussion of them. There is no institution of international law that has been so misused in this war as reprisals have been. Though this may be a question of the law of war, we must discuss them at this place, since systematic international law for the most part treats the theory of reprisals simply in the law of peace. To be sure, this misuse of the law of reprisal, as I have shown elsewhere,[1] is first and foremost the result of a military system that has adopted war with reprisals as well as terrorization as its guiding principle, and which disregards the restraints of law and morality. But this does not detract from the fact that the positive definitions of the right of reprisal are of a very defective nature, and that to a certain extent they thereby seem to open the way for transgressions against the law of nations as well as the dictates of humanity. It must therefore be one of the tasks of future international law conferences to define more carefully the limits of reprisals in peace as well as in war. Conditions, the nature and range of the admissible reprisals, must be carefully described; and in general everything possible must be done so that there can be no recurrence of the crass abuses that have taken place in this war in connexion with real or supposed reprisals. The regulations to be made in reference to the right of reprisal must tend to keep the application of this legal institution as much in bounds as possible in the future. For to the same extent that progress is made in the creation of a system of economic coercive measures to enforce international law, to that extent will reprisals in international law become more and more unnecessary. They are and ever will be an expression of self-help; but since international law solidarity is in the future in ever increasing measure to obtain validity, it will, it is to be hoped, make the use of self-help not only undesirable but in the course of time superfluous.

Embargo is usually counted as a further 'non-warlike means of self-help.' By it is understood the seizure of enemy merchant vessels. It is clear that this means reveals nothing of especial interest for the question under discussion. If the seizure of the property of the state to be coerced is decided upon, merchant vessels may naturally also be regarded as property, and, as in any

[1] Cf. my work *Deutschland und das Völkerrecht, Part I: Die Grundsätze der deutschen Kriegführung*, 1920, p. 34.

other case, this seizure may be changed to confiscation, i. e. to definitive taking.

Pacific blockade, the last of the means of self-help, offers more of interest. This coercive measure deserves especially to be seriously weighed alongside of the simple boycotting of the state to be coerced. It may perhaps be particularly employed to aid in making more effectual a boycott that, in itself, is not sufficiently efficacious. Moreover, a complete boycott will frequently include blockade without further question,[1] since by the latter is meant that exclusion from intercourse which is directed against the harbours and coasts of the state that is to be coerced. For various reasons special development of pacific blockade seems desirable as contrasted with the war blockade; not only because the former as here hypothetically described would no longer partake of the nature of self-help—and it will have to be the task of those who in the future give form to the new international law to extend as far as possible the domain where international law can be applied and thus more and more push self-help, i. e. war, as far as possible into the background—but also above all because a collective blockade by all the members of a league would be very much more effective than a blockade on the part of an opponent in war. If, then, we once possess an effective, practical coercive measure, like boycott in connexion with blockade, then will self-help appear of itself more and more useless.[2] It must be remembered, moreover, that the principles of pacific blockade have been thoroughly normalized by the Institute of International Law.[3] Naturally, the principles there laid down will have to be materially modified to conform to the new foundation to be laid.

Mention should here be made of the fact that a *Dutch Commission*

[1] On the boycott, cf. especially Bollack, 'Le boycottage, instrument de justice internationale', in *La Paix par le droit*, June, 1911; La Ferrière, 'Le boycottage et le droit international', in the *Revue générale de droit international public*, 1907, p. 288; and Séfériadès, *Réflexions sur le boycottage en droit international*, 1915.

[2] Once blockade is decided upon, other means of maritime commercial warfare will presumably also be made use of for enforcing international law.

[3] Cf. *Annuaire de l'Institut de droit international*, ix, pp. 275 ff. The objection that v. Ullmann, *loc. cit.*, p. 459, raises to the application of the pacific blockade, namely, that in coercive measures for settling a dispute without war it would have to be demanded that the action affect only the interests of the state to be coerced, disappears where blockade is established by the community. Non-participating third parties should reconcile themselves to the preponderating interests of the community, since this would also be their own interest.

has worked on the problem of the extent to which the organization of an international boycott as a guaranteeing measure would be desirable.[1] It correctly emphasizes the great value of the moral sanction and declares that nothing must be left undone to strengthen the same. Among the real guarantees, the economic ones would be preferable, since the expression of the military sanction, the international police, would be force of arms, therefore war. As an economic sanction in the truest sense of the phrase, it mentions the economic boycott internationally applied which means the stopping of all the foreign commerce of a certain state by the breaking of all commercial relations with that country. Doubtless this would be a final means of compelling a resisting state to yield. In order that coercive measures shall have a prospect of success they would have to be applied with greatly superior force. On this hypothesis an international boycott would be certain to succeed provided always that the country in question could actually be completely cut off, since nowadays dependence on foreign countries is in general very great. If the attempt were successful in actually cutting off a given state from supplies on every side, there would make itself felt in a very short time such pressing need of indispensable articles that the state would soon have to yield. Cutting off the avenues for the importation of goods from abroad has at all times been regarded as an effective means of forcing one's will on a hostilely minded state. Blockade, which for centuries has been counted among the means of carrying on war, has meant nothing else than to isolate the hostile state and to check as much as possible its foreign trade. That such a blockade was practised only on the high seas to prevent the importation of goods by sea was explained by the fact that on land a surer means consisted in the destruction of the enemy's defensive power and in the occupation of its territories. This was not possible at sea, since the nucleus of a state's power of resistance was on land and this could not be reached by ships. The purpose of blockade therefore was to weaken this power of resistance by indirect means. Blockade at sea and armed conflict on land are complementary, and this explains why when men first began to seek means to enforce execution of the rules of international law, the thought of economic isolation came spontaneously to mind and, what is more, of a *general*

[1] Cf. *Recueil de Rapports*, vol. ii, p. 129.

economic isolation, that is, on the land side as well. The report discusses several historical examples of such a boycott, as for example, that of China in 1905–1908 against the United States and against Japan, and of Turkey in 1908–1910 against Austria and Greece. These illustrations enable us to understand how the idea of applying the boycott as a coercive means of guaranteeing the system of international legal order was conceived. In general the sum of our experiences justifies the view that the boycott, if universally applied, would prove a never failing means of safeguarding the legal order against a disturber of the peace. On different occasions also *Congresses* have taken up the question of the organization of the boycott, for example, the World Peace Congress of 1906 [1] and the French Peace Congress in 1911 which discussed the proposal of Bollack to recommend the organization of a collective international boycott.[2] At the World's Peace Congress in Geneva, 1912, Bollack recommended 'a universal law for a customs boycott'. This boycott was to consist of a suppression of importation which the other lands were to proclaim against goods exported from the boycotted country. This prohibition was to be gradually extended until finally all the foreign commerce of the nation in question had been lamed.[3] Also at the Lake Mohonk Conference, 1915, the boycott was recommended by different parties.[4] Reference has already been made to the fact that, besides this, fifty-five American Chambers of Commerce, 1915, had expressed themselves in favour of the application of economic measures as a means of maintaining the international legal order.[5]

The commission is of the opinion that the measure would have to consist of a stoppage of all commercial intercourse of the

[1] The World Peace Congress in Milan recommended in 1906 to the Second Peace Conference as a means of guaranteeing the execution of an arbitral award: 'The economic isolation of the recalcitrant nation, the prohibition of loans contracted for abroad, the giving of security by powerful third parties, the voluntary deposit of sums of money or of territories belonging to nations in litigation, the temporary or permanent exclusion from the union of the delegates of the nation that had refused to carry out the sentence.'

[2] The Congress decided that under 'effective sanction those of an economic nature were to be considered as the most important; and, among these latter especially, the conception of putting under the ban the entire nation that rebels against justice.'

[3] Cf. Bollack: *La loi mondiale de boycottage douanier*, 1912.

[4] Cf. Report of the Twenty-first Annual Lake Mohonk Conference on International Arbitration, pp. 46, 72, 134.

[5] Cf. further the plan of L. S. Woolf, in *The New Statesman* of July 17, 1915.

country in question. For if merely the export trade were stopped, there would be danger that its effect would not be decisive. There is no ground for striking only at one-half of its trade. But it would not be necessary to go beyond the complete cutting off of intercourse. This means should only be applied in the most serious cases, as, for example, where a state refuses to submit to an arbitral award and seeks to create law through war. Once such a violation of the international legal order were confirmed, the interest of the whole community would demand that the disturber of the peace be brought to reason by every possible force. In case of non-recognition of an arbitral award, there is need of great circumspection in deciding whether the case calls for coercive measures, since not all awards are of equal significance, and coercive measures call for great sacrifices on the part of those applying them. It is therefore necessary that the participating parties be convinced of the extreme importance of the case. It might come to the point that the judge in pronouncing sentence should declare whether there should be a boycott in case of a refusal to carry out the arbitral sentence. Moreover, the boycott should become automatically operative if a state prefers war to the arbitral award, and, what is more, operative on the day war is declared. Also the court of arbitration should ultimately be empowered to decide whether the dispute is of such a nature that a refusal to submit it to arbitration should justify the application of the boycott.

The commission raises the question whether it be desirable to recognize this means in international law in the face of many objections to it, urging that it does not seem to correspond to the present-day law of war, according to which war is only declared by a state against a state. In view of this fact, the boycott which draws private parties into the war seems a step backward. But naval warfare is in fact directed also against merchant vessels. The right to capture merchant vessels and to decree a blockade originates in the same idea as the boycott, and should be subjected to rigid regulations. To be sure, in warfare on land the case is different, but even here the necessity of war has not required the retention of the former customs. Conversely, reference to this necessity of war might explain why, in naval warfare, the attempt was not made to break solely with the organs of the hostile state. Moreover, the application of the boycott would, as a matter of course, have to issue from the Governments. The measure is by no means in conflict with the inviolability of private property, since it merely prevents trade with its possessor. But to this extent it does cause injury to private interests and thereby indirect injury to the hostile state. The result therefore remains the same in either case—that both parties suffer injury. As a matter of fact, it is always the individual that suffers in the end. The present war is the best proof of this. Therefore it cannot be asserted that the proposed means would retard the development of international law instead of advancing it.

Another objection is that the means does not affect merely those against whom it is aimed and that to this extent it is a two-edged sword. This danger must, however, not be exaggerated. The notion that the boycott brings with it insurmountable difficulties for the nations that participate in it would only seldom coincide with the facts. It must be remembered that the exclusion would have to be carried out internationally and that the countries would naturally support each other ; also that the injury would be unequally divided among the countries, according to the amount of its commerce with the boycotted nation. Accordingly, an international commission would have to be appointed to apportion the varying damages of the countries among the boycotting states. There would also have to be some prospective compensation for injuries in order to anticipate unwillingness to use the means, especially in countries that are not immediately concerned in the issue.

The report of the commission also points out that this measure might ultimately exert a bad influence upon the development of the peaceful international community, since free international exchange increases the solidarity of the nations. A state that saw advantage in the carrying on of a war might also prepare itself beforehand against a boycott and thereby minimize its effects. By such an increase of its power to resist, the term of the boycott would be extended and it would be very questionable whether it would then be continued by the different nations with sufficient vigour. There would also be the danger that the present-day endeavour to become independent of the international community would operate against a policy of reconciliation and co-operation. The assumption that the establishment of the boycott would contribute to strengthening this endeavour seems justified. For these reasons it seems undesirable to adopt the organization of an international boycott for the guaranteeing of international law. A limited application of the same commends itself more. Even though the measure were perhaps not adapted to a just application and even though it might lead to an increase of economic opposition, the thought must not on this account be utterly rejected, and even a partial checking of trade must not be set aside. Rather the proper course would be to restrict the boycott to contraband goods. To be sure, the importance of the injury resulting from the breaking off of this trade would be far below that of a boycott embracing all goods, but it would yet have a certain influence. Even though the general resisting power of the state were perhaps but little weakened in this manner, nevertheless its defensive power would be weakened. A limitation of the number of contraband articles seems therefore desirable. To be sure, the same objections could be raised against the application of the sanction even in this diluted form as against the general boycott, but they would not be of the same validity here. And the measure would produce an effect even in this form if a state entered upon unallowed warfare and it were met with a prohibition against the export of contraband articles. An international regulation would therefore be commendable which would forbid the export of contraband goods to a state that began war in preference to submitting to the international legal order.

We will no doubt be constrained to agree with this splendid report on many points. The careful discussions therein contained deserve consideration. It rightly emphasizes that the boycott, if universally applied, would be an unfailing means of guaranteeing the international legal order. All the less can I therefore understand why the report at the end ascribes so great an importance to objections that are not at all conclusive, and recommends only a restricted application of the boycott whereby it would be deprived of a great deal of its effectiveness. To be sure, the possibility of a limited boycott according to the meaning of the report, that is one limited to contraband goods, should not be rejected. But one should by no means be limited to this form of boycott under all circumstances, but should retain along with it a possible place for the universal boycott, which might after all be effective in a far different way.

Tchéou-Weï has treated the question of a universal boycott with unusual thoroughness.[1] He distinguishes between 'popular or national boycott exercised by the people or the nation' and 'universal judicial boycott exercised by the states'. He recalls that China first developed this peaceful means of international sanction in the first instance against the United States in 1905, and that it was very effective. This boycott issued from the entire Chinese people and lasted more than a year. As further examples of such a national boycott, Tchéou-Weï enumerates the following cases :

China against Japan, 1908, on account of Tatsu-Maru.

Turkey against Austria, 1908, on account of the annexation of Bosnia and Herzegovina.

Turkey against Greece, 1909 and 1910, on account of Crete.

Greece against Italy, 1913, on account of the Balkans.

Anti-Greek boycott in Asia Minor, 1914.

Boycott of Tien-Tsin, 1916.

The author thus concludes his remarks :

> However it be, the effectiveness of the popular or national boycott is undeniable, and it is powerful especially if this boycott be combined with the international boycott exercised by the states with one accord and officially. In fact, if all the states and all the nations were to boycott simultaneously and collectively a state violating international laws or sentences, the menace would be terrible, the injury inflicted irreparable, the economic life of the rebellious state compromised to such an extent that the surrender of the recalcitrant state would be certain. Moreover, the indemnity that it would have to pay would constitute a pecuniary restraint which, carefully handled, could be made so effective that the rebel state would not dare to prolong its unreasoned resistance without exposing itself to collapse or bankruptcy.

Tchéou-Weï demands that with the national or popular boycott go hand in hand 'an international judicial boycott', consisting of :

1. Closure of the financial markets of the world.
2. Annulment of all loans already contracted abroad by the rebel state.
3. Stoppage of all commerce, all traffic, all transportation, &c.
4. Suspension or annulment of commercial treaties concluded with all the states.
5. Cessation of payments on all credits due to the rebellious state and its subjects by all the other states and their subjects.

[1] See p. 69 above, under No. 8.

6. Suspension or annulment of all commercial, industrial, or other advantages granted by the other states to the rebellious state and its subjects.

7. Suspension or annulment of all patent rights, of all trade-marks, &c., granted to the subjects of the rebellious state.

8. General interruption of all means of communication (rail-roads, fluvial and maritime navigation, passage of vehicles of every kind, mail, telegraph, cable, and wireless services, &c.).

Tchéou-Weï is of the opinion that the measures to be considered would be so numerous that they should be enumerated in an international penal code. He discusses further the doubts that have been expressed with reference to the introduction of the boycott, as, for example, the objection that the boycotting states would suffer great pecuniary losses and thereby inflict injury upon themselves. He urges against this that the losses of the boycotted state would be far greater ; and that, besides, the losses of the boycotting states would be borne by the boycotted state, being returned in the form of compensatory damages to the boycotting states. As security, recourse might be had to seizure and sequestration, embargo, &c., of the goods of the boycotted state and its subjects. Tchéou-Weï also does not grant the validity of the objection that there would be hesitation about applying the boycott as between states closely related economically. Whoever would oppose the terms of the international agreement would by so doing act in violation of a treaty and subject himself to the same penalties as the law breaker. Moreover, there would be compensation for all injuries, just as guaranties and subsidies as well as adjustments would be possible between the boycotting states. A still further objection was that there were states that had nothing to fear from a boycott. But in the complexity of modern economic life even these states would suffer under the boycott. One need merely think, for example, of the loans that great states have made to each other to recognize that, even in countries which from the standpoint of production seem self-sufficient, a boycott would be of very great efficacy, since every industrial undertaking, every financial operation, &c., would be cut off, to say nothing of other moral and material injury. And in case a state, in spite of all this, should not be willing to submit to law, recourse would simply have to be had to other coercive measures. That a powerful state could violently resist and declare war on the boycotting states Tchéou-Weï also does not admit as a valid objection; and this on the ground that too many other states would be opposed to the boycotted state. One state would surely not declare war on the whole community of states. The seriousness of such a crime and the coalition of so many states with their economic and military power would deter it from taking such a step. Besides, it would be for just such cases as these that the military sanctions are provided. But these should be used only as a last resort.

> The guilty state must be given the opportunity to repent before a decisive blow is struck against it. But if, in spite of the boycott, the condemned state should continue its defiance of the law and oppose the force of law, then this state becomes a common criminal, a danger to society in general and to each one of the associated states in particular; the common interest and international security will then exact severe punishment and radical repression of this dangerous state . . . No one will regret the destruction, ruin, misery, disappearance of the sovereignty and independence of the rebel state in consequence of its forfeiture of the right to be a member of the international juridical society.

I believe that one may, on the whole, agree to these proposals.

So much for the characterization of the above-mentioned individual means of enforcing international law. It may be that, in addition to these, other coercive measures may yet be proposed. The serious discussion of the subject has in fact just begun, and it is therefore to be expected that many new ideas will be suggested.[1] It is to be hoped that many practical ones will be among them. For the creation of a system of such coercive measures stands not only in the foreground of universal interest, but upon the manner of the solution of the problem will depend the value that will in the coming decades be set upon international law.[2]

It may be added here that when once men undertake the creation of coercive measures in international law, perhaps they will not stop until they shall have provided for the eventual *coercive execution* of the international *arbitral sentence.* I have before this war expressed myself decidedly *against* the necessity of coercive execution in international law.[3] But the situation

[1] In the Swiss National Assembly, A. Meyer has recommended the formation of an international society for the study of the question of the real guarantees.

[2] Cf. on this point the article cited in No. 1893 of the *Neue Zürcher Zeitung*, 1916.

[3] Cf. *Fortbildung*, pp. 373 ff.

has been constantly changing, as I have shown above. And if ever coercive measures be introduced it is not a long step to the thought of introducing them everywhere. Thus perhaps a coercive plan will be carried out against such states as shall refuse to carry out a sentence, although, as a matter of fact, such a case has not as yet occurred. But I repeat that this guaranteeing of coercive *execution* is of comparatively small importance. Arbitral decisions have thus far been universally carried out and it is to be hoped that this will be the case in the future. Nevertheless, one could prepare against any eventuality. The means that will be applied in such case will be in part the same as those already discussed above.[1] By analogy, therefore, all that has been said above of coercion in general may be said of coercive execution in particular.

There arises the further question whether one should be content with these economic coercive measures or whether, in addition to these, *military coercive measures* should also be provided. I have briefly discussed this point with reference to the League to Enforce Peace.[2]

> Naturally it would by no means seem to be the duty of the league of states to banish war by war. The military forces are to stand in the background only. But it would not do to omit all reference to this eventuality. For if ever a state allows matters to come to such a pass that it endeavours to avoid its obligations as against the league, then at least as a final resort the possibility of being able to bring military measures to bear upon the issue must be reckoned with. All states are to unite against the notorious lawbreakers, and thus the case might arise where military force would be necessary. It would therefore be a pity if the solidarity so happily proclaimed should go only so far and no further. But, as already stated, this should, as is the case with war in general, be only an *ultima ratio*.

It would in fact be adopting a half-way measure if a coercive system were adopted in international law without making any provision for the eventuality where military force had to be employed.[3] Doubtless the system of economic coercive measures must stand in the very forefront, and this must at the same time be so shaped that success may be confidently expected in the

[1] Cf. on this point especially the sanctions proposed by Dumas.

[2] Cf. the *Neue Zürcher Zeitung* of November 25, 1916.

[3] Kitzinger, *loc. cit.*, is not wrong in thinking that to persuade the most powerful states to submit voluntarily to such penal coercion will be the greatest difficulty to be overcome in going over to the coercive system. It is because I share this opinion that I started out from this point, that the formation of a special league

vast majority of cases. But I believe that the economic coercive measures, especially the boycott with blockade, &c., in the hands of a league of states will in fact be so effective that there will be no need of military ways and means. But if at any time recourse be taken to force, in case of necessity the programme will have to be carried out with all its attending evils against a perverse party. Under certain conditions it may be necessary to bring economic and military measures to bear simultaneously. In the end there might otherwise be no guarantees at all in the whole coercive system. To the external guarantees with which international law is to be invested might therefore in the future also be added that in case of necessity the community of states or league of states put in common at the disposal of the league the military forces with which to compel a recalcitrant state to observe international law. Without this military background the economic coercive measures, boycott, blockade, would, under certain conditions, find it still more difficult to achieve their object.

In what form and under what suppositions such military measures would have to be carried out is a question that cannot be entered upon in detail here, since it would be in part less an international law than a military-technical question. I should merely like to mention in brief that already before this war the application of violent measures for the observance of international law had come up for consideration. Attention is here called to the proposition then made by van Vollenhoven to establish an *international police force.*[1] I have come out against all these and similar proposals in turn, but to-day I believe that they should at least be examined with respect to their practicability.[2] Whether, then, one is to be restricted to the employment of an international

will be necessary to the extent that the states of the peace congress do not themselves create this coercive system. And for the same reason I regard it necessary to consider also military coercive measures. The expedients proposed by Kitzinger for avoiding these I do not regard as practicable.

[1] Van Vollenhoven, in the *Revue de droit international,* 1911, as well as in *De Eendracht van het Land,* 1913, and in *De Gids* of November 1910. To this proposal Lotsy has more recently come back in *De aanstaande Vreede en Prof. van Vollenhovens Denkbeeld tot instelling eener internationale politiemacht,* 1914. I pass over the rest of the *ante-bellum* literature.

[2] The proposal of van Vollenhoven referred especially to the failure to carry out the terms of an arbitral award. At the desire of the state that had won a decision, the powers to the treaty were to put at the disposal of said state a portion of their naval forces. Such an armed intervention was also to take place in case of the violation of the rights of neutrals.

'police force' in all cases, or whether and to what extent it would be preferable to go farther and put the military arm itself in the service of the cause of international law, the future will teach. However, I believe that it would probably be better in every case, when once military measures are considered at all, to draw the more far-reaching eventuality within the domain of the possible.[1]

Erich also rightly points to the fact that the execution of international decisions would not be the only task that the executive organ of the community of states would have to undertake in the interests of the same. In its further development

[1] On this theme cf. especially Rafael Erich, *Probleme der internationalen Organisation*, 1914, pp. 54 ff.; van Eysinga, 'La police internationale,' in *Zeitschrift für Völkerrecht*, 1911, p. 527; Dumas, *loc. cit.*, p. 157; Wehberg, *Kommentar zur Haager Konvention I*, 1911, p. 53; and *Das Problem eines internationalen Staatengerichtshofs*, 1912, p. 105; Lammasch, *Rechtskraft internationaler Schiedssprüche*, 1912, p. 223, and Zoller, *loc. cit.*, p. 138. The Hungarian Ödön Makai has also discussed the problem of international execution in the *Recueil de Rapports*, vol. ii, p. 38 ff. He distinguishes between whether execution should be effected through the apparatus already at hand or whether a new international organization for coercive means should be created. Van Vollenhoven and Erich represent the latter position—the creation of an international executive organization. Makai, on the other hand, demands for enforcement of the treaty obligations of a state that an international executive organization be created simultaneously with the development of the administrative council provided for by Art. 49 of the first Hague Convention. He has himself developed a scheme for such an organization in which the following points may be noted. The Administrative Council of Article 49 of the first Hague Convention is to be transformed into a 'Permanent International Administrative and Executive Council' with military and financial experts at their service. The latter constitute the military, the naval, and the finance commissions of the Council. The treaty powers authorize the organization of an international army and an international navy which are, however, not to be permanent. Every treaty power is to be a participating party to these organizations on a proportionate basis to be determined by the above-mentioned commissions. The finance commission has to do with meeting the expenses of war operations. In reference to the use to be made of the international army and navy, the author provides that after the treaty powers have duly informed the Council that a power has failed to recognize the validity of an award, and that, in consequence of the same, diplomatic relations have been broken off with the power that has broken the treaty, the council shall immediately put the army and, according to the necessities of the case, also the navy on a war footing. 'Once these measures have been taken, the international force undertakes the operations of war decided upon by the commission.' In case the entire force is not necessary, individual powers may undertake the operations of war in case the rest do not insist upon participating in them (!). 'The object of the operations of war by land and sea is to occupy and hold the territories, harbours, and colonies of the power that broke the treaty until the power in question submits to the authority of the court, executes the arbitral decision, and compensates the treaty powers to the amount of their expenditure.' It is obvious that this proposal points the way to Utopia, the ground of reality is left behind, everything is accomplished mechanically. In spite of this fact, I have not cared to suppress even this proposal as the reflection of a frame of mind.

the international executive body would prove to be a guarantee of a state of peace and international justice, a preventive against international violations of law.[1] Van Vollenhoven thought in the first instance only of an international navy which probably later was to be supplemented by an international executive army. Moreover, it may be said, that in *pacific blockade* an international police is already at hand. Attention is further called to the Danube Commission and the Congo Acts. Erich desires that the international fleet, as also the international army, be composed of forces from the various nations ; but in order to be able to perform their task in conformity with their purpose they should be as independent of the several states as possible, and should exercise their functions in the name of the community of states. A request from a state requiring assistance would constitute the condition of their activity. All this seems dubious. I believe in a co-operation of different national armies, as in the present war, rather than in an international army. In any event, the community of states would have to decide whether there was sufficient reason for intervening.

Assuming now that in the future success will attend the efforts to invest international law with 'real guarantees' in the manner here described, it follows that such a changed international condition may, of course, carry in its train a vast number of most important results. To be sure, war would not without further ado be removed out of the world by such a further development of international law. But there is no doubt that the probability of a preservation of the normal state of law, of peace, would be measurably increased at the moment when, to this international law, there were added at least to a certain extent the element of enforcibility. The probability of wars would therefore be pushed considerably into the background by such a coercive system. It may be said that the more coercive measures are created and the more effective they are, the more remote will seem the possibility of the outbreak of wars. The tendency, the real goal in all further forward steps in international law must obviously be to

[1] Gabriel Séailles, *Les Conditions d'une paix durable*, 1916, likewise demands : 'This international law should be guaranteed by a force that both commands respect and prevents violations.' He writes : 'If a judicial summons supported by a concert of the powers would not suffice, means of repression—breaking of diplomatic relations, economic boycott, sequestration of national properties, &c., would not be wanting before final recourse to arms.'

preserve *under all conditions* the state of law and therefore in the course of time *utterly* to eliminate self-help, war. However many objections may be raised against the possibility of an early realization of such a goal, from the standpoint of this present time, still this must never be lost sight of as the veritable ultimate aim.[1] For the efforts of international law in the last analysis are directed at naught else than the unconditional reign of law in the life of states and peoples, and if this goal is to be reached, then we will have to fight against self-help, war, the antipodes of right, and seek in the course of time to banish it utterly.

The system that supports war, the antipodes of international law, is doubtless the *military system*.[2] Among the general causes that have led to this war this system very obviously stands in the very front rank. Especially *the policy of the preparedness*, driven to extremes by this system, constituted an unceasing menace to peace. If one is bent on safeguarding peace and, by so doing, the state of law, then the excrescence of this military system must first be removed. In place of a supermilitarism that *menaces* peace[3] must come a reasonable defensive system that *serves* the interests of peace and not of war.[4] To this belongs primarily the ending of

[1] Otlet, *Les problèmes internationaux et la guerre*, 1916, p. 323, is right when he says: 'Law is the opposite of force. To the extent that the influence of the one increases, that of the other must decrease.'

[2] Further evidence on this point will be found in my larger work, *Deutschland und das Völkerrecht.* Cf. *Part I: Die Grundsätze der deutschen Kriegführung.*

[3] Fried, *Europäische Wiederherstellung*, p. 31, is right when he says the maddest product of imperialism finds expression in the race for preparedness that has for a generation given its character to our age. This, too, is a case of a justified institution transformed into an absurd degenerate form. No one would offer any objections to reasonable military measures of defence. The unnatural element of the present-day preparedness system lies in the fact that imperialism has made of a means of defence a forcible means of carrying out its imperialistic policies, a means that could not only be used for defence and protection but for attack and subjugation as well. Preparedness ceases to be a defensive measure but becomes a means of attaining definite aims set by imperialism. It is of the very essence of this system of preparedness, the value of which expresses itself in a constant superiority of strength as against the opponent, that the protection it affords the state engaged in the preparation is conditioned by the measure of the menace to the other states. Fried is also right in emphasizing (p. 58) that it was these preparations, and nothing else, that rendered vain the means for a settlement of the conflict according to the dictates of reason; indeed, that the system of mutually increasing armaments, which was so indissolubly connected with preparedness, seemed at a given moment to admit of no other way out than war, which, as alleged, it was intended to obviate. And yet, there are people to-day who in all naïveté believe in the wisdom of the saying: *Si vis pacem, para bellum.*

[4] Every state should be allowed to keep only as large a standing army as its safety in reason demands. Regard for its own security, and not the purpose of menacing its rival, must be the basic principle.

the exaggerated race in armaments. From the moment that international law is so constructed that its observance can be enforced there is surely nothing in the way of putting an end to this exaggerated arming. However sceptical I may have been on the question of an agreement on armament *before* the war, yet I believe that, once the international judicial system has real guarantees at its disposal, when above all else a powerful league of states comes into existence which assumes as its life work the enforcement of this judicial system, then also the moment will have come when the endless machinery that militarism had constructed can at last be cast aside. The institutions of the league will serve as a substitute for the armaments. *The end of the race in armaments will, however, also mark the actual end of the military system in general*, which morally has already received its deathblow in this war.[1] For when great armaments shall have ceased militarism will no longer be able to rear its head above diplomacy and politics, above law and morality, and will no longer be able to attempt to control the whole world ; but will, without further ado, be put back to its real, but essentially more restricted field—that of protecting peace and law. For a reasonable system of defence finds its *raison d'être* in being *not the antithesis*, but *the instrument* of the legal order and of peace. In order to bring it back to this task it will first be necessary to remove the present military system.

It is to be hoped that its removal will also have among its results the disappearance of the *militaristic mentality*, of that attitude of mind which is completely under the control of the catchwords and views of militarism and regards territorial conquests and annexations as the only guarantees of peace and law.

That the end of this war might prove to be the proper time to introduce the agreement in reference to armaments and thereby once for all remove the excrescences of militarism, I have already discussed in my *Denkschrift über die Grundlagen eines dauerhaften Friedensvertrags* (Memorial on the basis of a lasting treaty of peace).[2] The situation at the end of this war would be unusually favourable for the solution of this problem, since we would then be entering upon a new political era in which the bases of the political

[1] On this point, see Law of War, *infra.*

[2] Cf. *ibid.*, pp. 31 ff. Cf. also the report of the Dutch Commission on 'Limitation of armaments by international agreement,' in *Recueil de Rapports*, vol. ii, p. 165.

system surely will be wholly different.[1] The more the international legal order comes into the foreground the more reason is there for supposing that a step forward would be taken in the question of armament.[2] Accordingly, the hope that the peace congress will bring this problem nearer solution seems by no means exaggerated.

> If ever the time shall come when men must and can discuss with one another the system of armament that has prevailed hitherto, it will be at the time when the representatives of the states come together to discuss the terms under which, in the future, peace shall be kept between them. And whoever honestly desires a lasting peace will have to admit that the old-fashioned method of preparation cannot be continued without endangering peace anew. The hope that the Peace Conference will take up this question is all the more justified since there is hardly a demand of such far-reaching importance for the political, cultural, and economic development of the Europe of the future as this one . . . Under a system of mutual menace, where each state cherishes the misgiving that its neighbour is arming merely to fall upon it at the opportune moment, an honest peace is not possible.[3]

There must in fact be no illusions on this point, that as long as the militaristic system continues with its race in armaments, &c., serious progress in international law is out of the question. Among

[1] Especially so if a league of states to enforce peace will be formed.

[2] Of a different opinion is Strupp, who, in his *Neue Probleme des Völkerrechts*, p. 8, speaks of 'the no less than incomprehensible demand for disarmament after the experiences of the war, or at least of the limitation of armament by treaty'. This is not in accord with public opinion in Europe, which to-day everywhere demands an agreement on armament. As an example, attention is here called to the 'Union of Democratic Control'. 'Great Britain shall propose as part of the peace settlement a plan for the drastic reduction by consent of the armaments of all the belligerent Powers.' Cf. also G. Lowes Dickinson, *After the War*, 1915, who likewise demands an organization for the safeguarding of peace in the form of a league of peace, which is to be followed by a reduction of armament. Cf. further, Charles E. Hooper, *The Wider Outlook beyond the World War*, 1915.

[3] Milhaud expresses himself in the same manner: *Du droit de la force à la force du droit*, p. 113; 'The peaceful and juridical settlement of all international conflicts being thus assured, the limitation and the reduction of armaments become possible. In fact, everything is changed from the day when law instead of force is the *ultima ratio*, and when national armies are merely elements of the armed international force, a collective safeguard of law. From this time it will be sufficient that the force of the different nations, and finally the collective international force, be such that the people feel certain of their protection against every surprise attack or any attempt at a forcible stroke from any of the robber nations. It will then be possible to limit and even to reduce armaments on the condition of the limitation and reduction of armaments generally. It will be possible to make it compulsory on condition of making this obligatory limitation and reduction the subject of sacred and solemn agreements between all. It will be possible to guarantee observance of these agreements by the most formidable sanctions and to entrust the management of their execution to international commissions invested with the most extensive powers of inquiry and supervision. 'Neath the blessing of these incomparably strong and efficacious guarantees it will be possible gradually to reduce armaments . . .'

the 'real guarantees' that will have to be demanded in the interest of the enforcement of international law the eradication of the excrescences of the militaristic system stands in the very forefront. But perhaps we will to-day no longer be content with a mere 'paper' agreement in respect to armament, but will demand real guarantees in this direction also. As such might be considered an International Commission of Control, an international supervision of the manufacture of explosives and munitions,[1] of the manufacture of arms, of ships, the disposal of certain fortresses, &c. A treaty of peace that could not show stipulations along these lines, and of such a nature as not to admit of any doubts, would

[1] In the *Neue Zürcher Zeitung* of February 11, 1917, the demand is made that the materials absolutely necessary for war be put under common control. An association of representatives of the states would have to control and distribute these materials at one or more places. Explosives, munitions are such material. The superior force demanded by Wilson would have to rest on a *world monopoly of the production of munitions.* The individual states should, on the contrary, renounce the right to produce explosives. The sole right and duty to produce the same is to be granted to a neutral state and placed under the supervision of an authority in which all the parties to the treaty should have a representing member. This authority is simultaneously to exercise control and to manage and distribute the supplies. If the monopoly be violated, delivery of munitions to the state violating the treaty shall stop, and if the violation be not discontinued, the other states shall proceed to punishment, for which purpose munitions shall be put at their disposal. Cf. also on this subject the *Neue Zürcher Zeitung* of February 15, 1917, where a professional munition maker discusses the objections that might be raised to these proposals, and in turn makes the following proposals:

1. The manufacture of all explosive materials (including gunpowder) and of munitions is subject to international control and is to be restricted to this extent, viz. that each country be allowed to manufacture only as much as is absolutely necessary for civil purposes and military training.

2. The manufacture of purely military explosives is to be intrusted to several neutral states or to one state in small measure in order that, in case of the ultimate need of intervention against a rebellious state, they might be put at the disposal of the other states.

3. The control is exercised through an international institution (International Bureau for the Control of Munitions) with offices in a neutral state and affiliated branches in every country.

In the *Neue Zürcher Zeitung* of February 26, 1917, there is further proposed a reciprocal relation between the armament of a state and the tariffs to be charged on products of this state, in view of the relationship of export industry and militarism. The Peace Congress should fix its army budget for each state (according to number of inhabitants, extent of territory, &c.). This quota should be renewed or corrected every five years at international conferences. If a state on its own initiative increases its army budget, the other states should at once automatically increase the import duties on the products of the state in question by 100 per cent. It is self-evident that, along with this, the private manufacture of arms and ammunition would have to be forbidden. In the *Neue Zürcher Zeitung* of February 20, 1917, it is likewise shown that a power, against which no war party could make headway, could only be created by a reduction of armies. In the Berlin *Post* of March 5, 1917, all these proposals are designated '*political balloons*'. Sztern, in *Wissen und Leben* of March 1, 1917, also expresses himself as opposed to the real guarantees.

never be able to offer any guarantee that it actually is a peace treaty.

If now we assume that after the war a special league of peace will come into existence, then it is only natural that it will have to prepare to put an end to the system of excessive armaments.[1] The

[1] In *Wissen und Leben* of January 1, 1917, the author of *J'accuse* also points to this necessity. He correctly emphasizes that the world powers that would join the international league of peace would demand real guarantees for its peace of law. 'Above all, however, the powers that join the international league of peace will have to draw the most important and the most pregnant consequences from the new judicial organization: they will have to submit the question of armaments by land and sea to a treaty agreement for a simultaneous proportional decrease. *This is the most important real guarantee of the future league of peace.* On this point Herr von Bethmann has preserved silence. That is the point—the turning point—which will show whether Germany really, honestly, and uprightly wishes, hand in hand with the other peace powers, to tread the path of an international peace organization of civilized humanity, or whether she wishes to continue on her previous course of maintaining her position as a power by virtue of her own military force. A peace organization without a reduction of armaments by treaty is worthless and meaningless: the continuation of the competition of armaments will not only plunge the already bankrupt peoples completely into the economic abyss, but the race for armament would also conjure up anew all the dangers of the previous anarchy of nations, would again create only a latent state of war in place of actual peace. *An international organization of peace without limitation of armaments by treaty is like a knife without a blade and having no handle.* It is a mere figment of the imagination without value or substance. If, therefore, Germany seriously wishes the international league for the preservation of peace proclaimed by von Bethmann, let her declare that she also wants this most essential attribute of this league: *the reduction of armaments on land and sea by treaty agreement* . . . This is the touchstone of Germany's real will to peace. On this divide it will be shown in which direction Germany's streams flow. Here the guiding spirits of the German state will have to show their colours, whether they are endeavouring to secure now a *peace of necessity*, by reason of being forced to it and because there is no prospect of gaining an actual victory, or whether they desire a real *lasting peace* for Europe. On this question of armaments the spirits will be divided. *Hic Rhodus, hic salta.*' The author further shows that the consequences would also have to be drawn from the assent of the statesmen to the league of peace. 'Not only must the armaments of all those joining the league of peace be reduced, but the league of peace itself must be equipped with the prerogatives of executive power and the corresponding institutions in order to put its decisions into effect. How do you stand, Germany, on these questions? Are you ready not only to establish the league of peace, but also to make it so effective that its decisions will have to be respected by every participating member... From the answer to this question will be shown whether Germany is seriously bent on co-operating in the formation of a higher super-state of humanity.' In conclusion the author remarks: 'If it is true that the peace of Europe can only be guaranteed by pacifistic organization of the European family of nations, it was also true in 1899, as also in 1907 and the years that followed, above all in those last days of July 1914. If to-day international law disputes of the future can and should be submitted to arbitral decision, the Austro-Serbo-Russian controversy at the end of July 1914 could also have been submitted to the Hague Court of Arbitration for decision. For almost twenty years the German Government has rejected all pacifistic ideas, has constantly and scornfully contrasted such Utopias with the only justified "real politics", has set up inflexible opposition to all practical proposals of pacifist tendency,

eradication of the present militaristic system will constitute the *conditio sine qua non* of admission to the league of peace. This President Wilson expressly declared in his message to the Senate of January 22, 1917 :

> I am proposing that moderation of armaments which makes of armies and navies a power for order merely, not an instrument of aggression or of selfish violence.

And he has emphasized :

> There can be no sense of safety and equality among the nations if great preponderating armaments are henceforth to continue here and there to be built up and maintained. The statesmen of the world must plan for peace and nations must adjust and accommodate their policy to it as they have planned for war and made ready for pitiless contest and rivalry. The question of armaments, whether on land or sea, is the most immediately and intensely practical question connected with the future fortunes of nations and of mankind.

Law can only be assisted to victory by combating with every possible means its antithesis—self-help. And the same holds of international law and its antipode—war. Whoever is an adherent of the system of international law and desires its development must lend a hand, when it is a question of setting aside the system opposed to international law—the system of self-help, of war, that is, militarism in the form above described with its race for armament. Only in this way will success attend our efforts to give new form to international law! Anything less than this would be half-way work, which would be destined to prove fruitless. I believe I have pointed out in their leading characteristics the means by which this goal is to be reached of gradually setting aside this rival system and in place of it ushering in more and more the reign of law. *These means might prove helpful in the development of the system of international law, both of the old, which aimed at the development of the international law procedure, and of the new, which seeks to invest the observance of international law with real guarantees.* May the statesmen of future peace congresses use these means and thereby contribute to

and has seen the salvation of Germany only in the sharp-whetted sword and the shining armour. Only after the bloodiest war of human history had raged over the world for more than two years did the leading spirits of the German state recognize what the rest of the civilized world had recognized in peace, and had striven for with untiring energy in spite of all German resistance. That Germany's ways in these last decades were erroneous ones Herr von Bethmann now admits, at any rate if his utterances of November 9 are honestly meant.'

making it possible for international law to come out of this war as ultimate victor.

In conclusion I may perhaps be permitted to recapitulate my conception:[1]

1. Upon the termination of the war all those states that are seriously determined with every means to maintain the status of peace and desire, if need be, to enforce the observance of international law should form a league.

2. It should be the fundamental principle of this league that all international disputes among its members be submitted to an international procedure. Therefore, only such states can become members who pledge themselves:

(*a*) to lay all disputes in which they participate before an international court of arbitration, whether it be at The Hague or elsewhere, unless these disputes clearly concern their actual vital interests.

(*b*) to submit those disputes, in respect to which they made a reservation of vital interests, to mediation or to an investigating commission.

3. The members of the league should expressly place the fundamental principles of the league under their guarantee; in fact they should declare that they

(*a*) mutually guarantee their territorial possessions, inclusive of their colonies, as determined in the future peace treaty,

(*b*) mutually guarantee the observance of the fundamental principles of the league, as determined in the treaty of the league, in the Hague Conventions, or in other international treaty instruments.

4. Corresponding to this declaration of guarantees, the members of the league should obligate themselves to look upon all violations of the principles of the league as of general interest, since the observance of international law and the maintenance of peace represent a solidary interest on the part of all the states wishing peace and law, and since the violation of international law as well as a menace to peace would injure this general interest.

5. If a member should refuse to submit the matter in dispute

[1] [I believe that the programme outlined in these 14 points contains, even to-day, everything essential for the League of Nations, in spite of the fact that since then many more extensive proposals have been made.]

to international procedure and show instead a disposition to attempt self-help, perhaps entering upon hostilities and even warfare (thus violating the fundamental principles of the league), the league should first of all remind the offending state of its obligations and once more expressly call its attention to the consequences of violating those principles which it had itself accepted and, according to circumstances, fix a certain time within which the offending member is to conform to the law.

6. If in spite of this, the member of the league in question persists in refusing, it should be branded by the league as a law breaker before the whole world.

7. Without more ado, this mark of law breaker should be denoted by certain consequences, which I should like to designate as the moral sanctions at the disposal of the league. The league should above all

(*a*) pronounce the exclusion of the respective member from the league,

(*b*) break off diplomatic relations with this member.

8. If, in spite of all this, the member marked as a law breaker should persist in his intentions of disturbing the status of peace, the league should then resort also to economic means of coercion in order to compel the peace-disturbing member to maintain peace.

9. In order to insure in advance the effectiveness of such economic measures toward enforcement, it might be well for the league to demand, in the treaty of the league itself, that its members provide securities which would at once be confiscated in case of opposition.

10. In addition, the league should in this case also discontinue the economic and commercial, as well as the legal, relations with the law breaker and disturber of the peace. This discontinuance might be only partial or complete, according to circumstances. In certain cases it may be well to proceed only step by step in the application of economic means of coercion; on the other hand, the situation may demand immediate recourse to all the means of economic force.

In the latter case steps would be taken toward a complete boycotting of the state violating the law and disturbing the peace, by paralysing its entire commercial, financial, and industrial relations as well as its facilities for traffic and intercourse, such as its railways, its shipping, postal and telegraph systems, &c. At the same time all the treaties into which the law breaker and disturber of the peace has entered would have to be suspended, so far as these treaties affect them. The boycott could especially be also accompanied by the blockading of ports, coasts, &c., of the offending state.

11. Hand in hand with these measures for a partial or complete boycotting might go the seizure, sequestration, or confiscation (embargo) of goods which the offending state possesses in foreign lands. There might also be introduced corresponding measures opposed to the demands of this state.

12. Whether these economic coercive measures should be directed only against the law-breaking and peace-disturbing state, or also against its subjects, would depend upon circumstances.

13. Further, the league might, under certain circumstances, demand compensation from the state in question. At any rate, it is to be borne in mind that the offending state would have to be wholly responsible for the damages suffered by the members of the league and their subjects through preventive economic coercive measures. In addition, the league might eventually also impose punishment or a fine.

14. In case the employment of the above-mentioned economic means of coercion should not be effective, or if circumstances should otherwise make it appear desirable, corresponding military measures would have to be added to the above; such measures should prove so much the more effective, since the league would not only as a matter of course represent a much superior force; but since, in the future *peace treaty*,[1] the war preparations of the individual powers should be reduced to a reasonable degree, so that no single state would any longer be in a position to bid defiance to the might of the league. The observance of the prescribed limits of armament on the part of the individual states would of course have to be controlled in a suitable manner.

If these may be looked upon as the most essential principles by which the league of peace, yet to be established, should permit itself to be guided—I have intentionally avoided the consideration of too many details, since they would only complicate matters and make more difficult the realization of the idea—

[1] It is obvious that this matter should already be settled in the peace negotiations.

the question would still remain open as to how the relations between the members of the league and those outside the league would shape themselves. In this connexion I should like to emphasize that all those states which really earnestly desire peace, and which also seem to offer the necessary guarantees that they will adhere to their given word, should be eligible for membership in the league. Once being a member, it may be assumed without further question that such a state will also keep its obligations as a member of the league; that, having once entered, it will under no circumstances break the treaty. In view of such regulations, it is to be assumed that a great many states will join this league. So much the more, since the league would, for the small states especially, mean a powerful protection, which would in practical value vastly surpass the mere guarantee of neutrality. But one would nevertheless have to reckon with the possibility that individual states would remain without the league, whether it be for the reason that they narrowly adhere to the theory of might and refuse to submit themselves honestly to the law, or because the other members of the league, not placing the necessary confidence in the given word of such states, for the present refuse them entrance into the league. [This conception is, I believe, in complete agreement with the principles which have been expressed by President Wilson, Lloyd George, Lord Grey, Clemenceau, and other statesmen.]

Now what attitude would the league have to take toward such states outside the league? In my opinion it should be entirely analogous with the attitude toward the members of the league, but with this difference: that the requirement of the observance of international law and the maintenance of peace would, with reference to these states, not be based upon the treaty of confederation, but upon the general principles of international law, upon the existing conventions and the customary international law. The league might also, if need be, rightly demand of the states outside the league that they make use of the international procedure. With special reference to these very states, the league should, in case of necessity, seek to enforce law and peace; for it is to be assumed that just these very states outside the league might be the first to imperil law and peace. The league would be legally entitled to do so, since it would be acting as the mandatory of the community of states incorporated in the league, and the employment of the coercive means of international law would be all the more justifiable with regard to such states, since apparently this is the only way by which one might hope in time to bring them to the conviction that it would be to their own interest to subordinate themselves to the general legal order by attaching themselves to the league.

Thus it might be safe to assume that the principles of the league would not only from the beginning meet with quite general approbation, but also that the existence of the league would exert a favourable influence upon the entire international atmosphere which would manifest itself in the gradual entry of those states that at first stood aloof. And then when all of the states were once able and ready to join the international community as represented by the league, this league would perhaps coincide with the legal community which has hitherto been represented by the Hague Conferences. Such congruity between the league and The Hague might perhaps seem desirable at present for ideal reasons. For practical considerations it will, however, have to be looked upon as improbable and premature. To-day there is lacking the necessary basis for it—*confidence.* But I nevertheless consider the realization of the league as urgently necessary, even if the work of The Hague should be continued after the conclusion of peace, because it is by no means to be assumed that such radical innovations as I have here proposed could be brought about at the Hague Conferences within calculable time. A completely different atmosphere is needed for these improvements, one that is free from the difficulties encountered at The Hague. But, as I have said, this will not detract from the possibility that the league and The Hague might not find themselves in agreement at some future time. But one must by no means give up the plan of a league now on account of this eventual later agreement.

But perhaps the question will still be raised as to whether there is any possibility at all of the realization of the plan here sketched for a league of states which would, in cases of necessity, have to enforce the observance of international law and the maintenance of peace.

If I personally entertain the conviction that the prospects

for the realization of such a plan are by no means unfavourable, and that this plan is far from bearing an Utopian character the following considerations especially support me in this. The most important is of course the fact that the *leading statesmen of all states have manifested their firm intention* to start such a work of peace after the war. But I wish also to mention two facts which, in my opinion, likewise clearly speak in favour of the practicability of such a plan.

The idea that the world of states shall submit to a legal order with equal rights for all may be called a democratic one. At any rate, the democratic form of government is the one under which the realization of this idea will find the least obstacles. Whereas the idea of *might* finds expression in militarism and imperialism, the idea of *right*—the idea that right, in the life of nations, shall prevail over might—beyond a doubt finds its adequate expression above all in a *democracy*. Now there is no doubt whatever that the democratic idea has made wonderful progress in the world. And if there was anything which had to level the way for the advancement of this idea, it has apparently been the present war.[1] If there have been circles which have believed that this war would repel democracy, they doubtless have reckoned without their host. The future of the world does not belong to the powers of militarism and imperialism, which are hostile to international law, but it belongs to democracy. Democracy desires not only law, but also peace,[2] and one may therefore recognize in the growth of democratic power in the world a guarantee that law will more and more come into authority among the peoples. The great majority of states to-day is democratic. Why then should this majority not be able to achieve its desire for right and peace? Why should it not be able to bring to realization the demand for sanctions in international law, for a league to maintain peace?

I wish to emphasize here that the democratic idea not only

[1] This war has brought it about that, besides China, Russia [and now Germany and Austria also] have become democratic.

[2] In the beginning of March 1917 President Wilson said this war would never have broken out if all the European nations had had a democratic form of government. And in his message of April 2, 1917, Wilson says: 'A steadfast concert for peace can never be maintained except by a partnership of democratic nations. Only free peoples can preserve their democracy. . . . Peace must be planted upon the tested foundations of political liberty.' The purpose of war, Wilson points out, is the maintenance of the principles of peace and of justice.

requires a form of government, but above all *a state of mind.* This has recently been well pointed out by Egger :[1]

> Liberty is not only a constructive principle ; the making of peace is not only a technical execution ; liberty is not only a formula—it is a state of mind. The most beautiful legal order is useless, all peace treaties, all guarantees, all liberal constitutions are useless—liberty can only arise out of a liberal state of mind.

Yes ; in the end it is a matter of a liberal and democratic state of mind ! A progressive spirit cannot thrive where the minds of peoples are still under the spell of the slogans of militarism and imperialism. Where peoples have not yet wakened to freedom, the idea of law will also force its way with difficulty. There the cult of might signifies all. And in its retinue stands the idea of war, not that of peace.[2] Fortunately, however, this state of mind is in the modern world a vanishing quantity. The great majority of peoples are to-day of a liberal, democratic mind. In this fact above all we may recognize a guarantee for the realization of a league of peace to-day. Law and peace will prosper in the world in proportion to the progress of democracy and of freedom. And thus it is by no means a presumptuous hope that the time is not far distant when the international legal order, now so despised, will at last be honoured. Unless all is deception, the present war will bring the miracle to pass that in this world might shall no longer prevail over law.

[1] Egger : *Die Freiheitsidee in der Gegenwart*, 1917.

[2] It is characteristic that the thought that we are now about to have a series of wars finds expression right among the German historians, all of whom are to-day imperialists. The rest of the world, not thinking in terms of imperialism, wants no new wars, but an assured state of peace. Such a state will, however, not come from imperialism, which wishes for annexations, but from democracy, founded on law.

PART II

THE LAW OF WAR

THE LAW OF WAR

In the field of the law of war the relation between the ante-bellum postulates for the development of this sphere of law and the lessons of this war is relatively less simple than in the case of international law. The question whether the old postulates can still be retained after the experiences of this war is, in the case of the law of war, often very difficult to answer.[1] And the lessons which this war seems to hold for the future development of the law of war are quite naturally far more diversified and impressive than the lessons which it has brought for international law. These can really be summed up in the single sentence: In the future we shall have to seek to continue the progress of international law even *against* the will of opponents, and to enforce its observance by the creation of substantial external real guarantees. In fact, we find that through this war we are very much richer in experiences which ought to be used in the development of the law of war. Among these experiences there are even such as have a telling and revolutionizing significance for the whole province of war law and which therefore deserve to be considered first. While there are many postulates, known before the war, that still deserve to be retained and have

[1] Triepel, *loc. cit.*, p. 16, thinks it is most difficult to prophesy about the future of the law of war in international law; it is certain, however, that development can here only proceed slowly and fragmentarily—far more slowly at any rate than the great advance occurring through the Hague Conferences and the Declaration of London had led us to expect. It is doubtful whether the attempts toward codification will soon be renewed to a very great extent. Indeed, the number of problems the practical importance of which has been shown by the world war are essentially more extensive than the number of points of international controversy that had come up in earlier wars. The neutrals would also insist upon having many legal uncertainties conclusively cleared up as soon as possible, but on the part of the combatants the spirit of compromise would not be great. Confidence in the power of paper agreements has been too deeply shaken, the sins against the rights of treaties have been too great. It is true that confidence has been shaken. But among whom, and why? The remedy for this I have indicated above under the head of international law. It consists in a league of those states that wish the progress of law. The other states must, if necessary, be left behind until they have accustomed themselves to the general pace. Triepel believes that it may at least be said about the future of the law of war that the attempt to humanize warfare, in so far as this is at all compatible with the demands of military necessity, will not be discontinued, in spite of the many disappointments brought on by this war. I shall return to this subject later.

even increased greatly in inner importance through this war, it is also conversely true that many tendencies, which in the last decades were recognized as decisive for the formation of the law of war, have in this war been miserably wrecked.[1] Consequently, statesmen will at future conferences be confronted with the serious question, whether they shall continue upon the way hitherto trodden or whether they shall on the contrary enter upon entirely opposite roads.

In a critical retrospect of the results of the second Hague Peace Conference and the London Naval Conference[2] in respect to the law of war, I had given my opinions as to the wishes which from the legal standpoint (I have always kept this standpoint distinctly separate from the political) one might express for the future development of this subject. I believed at that time that I might say that there could hardly be a doubt from the point of *legal theory*, 'that neutrals especially should not become involved—or at least as little as possible—that the war should be confined to combatants, that private property of the enemy should be left intact, and that in the choice of military means certain humanitarian considerations are imperative. From *this* standpoint one would undoubtedly just as much advocate, for example, that mines be not employed, as one will agree on the subject that the right of capture of prizes is just as objectionable an institution as the injuring of neutral trade by relative contraband and the destruction of neutral prizes. And it will therefore scarcely be doubted that we should welcome it as a genuine advance in international law, if some day it should actually be declared : the right of capture and contraband are abolished, no more mines may be laid, no more neutral or private ships of the enemy may be destroyed.'

Thus I still wrote half a decade ago. To-day I should formulate my wishes quite differently. At that time, however, I already emphasized the fact that, besides legal and humanitarian considerations, others too, namely political ones, are bound to come

[1] The violation of the law is not identical with the making of new law, as I have shown in the *Schweizerische Juristenzeitung* of October 15, 1916, in opposing Eltzbacher. Also Triepel, *loc. cit.*, p. 8, writes correctly that one needs only consider for a moment the results of the view that the law of war has collapsed, in order to put it aside immediately as entirely impossible ; for if this view were correct, everything that was forbidden yesterday would to-day be allowed.

[2] Cf. my 'Zweite Haager Friedenskonferenz', vol. ii, *Kriegsrecht*, 1911, pp. 238 ff.

up for consideration in the development of law, and that it was here that the diverging elements in the views of the individual civilized states were reflected. Further, that it is just in the law of war that political, military, economic, and other considerations, as well as conflicts of interest, play an important rôle ; and that it is therefore exceedingly difficult to point out the way upon which one can attain legal progress. Eventually, one would have to resort to *compromises*. The courses which such compromises, especially in reference to the future reform of maritime law, would have to take, I then outlined as follows : As the *first* commandment, be it required that the neutrals must be affected by the war as little as possible. For this reason I especially demanded the abolition or restriction of the law of contraband, but also of other things as well through which neutrals might become implicated, and which stand in relation with the rules of contraband and blockade, as e. g. the destruction of neutral prizes. As a postulate for the future I designated the codification of the whole law of neutrality, both on land and sea. I proposed that any unjustifiable injury of neutrals should be looked upon as equivalent to a breach of international law. If this were once accomplished, maritime law would be divested of its worst defect. As a *second* commandment should appear the realization of the demand that naval war, as well as war on land, be restricted to the combatant states, and that the private property of the enemy be entirely let alone in the war. Finally, as the *third* commandment, should come the humanization of the methods of warfare. In this connexion I made special mention of aerial navigation and aircraft, and emphasized the fact that it would be an irremediable mistake if the states should lay upon the table the Hague Declaration concerning the throwing of projectiles and explosives from balloons.

The following examination will now show to what extent it is still possible to retain these postulates after the experiences of this war. Before I enter upon single questions of the law of war pertaining to land, sea, or air, I shall treat in a general way of the lessons which this war has taught us on the subject of the law of war. Not all these teachings are absolutely new. I have already pointed out that in many respects the war has also brought about a confirmation of principles, already represented before the war.

Even if it is natural, on the one hand, that the advancement and reconstruction of the law of war be urgently desired, it is nevertheless a fundamental principle, confirmed anew by this war, decidedly to guard against an *excess of regulations*, especially in reference to warfare.[1] One must not lose sight of the fact that in war we are not dealing with a legal institution,[2] but on the contrary with an act of self-help which can never be grasped by the law in its totality, and consequently as a whole stands outside the legal order. In the main the conduct of the war will at all times and places be dependent upon the necessities of the war, and nothing else. Legal regulation within such a state of self-help can therefore only be applied with moderation and only in very definite relations.[3] If this limitation is not regarded, the legal norms are likely to be violated.[4] The present war has doubtless produced distinct evidence for the correctness of this

[1] On this point cf. especially the discussions of v. Hartmann, *Militärische Notwendigkeit und Humanität*, pp. 10, 36. See also Alvarez, *loc. cit.*, p. 118; Strupp, *loc. cit.*, p. 10.

[2] Max Huber, in *Der Wert des Völkerrechts*, correctly writes: 'The idea of conceiving war itself as a legal institution and of regulating it in its course like a suit at court is an aberration of international law, resting upon Roman and mediaeval conceptions.' Among those who in recent times have recognized in war a legal status are Friedrich, *Grundzüge des Völkerrechts*, 1915, p. 126, and Bornhak, *Der Wandel des Völkerrechts*, 1916. War is a legal status, to be taken up and regulated by international law. 'War is in a certain sense a lawsuit among the members of an international community, in which the state puts forth all its might in asserting its rights, *as indeed all right* (*law*) *is an expression of power*. And the results of the war make the legal decision.' Lammasch, in his *Vertragstreue im Völkerrecht?* already opposed this view in reference to Kaufmann, for whom likewise war is a *legal* demonstration and 'the victorious war the verification of the idea of *law*, the last form that decides which of the states is *right*'. Lammasch correctly points out that politicians *à la* Treitschke and Bernhardi write thus, but not professionals in international law. 'In politics this idea may find relative justification as an opposite to *absolute pacifism*, which is equally one-sided. But this is not so in international law. For whoever makes might the norm of right places himself in opposition to the fundamental idea of international law, according to which all states, with the same premises, have equal rights.'

[3] Eltzbacher, in *Totes und lebendes Völkerrecht*, p. 21, correctly observes: 'International law has constantly imposed upon warfare only such restrictions, for reasons of humanity, as were possible without any considerable imperilling of the aims of the war. It was content with the proposition that the enemy was to be spared all useless sufferings as far as possible, i. e. that sufferings, which in n wise furthered the purposes of the war or that were immoderately great in proportion to their value, were not to be inflicted.'

[4] Of course, Prince Wrede (*Deutsche Revue*, October 1916) does not err when he writes that the sore point of the stipulations lies in the fact that military interest, closely examined at a peace conference, is *per se* a *contradictio in adiecto*. But the remedy for this lies in the very thing that I propose in this book: *The gradual absorption of the law of war by international law.*

observation. In future deliberations for the forming of the law of war this principle will therefore have to be kept in mind constantly.

But there is one other fact that one has learned to recognize more clearly than ever before through this war. I refer to the fact that the *legal conceptions* in individual countries and on the continents *diverge* so much in extremely essential points that *different systems of international law* may even be said to exist in different countries and groups of countries.[1] Such a divergence of viewpoints has been manifested especially between England and America on the one hand and the continent of Europe on the other. It was already known before the war that such opposing opinions existed, but it remained for the war to show us fully to what far-reaching results such adverse opinions could lead. This fact will have to be taken into account in the future. At any rate, it is questionable to-day whether there is really any purpose in only superficially glossing over such diverging opinions, or whether it is not far better to meet them openly.[2] Max Huber has recently called special attention to this point. He writes :[3]

> The law of war and of neutrality would have caused less disappointment if one had been more concerned about the actual defects in international law before the war, and if diplomacy had refrained from concealing important disputes by ambiguous explanations and by making treaty stipulations which admit of the most varied interpretations. . . . There are numerous stipulations, upon the issue of which it was evident to every intelligent person that the formula of agreement only apparently bridged over fundamentally antagonistic principles. . . . In the future it must be the mission of the science of international law to rid the field of all imaginary and ambiguous norms and to establish sure positions. Out of optimism and the wish for a rapid and extensive development of international law, it must in the future guard against being satisfied with incompleteness and uncertainties. It must inexorably destroy the false appearance which diplomacy, perhaps out of respect for public opinion, wished to awaken through the so-called progress of international law.

Besides the confirmation of such views and reflections, already expressed before this war, this war has also brought lessons that

[1] Cf. with this Alejandro Alvarez, *La grande guerre européenne et la neutralité du Chili*, 1915, pp. 43, 51.

[2] See what is said later on about the value of making reservations in conventions. Triepel, p. 27, also rightly observes that even in times of peace the progress of international law secured through treaties is made extremely difficult when different states, with completely opposing views on the nature of war, participate in the preparation of a treaty.

[3] Max Huber, 'Der Wert des Völkerrechts', in the *Neue Zürcher Zeitung* for November 19, 1916.

are absolutely new and speak more forcibly to mankind than any other.

It is a well-known fact that in recent years people on the continent of Europe had more and more accustomed themselves to look upon war as a *military war* in the narrower sense of the word, as a war which was not only to be fought out between military persons and which, by right, was not permitted to any extent to interfere with the rest of the population; but as a war which was also to be fought out entirely by military means and to have a military termination. This theory of war has now beyond a doubt suffered shipwreck in this war. But the two factors which have brought about this shipwreck and shown the modern world clearly what a monstrous nonsense such a resultant war is (a nonsense because it belies its own theories and leads nowhere in practice) have been *modern commerce* and *modern technical science*.

Modern commerce has shown that in the present age of commerce, in which millions of people live scattered about in foreign lands or move from place to place, it is impossible still to regard war as a matter which only concerns the military persons of the participating states. It has shown that not alone in the belligerent countries, but even in the neutral world, there is really no one who is not in some way or other affected by a great war. The mutual connexions between individuals in all walks of life are to-day so ramified and complicated that no one can entirely escape the effects of such a war. He who is not affected as a military person or as one who must enter into this war with body and soul will nevertheless be affected by the war in his family life, or his economic condition, or his social, spiritual, and moral relations. The attempts to curb or eliminate such effects have proved to be impotent. No one escapes these effects. It is therefore an empty theory that war is an affair of states, and that the carrying on of war concerns only military persons.[1]

[1] Burckhardt, too, in the *Politisches Jahrbuch der schweizerischen Eidgenossenschaft*, 1915, p. 4, writes correctly: 'The well-meant doctrine that war is merely a struggle between armed forces in contrast to the peaceful intercourse of the civilian population has proved itself an Utopia; the army cannot be separated from the people, nor the state from society; in spite of all theory war is waged between peoples, because all classes of the population must aid in the struggle, even though they do so with different weapons, inasmuch as they are all most intimately related to the state. No distinction can any longer be made between the state and the whole country; war is not only a military struggle between

In the age of commerce war is an affair of peoples who conduct it with all their physical and economic strength. It is not merely the affair of *one* people, but of *all* peoples who are either directly or indirectly involved, and all these peoples are therefore interested in preventing such wars as would make them fellow-sufferers in the age of commerce. No people should to-day dare to let itself be placed before the brutal facts of a war without opposition. All peoples to-day dare demand that their governments do everything possible to prevent war, since war has proved to be a matter not of states but of peoples.

But still more forcibly than modern commerce has *modern science* shown what an awful folly is committed by governments and their peoples when they undertake to conduct a war such as the present one in this age of technical science. It has already been predicted by several eminent persons that it will be science itself, military science, that will some day show clearly to all the world the absurdity of a military war in this present age. In this connexion we need only recall Johann von Bloch. In his famous book on war, which appeared about twenty years ago, he attempted to show (as Fried now emphasizes) that war between the equally armed great powers of Europe would present new facts, in consequence of the revolution in military science and of the economic as well as of the social development of Europe, facts which were unknown before and which make it seem questionable whether a war waged under such conditions could lead to any result whatever. Such a war between two almost equally strong opponents would necessarily have to end through the immobilization of the opposing powers, and chiefly because of the increasingly defensive effectiveness of infantry lying in the trenches. The consequent advantage for the defensive in the face of superior and numerically greater opposition would discourage any aggressive attack. This would show that the era

two armies, it is also an economic struggle between two countries.' Cf. also my article, 'Das Völkerrecht und der jetzige Krieg', in the *Politisches Jahrbuch*, 1914, p. 340: 'Now in all these relations international law has completely failed; yes, one may say that exactly the opposite has taken place of what was held to be the fact in setting up international norms. Never yet has a war been waged which has involved the civil population to such an extent, not merely of the belligerents but also of the neutral countries; yes, one may well say of the entire earth. Indeed, this is true not only as to all these peoples themselves, but as to their property and their cultural and economic condition as well.

of wars has passed.[1] Immobilization could only end through exhaustion of the belligerents in various degrees and through the final overcoming of the one who is most exhausted. The end of a war would be negotiations between the almost immobilized and extraordinarily disorganized opponents.[2]

[1] Cf. with this the article by H. G. Wells in the *Friedenswarte* of May 1916. In his *Europäische Wiederherstellung*, p. 66, Fried likewise points to the teachings of the present war concerning the changed effects of a war. The slogan of ' a brisk and merry war ' has been abolished once and for all, and with it the ideas of military romanticism and beauty. It is to be regretted that experiments were necessary to put aside this antiquated view. It was superficially thought that the institution which is still called war to-day was the same as that called war at an earlier period, because it was evolved from methods practised earlier. The war of the present day can no longer be compared with the knightly evolutions of earlier centuries. ' The tool that at an earlier day remained in the hands of man and was controlled by him has wrenched itself out of his hands. He is no longer the master of this institution, but its servant ; which, when once freed, he is no longer able to control. Herewith war has ceased to answer to the definition of Clausewitz, whereby war is a continuation, " only through other means ", of politics. For these means have proved themselves useless through the force of their effect. *War will henceforth no longer be designated as a continuation, but on the contrary as the professed bankruptcy of politics.*' Knowledge of this fact will become still more forcible when once the present catastrophe oan be viewed as a whole. Experiences will speak so eloquently that extollers of war will scarcely dare any longer venture to continue their dangerous business. Herewith the idea of imperialism has received a blow from which it will never recover. The dream of military romanticism has been dreamed to the end. But important, too, are the teachings which the war has brought us in its own *technical field.* Most of these appearances had already been foretold by Bloch half a generation ago, almost exactly as they have come to pass. He showed how the rapid development in the science of arms would completely exclude the application of the experiences of earlier wars, just as completely different tactics would have to be employed in consequence of the revolutionizing effects of arms. The necessity of intrenchments in rifle pits, which would transform war into a protracted siege, the superiority of defence, the great losses, the long duration of the battles, their uncertain effect upon the course of the campaign, and in consequence the long duration of the war itself, convulsing economic life in a manner hitherto unknown—all of this Bloch had set forth in detail. He pointed out the immense extent of the battlefields, the resultant difficulties of the maintenance of soldiers, the inadequate nursing of the wounded and the enormous loss of lives in these gigantic battles. On the basis of these predictions he reasoned that contestants would emerge weakened from such a war, that there would finally be neither victors nor vanquished, and only the complete physical and economic exhaustion of the belligerents could in dire necessity put an end to hostilities. Bloch has in the main been right ; this war has confirmed his teachings. He has not been understood, and we have preferred to be taken unawares by happenings which might have been anticipated if his teachings had been examined. Bloch will go forth as the real victor in this world war.

[2] Fernau, in *Wissen und Leben* of February 1, 1916, writes that the great fact taught by this war is the following : ' That modern wars, no longer bringing about any results, are in every way useless. They end with the mutual exhaustion of the combatants, and not, as formerly, in conquests and an increase of power. Their results are in no way proportionate to the terrible sacrifices which they demand.' With the knowledge of this fact war and all that pertains to it will be discredited by the nations ; and this is so great a moral achievement for the

Beyond a doubt this war has confirmed the views of Bloch in many respects. Most of his predictions have already been fulfilled. The size of the armies in itself prevents war from being conducted at the old pace. In fact war to-day has in essentials become a war of positions. It may indeed be considered symbolical that the opponents are compelled to hide from each other by entrenching themselves or concealing themselves in the water. Yes, to-day war must seek for itself a hiding-place. Nothing else can be done in the face of modern technical science, which in our day entirely rules warfare. There is no longer any military formation that can withstand modern technique. All inventions have been called into its service. Fortresses are no longer impregnable. Mountains are no more obstacles than rivers and the ocean. Even the air has been conquered by technical science. Distances hardly exist for modern artillery; it destroys the heaviest armour-plated turrets. Steamboats, railways, telephones, and the telegraph are in the service of the belligerents as well as automobiles and submarines. Aircraft, electricity and searchlights, explosives, poisonous gases, hand grenades, machine guns, flame projectors, mines, and torpedoes all play a rôle. These technical means defeat all struggle. Even the best-trained and best-equipped armies in the world can to-day accomplish nothing against these means. *Modern technical science has conquered military warfare and with it militarism itself.* That is the great lesson of the war!

The soldiers live in deep excavations (writes Max Müller),[1] silent and resigned; the armies of 1916 shield themselves against bursting grenades as primitive man formerly sought shelter in his cave from the elements and wild beasts. What a mechanical thing war has become! The soldier seems to follow every vocation save that of the warrior. He is road builder, carpenter, metal worker, artificer, engineer, he manipulates all kinds of tools, but no weapons! . . . To-day it is artillery alone that carries on war; with the same mathematical precision it tears the bodies of the brave and the dejected, shatters the nerves of the strong and the weak alike, and makes both the young and the aged tremble. A half dozen heavily calibred batteries to-day decide upon the victory and defeat of hundreds of thousands. 'We shall fight to the last man, to the last

human race that even the millions of lives sacrificed in this war are not too great a price. 'For, hitherto, war could only exist through the good repute created for it in homes and schools, in parliament and by the press. Let this good repute be destroyed, and no one will any longer recognize any advantages in war. Every one will abhor war, for it demands terrible sacrifices, brings no solution, and maims civilization.'

[1] Cf. the *Neue Zürcher Zeitung* for December 28, 1916.

horse.' How anachronistic that sounds in an age when it is no longer masses of men, but industries that war against each other! And yet, is it not man who has brought the technique of war to this degree of perfection? Will he in the long run let himself be ruled or crushed by this machine? How far is this 'materialization of war', this impersonalization of the soldier still to go? The first impression . . . is indeed that the technique of war will go on perfecting itself according to a natural law of evolution, and that a fourth or fifth year of war will bring forth new unknown progress in the means of offence and defence . . . the logical conclusion is: the war can still go on for years! We believe this is an illusion. Armies have to-day arrived at the limit of material preparation, which can perhaps still be exceeded quantitatively, but hardly qualitatively. Every age develops that military technique which is peculiar to it; our age developed its own in the last two years, since the long era of peace only offered imperfect opportunity to adapt in form and spirit the exercise of arms to the industrial existence of peoples. Just as the armies of knighthood were out of harmony with the age of trades and guilds, as infantry lost its dominating position with the introduction of metallurgy, and an army of mercenaries had to make way for the people's armies, so too our manœuvring armies of peace times were anachronisms. . . . The most perfect form of traditional preparation for war, the Prussian, was broken by the resistance of the Belgians and the French; a nation which was completely without an established technique of war, but embodied to a greater extent than any other the industrial spirit of the age, namely England, stands to-day as the most feared and most capable in war (with reference to duration). She holds in her hand the destiny of Europe. At the present time it depends entirely upon the modern point of view, upon patriotic discipline, upon the energy of the governments, as to whether all the belligerents should carry war preparedness in the industries to its logical conclusion. The armies at the front have ceased to be a mechanism in themselves; they are no longer the embodiment of 'a people in arms'; they are offshoots, a last expression of the high-strung energy of war-waging millions. Militarism had to take on this machine-like, soulless, anti-cultural form, in order that the nations might learn to hate it with all its horror and bloodshed. There will come a time when the human instinct for self-preservation will rise against this fatality, a psychological moment when the human will once more triumph over machinery.[1]

[1] Cf. further the article in the *Neue Zürcher Zeitung* for July 23, 1916: 'Ist das noch ein *Krieg*?': 'Is this not a war that denies and disappoints itself? It has been said formerly that war is a carrying out of a political struggle with forcible, i. e. military, means. Now all peaceful economic means are employed in carrying on war. In former times famine and pestilence followed upon failure of crops and poverty, against which no human power could prevail. Now want is consciously created by man and controlled like munitions and arms; it is sent this way and that way. Armies are no longer arrayed against one another for open designated places. Armies are no longer arrayed against one another for open battle. They entrench themselves deep in the earth or else rise in the air, shattering the earth beneath them and poisoning the air. One might think that war was now a technical undertaking with military means and an acute economic struggle, for which measures are taken in days and hours to disturb the lives of individuals and nations, the furtherance of whose welfare had formerly taken generations. We have had to learn anew.'

So it is indeed! This just and drastic description clearly shows that technical science has in a military sense already triumphed over war,[1] and, in so doing, has overcome the military system itself. *Commerce and technical science have to-day practically conquered military warfare. Militarism, which has prepared and brought about this catastrophe for Europe, is by this very war judged and condemned.* By this war it has shown itself *ad absurdum.* One may safely and rightly designate this result as the *greatest* of all the lessons of this war. Greater still will it be for those who know how to reflect upon this lesson and to draw the necessary conclusions from it. For we are to-day actually living in that psychological moment when the will must once more triumph over machinery and reason overcome the militaristic spirit.

The knowledge that the purely military war has outlived itself has naturally not yet reached every one, although I have no doubt that after this war it will become a common possession. It has, however, been quite generally recognized that it has become utterly impossible to *limit* oneself to a purely military war.[2] Naturally, there are still many to-day who will not admit that this war has *in general* proved itself to be an absurdity in our present-day relations. Triepel, for example, designates it one of the greatest tasks of the future[3] to find an adjustment between the two conceptions of war. He distinguishes between the one conception that war is a struggle between peoples, and the other that it is a struggle between states.[4] And he is of the

[1] Eltzbacher, in *Totes und lebendes Völkerrecht*, p. 16, also points out that the development of technical science has, so to speak, overcome the temporal and spatial limits of war. It has placed in the hands of belligerents means for destruction, in undreamed-of number and effectiveness; it has made it possible for them to place the industries of the whole world at the disposal of war. Besides, increased population and greater prosperity have also contributed to the force and weight of war. The modern spirit, too, more and more conscious of its purpose, has determined recklessly to employ all forces and means. *This* 'modern spirit' is identical with the spirit of militarism. This time, however, it may have reckoned without its host.

[2] Cf. with this the citation below from Burckhardt.

[3] Cf. Triepel, *loc. cit.*, p. 28.

[4] According to Nöldeke, in *Die Zukunft des Völkerrechts* (cf. the *Frankfurter Nachrichten* for July 15, 1916), the continental conception is the progressive one and the other is retrogressive. It is a question which of these views will in the future prevail in the law of nations. He writes: 'Upon this matter the views among us also widely diverge. Some are of the opinion that a compromise will take place between the two; yet it is very difficult to say in what manner such a mediatory view, if it is to be at all clear and definite, will be expressed. Others think that we should calmly accept the development of affairs, take our positions upon the ground prepared by our opponents, and draw the necessary conclusions

opinion that the conflict between these two theories will end neither in the complete defeat of the one nor of the other.[1] The conception of war in the form advocated by the English has certainly become untenable. On the other hand, that of the continental doctrine of international law is narrower and more formal than comports with either the realities of life or the aim of war. War is directed at the overcoming of the hostile state and nothing else. Therefore all that passes beyond this goal in injuries inflicted upon the enemy, that is, his land and his citizens, must be forbidden. However, it must be remembered that the state consists of people, not merely of soldiers. Already

from it. This would virtually amount to capitulation to the English viewpoint of war. It would naturally include a waiving of the freedom of the seas and the renouncing of the right of capturing prizes demanded by us and also expressly held by our government as one of the aims of war. For if, according to the example of our opponents, in the future we no longer wished even to recognize protection in war on land for private property, then the demand for the protection of private property in maritime war can no longer be upheld. The recognition of the English viewpoint must, however, still have far more incisive results for the whole economic relationship of nations after the war. And in this respect this recognition would harmonize very well with the views of our opponents, who desire as much as possible to prevent the resumption of relations between mutual dependents. For intercourse between individual peoples, as it existed before the war, is simply impossible if this English viewpoint becomes universally prevalent, or even if retained by England alone. Who in the future will venture to enter upon commercial relations with nationals of the states now hostile towards us, that will transfer his property to such states, or even begin commercial enterprises there, if he must fear that his economic existence is so seriously endangered? All more intensive commerce and trade between single countries are simply out of the question while such principles prevail. The natural development of mankind will, however, not permit such a state of things. But it is not we who are retarding the wheels of the world's history, by opposing the present powerful English idea of war; on the contrary, it is the theory represented by our opponents that is most discordant with all the demands of modern civilization and modern commerce. Thus the future of international law can only be directed towards the complete destruction of the English view of war, namely of all against all.' Were it not better to work for the complete destruction of war itself rather than to turn merely against the English theory of war?

[1] Niedner, *Der Krieg und das Völkerrecht*, 1915, p. 24, is of the opinion that in conducting war against economic interests it is not merely a question of the violation of single principles, but of the fundamental departure from certain previously accepted maxims, of the alteration of certain former fundamental theses of international law. Another conception of war is thus being accepted, another aim of war is pursued. This is assuredly incorrect, because one-sided. The aim of war is in reality always the same. Economic annihilation is not the object of economic war, but the overpowering of the enemy. The conclusion of Niedner that in the economic war all previous principles of justice crumble in ruins, and that the perpetrated violations of the rights of nations are no longer to be considered as such, is just as incorrect as his insistence that economic war corresponds to a more profound view of civilization and of justice. But I cherish the hope with Niedner that the conviction of the necessity of checking unbridled violence may again become the common property of civilized nations. Is this wish, however, to be realized only in the domain of economic war?

Moltke, seeing this, opposed the theory that the only task of war was the weakening of the *military* strength of the enemy, and laid emphasis on involving *all* the resources of the hostile government, its finances, railroads, food resources, even its prestige (!). If it is the purpose of war to bend the enemy's will by force, it then becomes necessary, yes permitted, to employ military means not only against the opposing army, but also against all the economic forces of the adversary. Up to a certain degree *every* war is a 'trade war'. A successful land war of itself destroys the greater part of the enemy's commerce during the war. Naval warfare has its particular weapons adapted to this purpose, and these can only be abolished with the abolition of naval warfare. Now since the economic strength of the state is composed of the strength of the individuals, it is inevitable that war should be directed against the economic interests and the property of individuals also, in so far as this is profitable and imperative for the attainment of the war aim.

It is evident from this exposition that even Triepel is already on the *road* that leads to the true knowledge of the teachings of this war.[1] The war that stands by the side of the purely military war (the 'war of state against state') should be characterized, not as the war of 'people against people', but as the *economic* war.

In fact, *economic war* stands side by side with military war. The particular task of naval warfare, as is well known, is to strike at the enemy's economic life. The aim of war is always the same—to impose one's will upon the adversary. But the methods employed in land and in sea warfare differ; and since both kinds of war present like claims to existence, their respective methods must have like justification. Wehberg is correct when he writes:[2]

It is impossible to reach an agreement in land warfare that the conquering of hostile territory beyond a certain small limited area should be forbidden, for that would signify the unattainableness of the war aim. Just as impossible

[1] Bornhak, in *Der Wandel des Völkerrechts*, 1916, p. 16, also writes that through the world war has come a reversal against former policies. 'Under England's influence, the principles of naval warfare which had been checked were again grafted upon land warfare. No longer was the mere subjection of the hostile armed force the goal of land warfare, but the destruction of hostile industries.' So the progress of centuries in international law is annihilated, previous international law torn to shreds, and the hands on the dial of the law of war turned back. Bornhak concludes: 'Economic, along with political and national opposites, govern the history of the world.... Therefore war, a purely military event, had again to become an economic struggle.' The question whether these teachings on war are not calculated to discredit war entirely Bornhak, of course, does not discuss.

[2] 'Das Seekriegsrecht,' in the *Handbuch des Völkerrechts*, 1915, p. 4.

is it that hostile commerce in naval warfare remain undisturbed, unless violence be done to the very nature of war on the seas. For in the one case the conquering of territory, in the other the greatest possible cutting off of imports, is the means by which the enemy is to be made submissive.

This argument answers also the reproaches against the so-called 'starvation war'. 'Starvation war' finds exactly the same justification in international law as military war. One must not be disturbed by catch-phrases in the service of an artificially stimulated war feeling. Economic and military war measures are equally justified in principle. These war measures naturally find their limitations, unless special standards forbidding certain means of war are involved, only in the rights of neutrals. If these are not transgressed, there is absolutely no objection from the standpoint of international law against the 'starvation war'.

In this connexion, this standpoint of principle had to be emphasized once more.[1] Moreover, states must as a matter of course allow themselves in economic war to be guided by the necessities of war, just as is the case in military war. In *both* cases all means calculated to subdue the enemy will be employed. Economic war can therefore not be limited to obstructing enemy *commerce*, but it must seek to strike a vital blow at the enemy's economic life. It is thereby unavoidable that private individuals be struck. The saying of Moltke was quoted above that war must be directed against all the resources of the hostile government, even against its prestige. That is then the standpoint which

[1] For all details on this subject, compare with my work, *Deutschland und das Völkerrecht*, Part I and ff. Allow me merely to call attention to the fact that the publication of the German General Staff, *Kriegsbrauch im Landkriege*, represents 'starvation war' as fully justified. And Niemeyer, *Prinzipien des Seekriegsrechts*, 1909, p. 17, even expressly states that in naval warfare life for the enemy must be made as intolerable as possible by all, even the most brutal means.' Burckhardt truthfully remarks in the *Politisches Jahrbuch der schweizer. Eidgenossenschaft*, 1915, p. 23: 'The destruction of commerce is at bottom a more humane method of warfare than the destruction of persons. And the conquering of the military strength of the enemy would in the last analysis be purposeless if the control of the economic resources of the country would not force the hostile government to surrender. It is for this reason comprehensible that every belligerent establishes for himself this aim . . . The power of the military resistance of a state is so closely interwoven with its economic strength that its industrial life is just as indispensable to the state for the continuation of war as the life of the soldier. Therefore the belligerent dare not be forbidden to attack also the economic resources of his opponent. . . . The starvation of the enemy, cruel as it is, is in my opinion in itself no prohibited method of warfare. It must, therefore, be regarded as permitted to injure the economic life of the opponent. The enemy is not bound to have any consideration for the enemy.'

German military literature throughout has accepted. Press statements which would now represent the economic war as unlawful must not lead us astray on this point.

In view of this state of affairs, it is from the very outset a hopeless undertaking if German literature on international law now opens a campaign against the economic war. Mendelssohn-Bartholdy, for example, attacks the 'conception of warfare of English law '.[1] He seeks historically to expose 'the grave falsifications and errors of a traditional policy, accepted apparently as though it were beyond the possibility of a doubt', and to bring to light the blackest motives 'out of which grew the right of capture and the war against the commerce of the enemy, the starvation war of the twentieth century'. But the English and American literature cited by Mendelssohn-Bartholdy shows plainly, in every instance, that, indeed in economic warfare long before the present war, it was a question not only of commercial war in the narrower sense, but also of war on enemy industries in general, and on intercourse with the enemy—a fact which the present war has lately made more strikingly evident than ever.[2] In view of such compelling facts it appears a useless task—this late effort to gather from old sources of information evidences of the perversion of the law of nations. Historical development cannot be undone by such a procedure.

Mendelssohn-Bartholdy writes in conclusion :

> But in the war which the peoples of Europe must now wage against each other it is one of the most tragic events that the Latin peoples, half under the impelling hand of fate, half as the willing sacrifice of their own spirit, bow down under the authority of the English idea of the state. Before this war the best French exponents of international law could say that under their guidance a new and more humane law regulating the relations of the individual to the war of states and their armies had been formed. In this war the Anglo-American conception, which makes war an annihilation of a whole enemy people and denies every progress of human thought, has already conquered the Allies and also forced Germany to go the road of retaliation that overtrumps evil with evil. Let us hope that after the war there may come that reaction of Russell, causing the triumph of the German idea of state and people. May the wars of the future, if they must come, be honourable battles of arms fought by valiant men, and not starvation wars directed against the women and children of the enemy.

[1] See Mendelssohn-Bartholdy, *Der Kriegsbegriff des englischen Rechts*, commentaries on the case of Panariellos, 1915.

[2] Cf. with this question Burckhardt, in the *Politisches Jahrbuch*, 1915, pp. 22 ff.

Mendelssohn-Bartholdy appeals in conclusion to the words of Shakespeare and of Ruskin, that not the richest and the shrewdest, but the bravest and the righteous must win in war.

And herein they [Shakespeare and Ruskin] have pronounced their verdict on the conception of war contained in English law, on the financial and economic war, which their people, *mercator populus*, is waging against us.

I do not believe it possible to subscribe to these statements. The teaching of this war is essentially different, as I shall presently show. In the first place we need not especially consider whether it is the English or the German conception of war that has been established by its events, but merely this question : Which form of waging war has proved most effective under modern conditions. It may be taken for granted that all the belligerents will seek to adapt themselves to this form, and for that no one can reproach them. If this form should be the economic war, that by no means signifies *a priori* a backward step ; for the economic war is certainly no more inhumane than the military, and its purpose is just as little the 'annihilation of a whole enemy people'. On the contrary, it also desires nothing else than to force the opponent to yield. Only the means are different ; the purpose is the same. Care should be exercised in manipulating such arguments as are employed merely to stimulate artificial feeling. Surely Mendelssohn-Bartholdy does not himself believe that the wars of the future will ever again be 'honourable battles of arms, fought by valiant men'. These times are for ever past. Therefore the appeal to Shakespeare and Ruskin seems dubious. The war of money and economic interests cannot be disposed of with such catch words.

Moreover, we are here not so much interested in the standpoint of previously accepted international law and the question of its possible violations. Far more interesting is the question of the teachings imparted by the present war and the practical application arising from them which will aid in the framing of international law *after* this war. And, considering the economic war, there comes to us from this war this great teaching : that in the present commercial relations of peoples, the economic war has a far greater importance than any one would formerly have thought possible. It may truthfully be said that the effect of modern commercial conditions on economic warfare is the exact opposite of what it has been on military warfare. If, by reason of the present commercial relations between the nations, the consistent carrying out of a purely military war has been proved to be an impossibility, these manifold commercial relations have, on the other hand, been the cause of the exceedingly effective commercial war. This war has shown that, given the present commercial situation, it would theoretically be possible to-day to conduct a war even with economic methods only, and nevertheless attain the war aim, namely, the forcing of one's will upon the enemy, just as thoroughly as this would ever be possible in a purely military war, by making use of military means alone. As a result of world commerce, economic warfare has obviously gained in importance and effectiveness, just as military war has lost in importance and effectiveness. *The future belongs to the trade war.* This deduction may with all definiteness be drawn even to-day from the events of the war, it matters not what its outcome may be. It may end as it will, the lesson that the *modern form of war is the economic war* remains indelibly written.

What conclusions shall we now draw from this teaching of the war? What practical applications grow out of this state of affairs for the future international development of law? That is the great question which to-day seeks an answer. Does it really suffice to stride along the former track, or must we on the basis of these experiences stake out new guiding lines for the future development of the law of war?

First of all, I should here like to interpolate that for a just objective judgement it is absolutely necessary to allow oneself to be guided solely by such considerations as are calculated to bring law nearer to its vital goal, namely mastery over might. This goal *alone* must be the standard point of view. In answering this question political considerations and points of view must become as though null and void. In international law it is not the single nation, no matter how it may be called, but the *totality* of nations in which is embodied the idea of law. In answering this question of the future, from which depends the welfare not only of *one people* but of *all peoples*, every one-sided national consideration is therefore to be unconditionally rejected.[1] One

[1] Compare with this my article on 'Der grundsätzliche Standpunkt für die

should therefore not give the preference either to military or to economic warfare because one form or the other best serves the interests of this or that country. International law does not aim to serve *one* country but *all* of them. Consequently, in setting up the guide boards for the future law of war, one dare not demand as a matter of preference the development of this or that mode of warfare merely because it would best serve the interests of this or that country.[1] The politician may engage in such speculations. For legal theory, however, which is to point out only the roads that lead to the real goal, namely the victory of law, these considerations can have no existence. It must renounce all such side glances if it is to escape the danger of wandering into forbidden ways.

These are basic viewpoints which must be accepted as the starting point without reservation if we are to answer the question, what form is the future development of the law of war to take in the light of recent experiences? In order that we may see this evolution with entire objectivity we must seek out an observation tower so high that every possibility of national prejudice vanishes, that the individual nations are no longer visible to the eye, and that only the great whole, the development of human international law, appears in sight. In order to see quite clearly the importance of an entirely objective judgement let us transfer ourselves a hundred years into the future of the history of the world. Surely no one will reproach the person who from this point of time surveys the present world war viewed by the light of its consequences, accusing him of having wished to draw his conclusions in favour of this or that military party of the past world war. Indeed, before his spiritual eye these parties vanish and, freed from all obstacles which stand in the way of the contemporary judge in his striving to gain an objective standpoint, he is calmly able to measure what influence the events of this war have had upon succeeding human development, what factors have influenced this development in a favourable, what in an unfavourable sense. From his tower he will doubtless be able

völkerrechtliche Betrachtung', in *Wissen und Leben* of July 1, 1916. This article forms the introduction of my book *Deutschland und das Völkerrecht.*

[1] Unfortunately at the Hague Conference, in many delegations, this point of view played the only deciding rôle. It is, of course, self-evident that to-day one cannot completely restrict one mode of warfare and allow full liberty to the other. Future developments must be left in the hands of the future.

to estimate the teachings that this war has imparted more justly than we to-day are in a position to do. He will surely not attribute the historical fact of the fiasco of the purely military as against the economic war to the credit of this or of that past military party, whose names are for him without any meaning whatever, but he will view them, just as I have here proposed to do, purely *in the light of the development of the idea of law.* And seen in this light he will perhaps find that the so-called historical fact has in no sense of the word been a misfortune, but that it was throughout adapted to further very materially the development of international law. For, leaving quite out of consideration the fact that economic warfare as the more humane involves a forward step, as against the more mediaeval military warfare, it is quite evident that on the route leading to the gradual elimination of self-help, of war—in a hundred years we shall recognize this still more clearly [1]—above all the purely military war retreats more and more into the background.

This needs some explanation. I have called the real goal the victory of law. And I have already shown that this victory involves as its necessary presupposition the maintenance of the normal condition of law—a state of peace. The gradual elimination of self-help, of war, which is the negation of the way of law, appears, therefore, to be the most important task, the supreme command, if we are ever to come nearer to this real goal. I am not Utopian enough to believe that wars can be abolished within any time limit that can now be set. But that does not invalidate my claim that the real goal of international development is the setting of *international law* on the pedestal now occupied by *war.* In surveying the route for the further development of international law, this final goal dare never be lost sight of. Even if for the present we merely make wars more difficult, less frequent, that is at any rate a gain. But as already said, this nearer goal, attainable to-day, must not blind us to the final one.

Now this final goal is the same for the law of war as for international law. In speaking of international law, I have already said that we must always strive that law in the life of nations

[1] A backward glance would surely also reveal what terrible folly the competitive armaments of the last years have been, a folly that led nowhere and which not only was unable to prevent the fiasco of the military system, but, on the contrary, hastened it. Perhaps such a retrospective look would also show how this system was discarded as antiquated soon after the war.

steadily gains ground. This gain is made at the expense of self-help. By building up the law of nations, especially through the creation of methods of international coercion, the domain of international law will naturally be extended and that of self-help diminished. Law takes the place of self-help; international procedure, international compulsion, the place of war. Thereby not only war, but with it also the importance of the law of war, would be pressed more and more into the background. Thus we arrive at the *gradual absorption of the law of war by international law.* And we cherish the hope that, as the final result of this development, the time will come when *international law will completely usurp the place of the law of war.* Should the final goal be attained, and right celebrate its victory over might, this absorption would then be complete.

We are certainly to-day still far removed from the attainment of such a goal. But, as I have repeatedly emphasized, it is always desirable to seek not to lose sight of the basic tendencies in coming developments. No harm can therefore result from holding before our eyes at this present time the circumstance that international law is continuously to gain ground over the law of war and finally absorb it; for from this fact flows as a matter of course a series of consequences helpful for the future development of the law of war.

Of what then do these consequences consist? What shall we deduce from the teachings of this war, above all, concerning the value of the economic in its relations to the military war, in the face of a goal that points to the gradual absorption of the law of war by international law? The first conclusion from this state of affairs would seem to be that we should seek to further the development of the law of war and of international law along lines approximately parallel. Such a parallel development would, in my opinion, most readily lead to a gradual absorption of one by the other.

What do we understand by a parallel development of the law of war and of international law? The new starting point in the development of international law which we found to be the result of this war, consisted first, in the necessity of creating a system of substantial external guarantees for this law. Further, we have planned the extension of this new system of coercive measures in the following form: first of all, a series of economic coercive measures would have to become effective, and only if these economic measures failed should military coercive measures be employed as *ultima ratio.* Should not this method of building up the system of *international law* be also a guide post for the future building of the *system of the law of war*? Why should the development of the law of war not proceed along lines parallel to those of international law? And would not such a parallel development actually be the best transition to the gradual attainment of the final aim, which consists in an absorption of the law of war by international law? This calls for further explanation.

We have seen the characteristic trait of international procedure, as well as that of the system of coercive measures of international law, to be the 'co-operation of third parties', in which is expressed international solidarity. The opposite of this is self-help—that negation of law in which isolation expresses itself. The methods of law and those of self-help evidently run so far parallel that in both cases economic and military measures are to be distinguished, though existing side by side. For international law we have placed economic and military coercive measures side by side. And in the law of war we distinguish between economic and military warfare. Therein lies, as already stated, a certain parallelism. But what should hinder this parallelism from going a step farther? For international law we have characterized the application of military coercive measures as the *ultima ratio.* Economic coercive measures are under all circumstances to be given the preference. Military compulsion is to be used only if economic compulsion does not suffice to inspire respect for the law of nations. Why should not these principles, which in the 'co-operation of third parties' find a place in international law, be applicable in self-help, in war, to a certain degree? That at any rate would be the *most significant* progress which at present could be made in the law of war. And, as our observation has shown, it would be such a forward stride as would be thoroughly in harmony with the experiences of the present war. For this war has taught us to ascribe to economic warfare a materially greater importance than has previously been attributed to it. Why should we not strive to apply the above-mentioned system of international law to the law of war, by conceding as a matter of principle the preference to the economic war, that of trade, thus introducing gradual changes even in self-help? Only in those cases in which the first stage of self-help, the economic war, has not led to the goal, is the actual military war to be recognized as permissible. Such a parallelism in the development of international law and of the law of war would not only arise automatically from the teachings of this war, but it would also be of supreme significance, as I have already indicated in referring to the real purpose of the development. For such a development of the law of war, in which the road of self-help at first coincided with that of an intensified war of trade only, would also be at the same time the destined way leading to the point where it would be possible to desert the way of self-help entirely, in order to proceed only on the way of law. Will the time ever come when we shall wage *wars without weapons, wars of trade only*? That is the distant vista, the perspective, which is here revealed. The system here proposed would be the *transition, the bridge*, but likewise a bridge leading to a later warless era, *in which the coercive measures of international law would entirely usurp the place of wars.*

From such a train of thought there would proceed for the present age, first of all, the postulate that, in the law of war of the future, economic warfare especially should be further developed. This method of warfare should not only be further developed, but this development should also take a direction to some extent parallel with that of the economic coercive measures of international law. This would of course by no means hinder the further building up of the law of war. The essential thing is that the economic war, the intensified war of trade, be placed more in the foreground, and the military war, the resort to *all* means, be expressly given the character of an *ultima ratio.* The chief difference between the application of economic coercive measures according to international law and the economic war would above all consist in this: The former would proceed from the international community, the confederation of states, the league of nations, the latter on the contrary from the state alone that had declared war. In other words, the former way would be the way of law, the latter that of self-help. However, in other respects the coercive measures to be applied in both cases might coincide throughout. The same comparison would hold, more or less, between the military coercive measures of international law and the military war.

If I have here wished to stake out a general line of direction which, in my opinion, after the experiences of the war, should not, in the interests of the progress of law, be entirely overlooked in the future development of the law of war, I am nevertheless subject to no illusions as to the immediate possibility of realizing such theoretical propositions. Even if the attempt to guide the development of the law of war into the channel that I have indicated should fail, there is certainly no harm done in at least pointing out possibilities of the sort. As already stated, such possibilities furnish an opportunity to again become conscious of the real goal in the setting up of international rules of law, and accordingly to test and perhaps subject to revision the basic tendencies by which the further progress of the law of war ought to be governed. If we seriously consider what has here been said, we will surely not persevere in merely proceeding along the beaten track, but we will doubtless seek new roads.

Before I proceed to draw definite practical applications for land, sea, and air warfare I must here insert a further basic observation. The future form of war law as well as of international law is under all circumstances to signify a *forward*, never a *backward* step. It is, as I have already indicated in the introduction, by no means superfluous to doubly underscore this basic remark. There are unfortunately to-day no lack of tendencies that would turn the law of war back once more to the standpoint of the Middle Ages, as is shown by the already mentioned article of Eltzbacher's as well as by many other war publications. From the perpetrated violations of international law in this war they have drawn the false conclusion that the further development of international law must proceed in the sense and in the direction of these violations. To a certain degree they have done this in order to give a belated sanction to the perpetrated violations. Yes, they have even gone so far as to pretend to ascribe a character directly formative of law to the very violations of law. Herein these teachers of international law have fully misunderstood the lessons which this war has taught us. We should certainly take to heart the teachings of this war in the future development of international law. Under no circumstances is a breach of international law an act by which law is created.[1] *Injustice remains injustice*, and no dialectics can change that fact. The new inter-

[1] Laband also emphasizes that it is unnatural to transform acts of violence of the war into acts creative of law. Cf. further Friedrich, in the *Grenzboten* of October 1916. See also below, p. 133, note.

national law can only be created after the war by law-creating factors, namely the states. It is by no means already here. The tendencies which are to blaze the way in this creation of law will assuredly never be the same as those which have made themselves so conspicuous in this war through their contempt of accepted international law. The way of law must under all circumstances lead *upwards*. The teachings of this war are particularly adapted to-day, more than ever, to bring out in bold relief this road leading upwards.

It seems to me that in what has been said there are concentrated some of the most important general tendencies that ought, according to my opinion, to be considered in the new building of war law. Without discussing in detail all the various departments of the law of war, in what follows I shall seek to show, by at least several examples, how a practical application is to be made from the above principles.

Let us examine first of all *land warfare*. The point of departure for our consideration is above all the Hague Convention on Land Warfare, which is a comparatively complete codification of existing law on land warfare. We must concede that this convention has on the whole stood the test.[1] Moreover, it conforms to the exigencies for which allowance must be made in the regulation of war law, for it refrains for the most part from too far-reaching restrictions through which the freedom of the belligerents would be shackled.[2] It seeks rather to adapt itself to the needs of warfare and to leave sufficient free play to military necessity.[3] It is true that in particular points the convention has been found wanting. That has been especially the case, as we have seen, where it has attempted to protect the non-combatants against the consequences of this war, in as far as their lives, their property, their safety, and their honour were concerned. It is just these endeavours that looked towards the humanizing of war that have, unfortunately, completely failed.[4] What conclusions then shall we draw from this fact ? Shall we seek to abolish the

[1] Cf. with this statement my treatise, 'Das Völkerrecht und der jetzige Krieg', in the *Politisches Jahrbuch*, 1914, p. 337. Likewise Triepel, p. 19.

[2] No one can maintain, for example, that the prohibitions against bombarding unfortified and undefended places, against plundering, &c., are too severe.

[3] For more detailed information on this point see my larger work, *Deutschland und das Völkerrecht*, in *Part I*, pp. 60 ff.

[4] Cf. with this statement Preuss, in *Das deutsche Volk und die Politik*, 1916.

pertinent provisions of the convention or shall we strengthen them; or shall we let things remain as they are? This question should be answered in the light of the principles which I have developed above.

First of all it is clear that after the experiences we have had under present conditions the aim of an absolute militarization of war must be definitely rejected. Burckhardt writes:[1]

> The limitation of the struggle to the purely military side has hovered before many a theorist as the ideal of the 'civilized' war of the future: private property should be secure on both land and sea, the private exchange of wares should continue even among the belligerents; war should be conducted only between the states by their armed land and sea forces, but not by the citizens of the hostile states. To-day this ideal is perhaps without a single disciple, not because it is too far removed from harsh reality, but because it has been shown to be artificial, even unnatural. Not only is the commerce existing between adjacent or neighbouring states hard hit under all circumstances by military events, but it would, moreover, be highly contradictory if, from feelings of consideration, a state should have to spare the commerce of the enemy while it was mowing down his youth by thousands; if it should have to permit its subjects to send exports to the enemy while it bombards his ports and occupies his territory.

We can scarcely consider an essential strengthening of the pertinent regulations after they have so fearfully failed. But shall we therefore now give up these regulations? Shall we proclaim the war of all against all, and in the future renounce the protection of private individuals in war?[2] That also appears

[1] Burckhardt, in the *Politisches Jahrbuch der schweizerischen Eidgenossenschaft*, 1915, p. 22. Niedner, for example, writes, *Der Krieg und das Völkerrecht*, 1915, p. 15: 'The former prevailing conception of the European civilized states, confirmed by practice, was to the effect that war between two civilized states was merely the conflict of their armed powers, with the aim of compelling the hostile state to surrender.' According to Bornhak, *Der Wandel des Völkerrechts*, 1916, p. 15, it is an essential principle of war law that the only purpose is the defeat of the enemy's army by one's own military forces.

[2] Eltzbacher, *op. cit.*, p. 29, justly emphasizes the fact that the development of warfare and of international law in favour of the civil population coincides with the general progress of mankind. But so much the more hazardous are the conclusions which he ventures to draw from the events of this war. He stresses the fact that modern warfare is characterized by its unscrupulous prosecution of the war aim, and that it has therefore renounced the right of allowing itself to be guided, in its treatment of the hostile civil population, by any other principle than the will to victory. 'A warfare inspired by this spirit dare show no hesitation in view of the fact that war has become more and more an affair of the people, that it has come to depend more and more on the number, the economic resources, and the confidence in victory of the entire people. As the military achievements of the adversary struck deeper root into the collective strength of the people, it became increasingly important to break this strength by all the means at disposal. Thus the war against a hostile army had to become a war against a whole hostile people. If, however, the waging of war once took this step, international

to me to be a hazardous conclusion, which conceals in itself a danger against which I have already sounded a note of warning; namely, that of retrogression in international law. There remains therefore only the third possibility, that we seek to hold fast to the principles of the previous codification. Here again we must hesitate, after seeing how these principles have suffered shipwreck in the practice of war.

In my opinion the following must be said in answer to the question. Certain limits for the humanization of war have been

law had to follow.' According to Eltzbacher, international law has already followed. 'The previously accepted principle that war may be conducted only against the enemy's armed forces, and that the civil population may only in a few definitely defined cases be subjected to the hardships of war, was therefore antiquated. The present war has cast this principle aside. It has been violated not only in individual cases, but it has forever and completely collapsed. It will no more be observed in future wars. The break with the past is irrevocable.' Events, however, do not move with such rapidity. The assertion that international law has already been transformed is wide of the mark. Violations of law do not create new law and waging war is not yet international law. This theory is evidently only concocted to serve the purpose of justifying the perpetrated violations of the law of nations. Well has Lammasch said, that a violation of international law can receive no recognition in the system of international law nor the negation of law in the legal order. But *de lege ferenda* the case is also otherwise than Eltzbacher thinks. He demands that *international law bow before militarism.* There is, however, a *second alternative*, and that reads: *militarism must be abolished, in order thereby to enthrone the law of nations.*

It will perhaps be of interest in this connexion to give still further conclusions of Eltzbacher. He writes, p. 53: 'Not until now has the idea of the struggle against the whole enemy people, through which the basis of its means of waging warfare is destroyed, been grasped in its enduring significance. The fight against the enemy people has become a common possession, a technical means, which from now on ministers and generals of average capacity and strength of will will make use of with impunity. This greatest military means of modern times, which is infinitely more terrible than 42-centimetre guns, U-boats, and airships, will in the future conquer for itself a still greater domain. In the sharpening struggle for existence, the nations must more and more subject all their powers to the service of war; consequently it will become increasingly important for each side to weaken the strength of the people of the adversary. At the same time, the increasing interrelation of the economic interests of the world and the growing dependence of peoples on each other, lend to the attack on the strength of the enemy people more roseate prospects of success. The economically progressive nations, which send many men abroad, invest great sums in foreign countries, import quantities of raw materials from them and in exchange deliver their manufactured wares, offer to such an attack the largest exposed surface. Therefore the fight against the civil population will be a singularly effective weapon, particularly in those wars in which backward peoples seek to prevent progressive ones from rising.' From the arguments of Eltzbacher we must, in my opinion, draw quite a different conclusion, and this runs: Abolition of the entire military system and *the substitution of economic for military warfare. That* appears to me to be the compelling conclusion to be deduced from what Eltzbacher says. He himself writes on page 64: 'Complete liberty of attack on the economic life of the enemy is to-day permitted. Everything may be done that will aid in shattering the enemy's economic foundations, on which his power of waging war rests.'

drawn. We dare not expose the previous achievements in this direction to destruction,[1] but neither dare we fetter the waging of war, whether it be by military or economic means. Let us therefore go no farther than we have already gone. At any rate, we should not now attempt to restrict the war on trade by one-sided regulations, since to-day it is recognized as having equal rights with the military war. The circumstance that commerce and industry are both attacked by war can have only a *prophylactic* effect. It will increase the number of the opponents of war quite materially.

On the other hand, all those regulations which have been made for the protection of individuals should not only be maintained, but above all they should be *more clearly defined.*[2] We should be decidedly better able than heretofore to hinder the future violations of the law of war by a closer study of many questions, as, for example, that of the participation of non-combatants in the struggle or in hostile acts, the protection to be afforded to private individuals and their property and interests in the belligerent states, the question of reprisals, the rights of requisition and levying contributions, the holding of hostages, the punishment of the interned and prisoners, and so forth. These are questions which stand in a comparatively loose relationship with the attainment of the military or the economic aim of the war, and which therefore make it possible to let the voice of humanity be heard without hindering the progress of the war.[3] A service can be performed to both warfare and humanity by a clear rewriting of the law. Let us take, for example, the question of reprisals, which have played so disastrous a rôle in this war.[4] It is most necessary to issue more accurate regulations, so that we may never again experience a repetition of the events of this war. The same thing is true of numerous other questions, the solution of which would be to the advantage of private individuals. Here we have before us the field where a legal standardization appears not only desirable but possible, whereas in respect to the regulation

[1] Triepel is also of this opinion, *ante,* p. 109, note.

[2] Triepel, p. 19, for example, justly points to the gaps of the Geneva Convention, particularly in regard to the sanitary personnel.

[3] Triepel, p. 29, justly emphasizes that it remains the task of international law to balance in its universally applicable decisions the interests of a warfare impelling to victory and the need of protection of the peaceful citizen.

[4] Fuller details on the war of reprisals will be found in my repeatedly mentioned book, *Deutschland und das Völkerrecht.*

of warfare proper we would perhaps do well to exercise more restraint than before.[1]

Just as the regulation of land war will to-day be regarded with somewhat different eyes than before this war, so to a materially greater degree will *naval warfare* have to submit to a revision of many views expressed before this war. Many of its institutions will doubtless need a thorough revision.[2] Many postulates set up before this war must be abandoned without more ado. This, as we have seen, follows necessarily from the fact that after this war international law will be given an entirely new character. Before the war it was supposed to be built chiefly, yes exclusively, on mutual *confidence*. Now, with this confidence lacking, we shall no longer be content with a building standing on such a weak foundation, and we will desire that coercive measures be introduced into international law. That of course changes the whole state of affairs, though this is less the case in the domain of land warfare, in which we already have a complete code of war law, and in which the previous outlines can on the whole be preserved.[3] The same cannot be said of naval warfare, in which we have a series of institutes which stand in fairly close connexion with the proposed system of coercive measures. As long as we believed that we could dispense with coercive measures in international law, and still thought of the possibility of a war of a more or less exclusive military character, so long did the postulates which I cited at the beginning of this section appear capable of realization.[4] One could at that time still plead for a complete abolition of the rights

[1] Triepel also justly demands, pp. 21 ff., a revision of the 'clause of general participation' in the Hague Conventions. In the event of war, one should grant to the treaty power engaged with several adversaries, who are not all parties to the treaty, the right to decide for itself whether and in how far it wishes to have the treaty applied. We must also agree with Triepel when he objects to the many *reservations* attached to the conventions. Under certain circumstances one should absolutely refuse to sign a treaty weakened by numerous reservations, for the reservations are a sure sign that the time is not yet ripe for a codification, and it would therefore be better not to attempt it. Another possibility would be, however, that those states which are agreed conclude a treaty among themselves.

[2] Burckhardt is also of this opinion, 'Wandlungen des Prisenrechts im europäischen Kriege', in the *Politisches Jahrbuch der schweizerischen Eidgenossenschaft*, 1916, p. 117. He is of the opinion that the present war has shown that a mere modification of the existing institute on the right of capturing prizes will not lead to any satisfactory result. An entirely new law must be created. Since I cannot at this place enter into the discussion of individual problems, the reader is referred to Burckhardt's criticism of prize law.

[3] Strupp, *Neue Probleme des Völkerrechts*, p. 10, is of the opinion that action in the domain of land warfare will be almost wholly revisionary in its character.

[4] Cf. above, p. 110, and my *Zweite Haager Friedenskonferenz*, vol. ii, pp. 238 ff.

of contraband and the capture of prizes. This appears to me questionable to-day,[1] for to the degree that we introduce coercive measures and bring the economic war to the foreground, to that same degree do we interfere with the waging of war if we abolish these institutions. It is just this that we wish to avoid, as I have repeatedly explained.

The salient point in the question concerning the retention, abolition, or modification of the institutes of naval warfare must evidently be, whether they are really adapted to making possible the attainment of the essential war aim. If so, they will presumably be retained[2] and merely adapted to the modern method of waging war. The war aim, as we have seen, is always the same, in land as well as in naval warfare, in the military as well as in the economic war—to force one's will upon the opponent. But this can be accomplished by economic as well as by military means, and in naval warfare the former play an especially important part. Consequently it appears impossible that in the future we should dispense with these means. Rather the nature of future warfare depends in great part on the manner in which the application of these means takes shape in the war law of the future. And linked with the shaping of future warfare is also that of international law.

In the foreground of our interest stands to-day without a doubt one of the most effective means of naval warfare, the institution of the *blockade.* As in many fields of international law, so also in regard to the right of blockade, there has been for years past a divergence of opinion between the continental system and the Anglo-American practice. According to the latter system, the consequences of a violation of the blockade are meted out to every ship which sails to a blockaded port. (Theory of the continuous voyage.) In the Declaration of London an attempt was made to reconcile these divergences by a compromise, but the Declaration of London was never ratified, nor were its regulations by any means

[1] Strupp, *loc. cit.*, p. 11, says: 'It will no longer be merely a question of legalizing submarine warfare, but above all of limiting materially the right of blockade, of defining the position of the enemy's merchant marine, and of abolishing the right of the capture of prizes.'

[2] Niemeyer, *Prinzipien des Seekriegsrechts*, pp. 19, 22, emphasizes that the unlimited form of all serviceable military means, inclusive of the right of capture of prizes, is in accord with the principles of naval warfare. I believe that to-day we can say with greater accuracy the unlimited form of all serviceable *economic* means.

complete. Consequently the divergences still exist. Besides, through this war the views concerning the conception, the extent, and the methods of the blockade have doubtless undergone a very essential modification. The conception of the blockade appears to-day to be very materially enlarged. In its legal aspects we can scarcely go back to the old institution. In addition, we must remember that if coercive measures are once introduced into *international law*, we might have to wield the boycott along with the blockade, not only in war law, but also in international law. Consequently this institution takes on not merely a new significance, but it may perhaps assume quite a different appearance. All of these facts which I have mentioned must be borne in mind in the building of the maritime law of the future. Of course the right of blockade must be so fashioned that it comports with all modern needs and the experiences of this war, and so that it conforms to the alterations in the methods of waging war. We dare not seek to emasculate the blockade.[1]

It is doubtful whether the states would still be willing to-day

[1] Eltzbacher, *op. cit.*, p. 71, is of the opinion that, even if it has not brought about an effective blockade, from now on a belligerent state can forbid neutral ships to enter the harbours of the enemy, if it is of the opinion that the hostile state might use them to carry on world commerce. It might also attach conditions to the permitting of the voyage, e. g. that men of military age of the enemy state be surrendered, that wares destined for the country of the enemy be handed over, that the searching of the mail be permitted. On this subject compare Burckhardt, *loc. cit.*, 1915, p. 62. Among other things, he justly points out the fact that in London the important question remained unsettled as to whether the blockade might be carried out by the laying of mines. Convention VIII contained merely the unsatisfactory stipulation that it was forbidden to lay automatic contact mines before the coasts and harbours of the enemy ' for the sole purpose of hindering commerce '. It is worthy of note that at The Hague Germany declared that she would accept this article only with reservations. In the *Politisches Jahrbuch*, 1916, p. 5, Burckhardt summarizes the experiences of the war in reference to the blockade, saying that the methods that modern military technique has employed to effect it must be called into question ; and that, on the other hand, it frequently happens that the blockade of a limited section, or even the whole of the enemy's coast, is rendered purposeless by the ease with which non-blockaded ports can be pressed into service. We already knew before the war that, on account of mines, torpedoes, &c., the blockade could only be carried into effect at a rather remote distance from the coast ; now we know in addition that it is no longer possible to blockade hostile coasts by means of permanently stationed ships on account of the submarine boat danger. All these experiences assuredly speak in favour of a thorough modification of the present law of blockade. Burckhardt, *loc. cit.*, p. 115, demands the complete rejection of the right of blockade ; when limited to the coasts of the enemy it has proved to be ineffective. I am also of the opinion that the conditions of the blockade must undergo a complete change, but do not think that on this account the institution as a whole ought to be abolished. On the contrary, the blockade in the future may prove to be a thoroughly effective weapon.

to consent to a complete abolition of the *law of contraband*, as at the second Hague Conference.[1] This institution stands in too intimate relations with the economic war and with the blockade to be so lightly dispensed with. And it can doubtless be of the greatest influence on the attainment of the economic war aim. I believe, therefore, that we shall have to count on maintaining the institution as a whole. Nevertheless, we hope that for the sake of the neutrals there will be prescribed definite limits in the regulations concerning relative contraband, unless, indeed, in the future we are to restrict ourselves to absolute contraband. Moreover, I should not consider it a misfortune if in the new regulations we do not go back to the Declaration of London, for its provision signified, as I have already explained, a backward step.[2] At that time I characterized as the goal of a regulation of the law of contraband the defining and limitation of its meaning. This is still the desired goal. It is possible to conduct an effective naval warfare, and nevertheless out of consideration for the neutrals to hold fast to the postulate of a definite limitation of the law of contraband.[3]

[1] Cf. with this my *Zweite Haager Friedenskonferenz*, vol. ii, p. 212. The proposal for the abolition emanated from *England*. Sir Ernest Satow declared: 'We regard, then, our proposition to abolish contraband of war in every sense of the expression as the only step in advance which has been made in our day for the development of the true principle of the Declaration of Paris.'

[2] Cf. with this my *Zweite Haager Friedenskonferenz*, vol. ii, pp. 225 ff. Von Bar, in the *Deutsche Revue* of December 1909, expressed himself to the same effect. This retrogressive action at London in part made it possible that in the practice of this war the conception of contraband could be subjected to such an elastic interpretation.

[3] Eltzbacher, *loc. cit.*, p. 71, is to be sure of the opinion that, from now on, a belligerent state, without paying any heed to the former principles of conditional and absolute contraband, may take from neutral ships wares destined for the enemy, without regard to their nature, and without reference to the question whether they are going directly to a hostile or to a neutral port, in order from there to be sent further by land. Of course this view calls for no serious refutation. On the contrary, what Burckhardt writes, *loc. cit.*, 1915, p. 69, is very much to the point: 'What (in the Declaration of London) was proposed as a common law of nations has not stood the test. In the first place, it is dangerous to allow so much scope to the belligerents in the definition of what is to be contraband and what not; and, in addition, the rules concerning neutral or foreign destination and the presumptions established to determine it, leaving quite out of consideration a certain lack of clarity in their formulation, are so subtile that they fall to pieces when the attempt is made to apply them. In particular, the distinctions concerning the destination of contraband seem to us to be of almost unbelievable shortsightedness. The present war has shown that it is impracticable to distinguish between objects destined for the use of the state and those for private consumption. What is once in the country belongs to the whole people and is at the disposal of the state. . . . Further, it is impracticable, in respect to the importation of relative contraband, to distinguish whether the ship unloads its

Many a progressive step could perhaps have been achieved before this war which will now be more difficult of attainment. Such a one is the abolition of the *right of the capture of prizes.* At the second Hague Conference England would have been inclined to make concessions in this direction had Germany been willing to meet her half way on the question of the limitation of armaments.[1] This progress was at that time completely thwarted

wares in a neutral or in a hostile port. . . . The right of taking prizes is not justified as a means of injuring merchants or of putting the commerce of the opponent at a disadvantage, but only as a means of weakening the power of resistance of the hostile country. It does not fulfil its purpose if commerce can be carried on through other countries. It is readily conceivable that England would feel itself placed at a disadvantage by a regulation limiting the right of taking prizes, since as an island it will never be in the position of having to provision itself by way of a land route leading through other countries. In regard to an inland state also, such as Switzerland, the declaration of naval law is unjust, since it permits the confiscation of objects destined for inland states, in spite of the fact that the ship is bound for a neutral port. If, therefore, an inland state is at war, it can never import relative contraband by way of a neutral port. The London Declaration of naval rights is therefore defective, and it is not surprising that it failed when it came in contact with harsh reality.' In the *Politisches Jahrbuch* of 1916, p. 5, Burckhardt also points out that the Declaration of London suffered from an unfortunate lack of clearness in its basic ideas. Cf. further Zoller, *loc. cit.*, p. 83, and Frantz Bernard-Beaumaine in *La paix par le droit*, 1917, pp. 49 ff.

[1] Cf. with this my *Zweite Haager Friedenskonferenz*, vol. ii, p. 127: 'The decisive factor in the position taken by the English delegation was the impossibility of separating the question from that of commercial blockade, as also the circumstance *that the hindering of commerce seemed less cruel than the customary war massacres.* The English Government nevertheless declared itself ready to examine the question of the conclusion of an agreement to abolish the right of capture, if such an agreement would also promote the reduction of armaments.' Sir Ernest Satow declared in the session of July 5, 1907: 'If a change should ever be effected which would favour reduction of armaments, our government might perhaps examine the question anew. If, for example, on the one hand, the nations should for the most part show themselves disposed to reduce the effective of their naval and military forces, in such a manner as to diminish to an appreciable degree the fear of the evils which war might inflict upon them, and to render war improbable by the very fact that aggression had been rendered difficult; and if, on the other hand, it became evident that the conclusion of an agreement for the abolition of the right of capture would facilitate this change, and that the absence of such an agreement would hinder the realization of it, the government of His Majesty would doubtless be disposed to admit that the benefits to be derived from the change were superior to the objections which, as a matter of principle, might be opposed to it.' . . . Burckhardt, *loc. cit.*, 1916, p. 115, is of the opinion that the right of capture has lost its justification if it only serves the purpose of injuring single enemy merchants, but does not affect the life nerve of the economic life of the enemy. This argument, however, might just as well be applied to all the activities of war. Burckhardt, moreover, rejects the rights of blockade as well as of contraband and capture. He admits that the means of attack open to the belligerents at sea would thereby be pruned down to an extraordinary degree, but measured by the law as it existed before the war, less than one might think. I doubt whether we shall succeed in abolishing the institutions of naval warfare within an appreciable time. I do believe, however, in a *new order* which will be built upon a modernized right of blockade. In what

by the resistance of Germany to every discussion of the problem of armaments. To-day it must appear questionable whether England would be inclined to make concessions in this direction.[1] The more we strengthen the character of international law by coercive guarantees, and the more, on the other hand, the law of war tends toward economic war, so much less can we count on commercial war being able to renounce the previous methods of warfare. However, the creation of a league of peace with an agreement concerning armaments might still bring progress in this direction. If we succeed in abolishing the military system, then perhaps the right of capture will also disappear.

A further problem is the question of the laying of *sea mines*. The Hague Conferences left this problem unsolved. The Comité d'examen of the second Conference had worked out a project. This did not propose entirely to forbid the use of mines ; at any rate not their use for the purpose of injuring the armed force of the enemy. But it proceeded on the theory that the use of this weapon concealed in itself dangers for peaceful navigation. In order to protect the principle of the freedom of the seas, this peaceful navigation had the right to demand that the high seas, open to all nationalities, should not conceal any secret machines of destruction in places where they were not expected, and where the necessary precautionary measures would therefore not be taken. International law must seek, said the committee, to reconcile the principle of the freedom of the seas with the demands of war and national defence. The attempt to secure for peaceful trade an effective protection must be the point of departure of these deliberations. The entire prohibition of mines is not to be hoped for, perhaps not even to be desired. I believe that to-day we can still acknowledge these principles to be correct. We hope that it will be granted to future conferences to succeed where the second Hague Conference failed :[2] so to regulate the use of mines

manner and to what degree the rights of contraband and of capture will be preserved is, of course, to-day an open question. I for my part hope for a regulation in the sense of my above given explanations.

[1] Cf. Zoller, *loc. cit.*, p. 81.

[2] There were at The Hague two opposite tendencies in particular in reference to the places where it was to be allowed to lay anchored contact mines. Whereas the one side wished to establish definite limits within which the use of such mines should not be prohibited, the other side, on the contrary, demanded for the belligerents the right to make use of anchored mines without any space limitations, even on the open sea, within the sphere of their immediate activity. The *English*

that peaceful navigation will not be affected by it. I wrote at that time concerning this question: 'For the neutrals—and these are *in dubio all* the treaty powers—it is and remains an incontestable demand of justice, that they at least are not to be molested by war, even if other states believe that they must settle their affairs that way. The greater the number of states which *seriously* desire an enduring peace, the nearer will we come to the time when the neutrals, or, what will then be the same thing, the community of states, will simply demand a guarantee against damages on the part of the belligerents. Common interests should and will bring the neutrals closer and closer together in war, in order to take common action for their protection. If two treaty powers become involved in a war, all the remaining parties to the treaty form in opposition to them a natural group of interested states. They form also a legal community, and they should therefore stand together for the strict observance on the part of the belligerents of the conventions concluded in common. That is no more than their just right. They would doubtless also have upon their side the power necessary to enable them to accomplish this effectively. Not until the feeling of solidarity among the treaty-making states shall have so far progressed that they are ready under all circumstances, without regard to any temporary political alignments, to stand common guard over the rights of nations, will the time have come when the difficult subjects, to which the question of mines also belongs, will be ripe enough for a really successful judicial treatment.[1] The task which I had here allotted to the Hague community of states will be solved, I hope, by the future league of peace.

I must here put in a word in regard to the *submarine boats*. These constitute a *new* weapon, and new regulations must therefore be made concerning the use of this weapon in the naval law of

standpoint, according to which unanchored mines were to be entirely forbidden, as well as anchored ones on the high seas outside of the territorial limit, was the most progressive. Germany was willing to concede the first point, but persisted in her opposition to the second. Cf. my *Zweite Haager Friedenskonferenz*, vol. ii, p. 109. Eltzbacher, p. 71, says: 'The belligerents are to-day no longer prevented, not even out of regard for the rights of neutrals, from laying mines before the enemy's coasts and ports, if these mines are exclusively for the purpose of injuring maritime commerce. They are under no other obligation than to give due notice of their intended action.'

[1] Cf. my *Zweite Haager Friedenskonferenz*, vol. ii, p. 123. Cf. further *Fortbildung*, p. 499, and Hilty, in the *Politisches Jahrbuch der schweizerischen Eidgenossenschaft*, vol. xiii, pp. 63 ff.

the future.[1] In formulating these regulations the same demand must be made of the submarine boats as in the case of mines: their use dare not degenerate into the endangering of peaceful navigation. Certainly the law of war must not put chains upon the waging of war, certainly the attainment of the war aim is not to be hindered by rules of law, yet the use of mines and submarines can very well be so regulated that, to the limit of their capacity, they may be made to serve the aim of war, and yet avoid exposing neutrals to unnecessary perils and injuries. In formulating laws of submarine warfare, the experiences of this war will cause this point to be emphasized above all others, namely, that by mere terrorizing the war aim can never be attained. Only that which may be decisive for the termination of the war serves the war aim. Terrorization merely intensifies warfare without actually being of service to its aim. That of course is not merely to be said *de lege ferenda*.[2] As long as there is a lack of special provisions for submarine warfare, it is subservient as a matter of course to the previously accepted international law. To the extent that submarine warfare disregards these provisions, it violates international law.[3] Of that there can be no doubt. New law in this domain may appear desirable, but it does not yet *exist*. It is yet to be created. As long, however, as it does not exist, the old law is still valid. He who does not regard this transgresses against the legal order. *For law must remain law.* Surely no one would desire to make the new law synonymous with terror. We would so shape it that, like all others, the new weapon be limited to the

[1] Cf. with this question, for example, Teich, 'Neue Völkerrechtssatzungen', in the *Kölnische Zeitung* of December 28, 1915. Further, Bornhak, *loc. cit.*, p. 80, Eltzbacher, *loc. cit.*, p. 66, *Zeitschrift für Völkerrecht*, ix, pp. 20 ff., 135 ff.; and the writings of Meurer, Frank, Steinuth, Hollweg, Frankfurter, &c.

[2] The Austrian Vice-Admiral Kailer von Kaltenfels gave expression to his views on the future of naval warfare through the columns of the *Berliner Tageblatt*: 'The combinations in the world war now raging give to the powers of the Entente such an enormous superiority in the forces of naval warfare that the necessity of submarine warfare for the Central Powers arose automatically. It is difficult to make predictions as to the form that it will assume in the future. Probably at the peace conference or at international negotiations, England, France, and America will urge the passing of international legislation by which the submarine weapon will be restricted in the future and its effectiveness rendered difficult. This is of very great common importance for the powers which have at their disposal great fleets of battleships. In these conferences the small states, for whose defence of course the submarine weapon is of the greatest significance, must vigorously support the side of the Central Powers, in order that in future naval wars the position of this decision-bringing weapon may be assured.' It is scarcely to be assumed that any state on earth will take the side of the Central Powers on the submarine question.

[3] For further details, see my larger book, *Deutschland und das Völkerrecht.*

urgent necessities of war and be confined within the bounds of regulated law.

Finally, a brief word on *aerial warfare*. The same may be said of aerial as of submarine warfare. The invention of aerial navigation and of flying has proved to be of the greatest importance in warfare. Aircraft to-day appear indispensable for reconnoitring. On the other hand, it is evident, after the experiences of this war, that the throwing of bombs from aircraft, in contravention to the law of nations, is unable seriously to further the war aim. It can only serve to terrorize. Innocent private individuals are for the most part the victims of this aerial warfare. Military necessity cannot be used as the basis of the argument of the advocates of this method of warfare. And this demonstrated fact therefore justifies us in holding fast, also after this war, to the postulate, that the declaration concerning the throwing of projectiles and explosives from balloons be renewed in a form corresponding and adapted to the newest technique ;[1] and this not merely *in spite of* the events of this war, but also *because* of these events. For they have shown plainly enough the uselessness of this procedure and have proved to the whole world that the warfare in the air is really nothing but a *war of reprisals* lacking every inner justification with respect to the attainment of the real war aim. Reprisals never serve the aim of war, merely the causing of terror, of war sufferings.[2] And therefore in the war law of the future we must with all our energy attack *this whole system of reprisals*. We hope that aerial warfare will finally

[1] On this point, cf. my *Zweite Haager Friedenskonferenz*, vol. ii, p. 10. See also Zoller, *loc. cit.*, p. 32. ' So excellent and valuable for reconnoitring as the work of the airmen was in the European War, so slight, yes directly insignificant, were their achievements in so far as they attempted to carry destruction into the hostile ranks.'

[2] Eltzbacher is of the contrary opinion. He says on p. 67 that many kinds of activity are permissible, the purpose of which is to *shatter the spiritual foundations of the enemy's warfare*. Among these activities he counts the bombardment of undefended coast cities by warships, because such bombardments are not merely adapted to disturb the enemy's economic life, but also to fill the enemy population with a very special terror. ' For the same reason no reservation should be imposed on the hurling of bombs from aircraft. In respect to such attacks the distinction between fortified or defended places on the one hand and unfortified or undefended on the other is quite purposeless. For in the great majority of cases bombs are thrown not to help to conquer a place, but to disturb the enemy's economic life and, above all, to create despondency and war weariness in the hostile population. There effects are also attained by bombs which fall upon defenceless places.' These words need no commentary. Future creators of international law will surely know how to distinguish between an economic war and a war which needlessly seeks to sow terror.

vanish with this system. We also hope that modern war law will again confine aerial navigation and flying exclusively to the service of reconnoitring and thereby fulfil a postulate which I once characterized as one of the most important which could be presented to the Third Hague Conference.[1] It has recently been justly said that, judging by the experiences of this war, aerial warfare may be forbidden without disadvantage to the belligerents, but with great profit to the civil population.[2]

Presumably the most difficult problem of all will be the bringing into accord the *interests of the neutrals* and the needs of modern economic warfare. Even before the war I pointed out the postulate which should be placed at the head of the list of demands respecting the building of war law, namely, that the least possible injury be inflicted upon neutrals.[3] Burckhardt has lately justly emphasized that, however comprehensible it may be that the belligerent should aim at forcing the enemy government to yield by mastering the sources of its economic life, the means employed are, nevertheless, not a matter of indifference, since their choice determines whether the interests of neutrals should suffer much or little.[4]

How can this postulate be made to harmonize with the doctrine of military necessity which demands the attainment of the war aim by the aid of any and all means ? Eltzbacher is of the opinion that the position of neutrals before the law has grown much worse in the present world war. Many rights of neutrals were so generally and regularly violated that they can no longer be considered as existing.

> Since they have been so overridden to-day, future wars will no longer recognize them. The new convictions of what is right and just have swept old rights aside. The breach with the past is irreparable. The position occupied by former law, in particular Articles 2 and 4 of the Paris Declaration of maritime law, has been usurped through a revolutionary remoulding process by a new unwritten law which permits far deeper attacks upon the existence of the neutral states. The present time is unfavourable for the rights of neutrals.

[1] Cf. my *Zweite Haager Friedenskonferenz*, vol. ii, p. 248. Consult the same work for a further statement concerning the then existing status of the problem.

[2] Zoller, *loc. cit.*, p. 33.

[3] See above, p. 111.

[4] Cf. Burckhardt, 'Das Recht der Neutralen auf Verkehr mit andern Staaten', in the *Politisches Jahrbuch der schweizerischen Eidgenossenschaft*, 1915, pp. 22 ff. Burckhardt justly starts out from the viewpoint that war is not merely a military struggle between two armies, but also an economic struggle of country against country. This fact dare not be left out of consideration in judging the behaviour of the belligerents.

According to Eltzbacher, only certain states, whose participation in future wars is very improbable, such as Switzerland, Holland, Norway, will reap a permanent advantage if commerce and the other neutral interests are assured by international law.

Most states on the contrary find occasion to become enthusiastic over the rights of neutrals only if it is probable that they themselves will be neutrals in the wars of the immediate future. If England, the United States, Russia, Japan,[1] say to themselves that in the wars of the coming decades they shall presumably be mere spectators, they will advocate a secure legal status for neutrals because they hope to derive profit thereby for themselves. If, however, these states say that a near or somewhat more remote future will see them involved in a war, they will not bestir themselves to secure the adoption of laws which might hinder them in carrying on the war. . . . An age of world wars seems to be dawning and every great state must count on being drawn into them. International law is based ultimately on the will of the great nations. Without their support no institute of international law can be maintained. At a time when the inviolability of neutrals is merely a burdensome fetter for the majority of the great states, the position of neutrals in international law must of necessity grow worse.

I believe that not only the neutrals, but also the citizens of most of the belligerent countries will reject such a conception. If violations of law have been committed, these bear witness, not to convictions of newborn rights, but to the fact that wrongs exist. And the claim that nations become enthusiastic for the rights of neutrals only when there is a prospect of gain in store for them does not bear testimony to any particularly high degree of respect for law. But we neutrals are convinced that there are states which do possess this high respect for law, and which will, therefore, vigorously support the rights of the neutrals ; indeed this is so much the more the case, since to-day the prevailing thought of the whole world is directed to the hope that we are entering upon *a period not of world war*, but, on the contrary, of *an enduring peace*, a peace which can rest only upon a high regard for law.

Burckhardt[2] writes concerning the consideration which the belligerents ought to show for neutrals :

The rights of neutrals should reduce the disadvantages accruing to them from the war to a definite minimum. At the same time they offer the belligerents a certain guarantee against wilful damages by the enemy, especially economic isolation, from which, according to the circumstances, now one party, now the other, can reap advantages. They form a sort of silent convention as to what is

[1] Not Germany ?

[2] Burckhardt, *loc. cit.*, 1915, pp. 24 ff.

admissible among the belligerents, and upon which both sides should be able to rely. Consequently, the principles concerning trade between neutrals and belligerents should be clearly formulated and during the war should remain unchangeable. . . . The indefiniteness and the remoulding of the laws of neutrality *durante bello* has contributed much to the growing bitterness and intensity of war at sea.

Burckhardt recently demands[1] that future law be directed towards final regulations of the trade of neutrals during war times as an affair of the neutral states themselves, of state communities as such, and that it be not left to chance or to the ability of single merchants as to how far this law be maintained. The commerce of the neutral countries must either be permitted or forbidden. What is adjudged permissible must be recorded as a right of the neutral state and be respected by the belligerent. What is forbidden must be forbidden to the neutral state, that is, the obligation of suppressing forbidden trade must be made incumbent upon it. It is a question of the economic functioning of the country or of a right of the state, if the limits of its permitted commerce are defined. It is not merely a question of the private interests of a larger or smaller number of merchants. The neutral state must be able to count on its permitted trade not being cut off, whether it be carried on by private, subsidized, or purely governmental mercantile fleets. On the other hand, whatever is characterized as unallowed support of the enemy should be entirely forbidden to the neutral country, not only to the state as such, but also to the private citizens of the country. Just as little as the state and its nationals admit of separation in cases of legal rights, just that little do they also admit of separation when obligations are involved. The state is responsible for its nationals in so far as it can determine their conduct, and to-day it can determine very definitely what it wishes in respect to exports and imports.

I believe that probably all the neutrals will concur in the wish here expressed. In this question we need clarity above all things. Clauses open to double interpretation, such as have prevailed up to the present, must be done away with. There can be no doubt that the previous regulations were unsatisfactory and contradictory, and therefore we can assuredly give expression

1 Burckhardt, 'Wandlungen des Prisenrechts im europäischen Kriege', in the *Politisches Jahrbuch der schweizerischen Eidgenossenschaft*, 1916, pp. 111 ff.

to the hope that in the new formation of international law there may be clarity in this matter also.

In regard to the question as to what commerce should be permitted to neutrals and what commerce should be prohibited, Burckhardt thinks that neutrals should be forbidden to deliver munitions to belligerents, that is, they should also be under obligations to prevent such supply on the part of their inhabitants. On the other hand, the import and export of other wares into and from belligerent states should in general be permitted. In my opinion, the solution of this question will depend essentially upon the future form of the law of contraband. I have already said that fixed limits and restrictions of this law would be desirable.[1] The future laws of neutrals with regard to commercial intercourse should also be made to correspond with these limits. Burckhardt pleads for the permission of all trade with the exception of munitions, that is, of absolute contraband. If relative contraband were abrogated, this result could perhaps be obtained. At any rate, Burckhardt correctly points out that it is impossible in practice to prohibit supplies for the enemy forces and permit them for the civilian population; that one only has the choice of permitting both or of forbidding both. Just as unpractical, he thinks, are the restrictions of the prohibition of trade to enemy territory; here there would be only these alternatives, either to permit neutrals to export to and import from the enemy country too such wares, or to allow the belligerents to tie up also the trade by way of the bordering neutral states; this latter interference would be opposed by the right of self-government of neutrals. This view, too, is certainly correct, and one must hope that a satisfactory solution can be found for this dilemma.

The above discussion shows that a more definite restriction of the rights and duties of neutrals is in fact to-day more than ever an urgent necessity and it is to be hoped that it may come to pass soon after the war. The best way to reach this end, in which all are equally interested, would be through a *co-operation*

[1] I cannot agree with Burckhardt's view that the abrogation of contraband which England has proposed would only be acceptable on condition that trading in actual munitions be suppressed. If there is no longer any contraband, then all commerce must be free. It does not seem necessary to me to discuss the consequences of this freedom of trade. The delivery of munitions, as we have seen (see above, p. 96), may also be of importance from the point of view of a guarantee of peace, of a preventive against the making of war.

of neutrals. Without a doubt the tendency toward such co-operation exists to-day. More than once, as we have seen, the cry has gone forth for a *federation of neutrals.* But even if such a league should not be actually formed—and perhaps it does not need to be formed in view of the league of peace to be established which in itself represents such a federation of neutrals—nevertheless a great service would surely be rendered to their interests through a co-operation of neutrals for definite purposes, as, for example, the creation of a law of neutrality and a law of war corresponding to the interests of neutrals.[1]

In this connexion there is still another problem that needs brief consideration, the postulate of *the freedom of the seas,* which has come into such prominence lately. This postulate has recently been brought forward upon every occasion, especially from the *German* side ; but in *America,* too, it has been a topic for discussion. It should be noted at once that this subject naturally deserves consideration in this work only in so far as it actually has to do with efforts in the interests of *international law.* International law must not be converted into a mantle for the concealment of political efforts. If, then, it should merely be a matter of attaining the political end of a naval supremacy, a struggle for the lordship of the seas, from the standpoint of international law this claim would *a priori* have to be waived, because international law is reared upon the idea of equal rights for all states and consequently is not to be abused by favouring any imperialistic tendencies whatsoever. In taking up the question of the actual purport of this postulate of the freedom of the seas, all political discussions or considerations, of whatever nature they may be, have to be kept in the background. What does the freedom of the seas signify in the sense of *international law*? Does it perhaps already exist, or, presupposing that there is indeed a justifiable claim at hand, must it first be created ?

Before I attempt to answer these questions from my own point of view, I should like first to allow a few others to express themselves upon the matter.

[1] Cf. with this my article of July 1914, on this subject, printed in the Appendix of my *Die Gestaltung des Völkerrechts nach dem Weltkriege,* p. 250 *et seq.* It is omitted in this translation. See also pp. 45 ff., above.

Let it be observed, that on August 19, 1915, the German Imperial Chancellor stated :

> For our own protection and welfare as well as for other nations we must win the freedom of the seas, not to rule supreme over them, as England wishes, but to place it at the service of all nations in equal measure.

In a letter to the press for August 25, 1915, Sir Edward Grey is said to have declared :

> It would be wise after this war to make the freedom of the seas the subject of discussion, definition, and agreements, but not as something separate, and not as long as there is no peace and no assurance against war and German methods on land. If guarantees against future wars are to be created, they must be equally effective and compelling guarantees, binding Germany as well as the other nations, including us.[1]

But what does one imagine this 'freedom of the seas' to be? The English Admiral Sir Cyprian Bridge answers the question of the meaning of the German demand of the freedom of the seas thus :[2] behind this demand there is concealed nothing else than the increase of the German naval power at the expense of the English. Earlier it was willingly recognized in Germany that the English Navy was effectively policing the seas. But since the growth of the German navy, what was once looked upon as a protection or as a support became viewed as an obstacle in attaining political ends. Thus arose the cry for the freedom of the seas. First and foremost is the demand for the abolition of the right of capture. But this [according to Admiral Bridge] is easily reconcilable with regard for the interests of neutrals.

In contrast to this, a former *German* marine officer[3] writes that by freedom of the seas is meant an international agreement, *whereby sea trade in times of war would be secure against the seizure of goods and trading vessels.*

> Such an international agreement would correspond to that generally recognized stipulation according to which private property is also protected in the enemy country as long as the owner enters upon no hostile activities and if the object is not a direct hindrance to military operations.

[1] Cf. further, the statement of Lord Robert Cecil of October 14, 1915 : 'To secure immunity of private property at sea was the principle of the naval policy of the government from 1906 onwards, and, according to Sir Edward, it is their policy still, though the war may have temporarily postponed its prosecution.'

[2] Cf. *Pall Mall Gazette* for November 8, 1915.

[3] Cf. the *Neue Zürcher Zeitung* for January 2, 1917.

The right of pillage is definitely abolished. The observance of these principles is often very difficult on land. At sea the situation is far more favourable. It is evident that an agreement recognized by the joint sea powers which would warrant the security of vessel and cargo against seizure on the part of the enemy could easily be controlled. But the elastic conception of forbidden goods would have to be eliminated. Such an agreement would have great economic advantages for all trading nations, especially England, which is obliged to maintain a great naval force for the protection of its commerce and imports as long as the right of capture exists. England would, therefore, first and foremost have to recognize the freedom of the seas. But in politics the decisive thing is unfortunately the striving after power. For more than a century England has been in possession of the supremacy of the seas, and was consequently able everywhere to impose its will without meeting any opposition ; on the Continent it favoured a balance of power. In times of peace the smaller states had not suffered under the English world-hegemony, since in times of peace the seas are free. It was this war that first showed neutrals that they, too, are injured by the right of capture, that freedom of the seas would be a blessing for all mankind. The fleets could then be materially decreased.

In consequence of this exposition, the Englishman J. Grande found it necessary to go to the bottom of the exact meaning of the expression 'freedom of the seas', as it is understood by Germany.[1] He thinks it evidently does not mean that all nations,

[1] Cf. the *Neue Zürcher Zeitung* for January 5, 1917. The same writer points out in the *Neue Zürcher Zeitung* for February 10, 1917, that Germany has not the slightest occasion for complaint. Before the war its maritime commerce had grown to gigantic dimensions and the German shipping companies had prospered immensely. It was most improbable that England, which almost alone of all seafaring nations opens its harbours to foreign ships without duties or taxes, would do anything at all toward placing obstacles in the way of international trade. As long as England was the greatest power at sea no danger existed for the world. But, after the experience of this war, what neutral power would like to see the supremacy of the seas in German hands ? When one speaks of the 'freedom of the seas' it can only be in reference to the relations of war. 'The idea is, that enemy private property on the seas must not be seized or destroyed. As the present occurrences show, this would annul one of the main effects and functions of maritime power. If such a change were made, then Germany could import and export goods almost as in times of peace. It is, therefore, not strange that Germany, weak in maritime power, should wish to deprive it of its chief weapon, while all the advantages of land force in which it is strong would remain in her hands. The downfall of Napoleon is to be attributed in the main to English supremacy at sea. At that time it was maritime power that liberated Europe, and

the small as well as the great, are equally entitled to use the sea for their trade and other purposes, since this right has existed for a long time, and has been guaranteed by England and Holland for the good of all nations. English naval supremacy has therefore never stood in opposition to this principle of the freedom of the seas. It has acted as a police force to the advantage of the merchants of all nations. English naval power has rescued Europe from Napoleon and it will also bring to naught the dream of a German domination. For the Germans it is not at all a matter of 'equal privileges at sea' or of 'the security of unrestricted communication by sea', since these conditions are already fulfilled. Germany has a quite different interpretation. It only wishes to destroy the great obstacle which prevents it from carrying out its plans for political and economic domination. Its purpose is to cripple the efficacy of sea power, while military land force is to remain unrestricted and undiminished. Seafaring peoples are no longer to be permitted in times of war to attack the sea trade of their enemies. Land forces would be, however, in a position to invade other countries, to devastate them, to levy war contributions, &c., while enemy property at sea would be declared inviolable. Balfour has described the results of such a condition as follows:

> Navies would still continue to be indispensable, but their relative value would be changed. They could no longer be employed in exercising pressure upon the enemy, except in union with land forces. The only nations to benefit would be the nations with great armies—the military monarchies. Commerce at sea would remain free, but overseas invasions would be permitted. The proposed change would therefore not merely diminish the value of sea power, but it would diminish such power especially for non-military states such as America and Great Britain.

England would therefore never consent to a peace which would

it will do the same thing in this war. "To cripple naval power and permit land power to remain unchecked", said Balfour, former First Lord of the Admiralty, in a conversation with an American journalist, "is certainly the greatest injury that international law could inflict upon humanity." . . . And who would guarantee that a power like Germany, advocating the theory of military necessity, would adhere to a convention concerning the freedom of enemy commerce? It is therefore most unlikely that England would give up its interests as an insular state and sacrifice the cause of freedom of the whole world, by depriving maritime strength of its chief weapon.' Cf. further the article in the *Kölnische Zeitung* for May 20, 1916, on the freedom of the seas, in which is quoted Balfour's conversation of May 19, 1916, with the American Marshall, which shows clearly the English conception and emphasizes the common ideals of England and America.

cripple its authority at sea and betray the cause of freedom and free development in the world. If power at sea ceased to serve as an actual counterpoise against power on land, then the cause of freedom would be in a desperate condition.

It can already be seen from this discussion of Grande's that political considerations in the problem of the freedom of the sea may play a rôle. German expressions upon this subject can only confirm this impression, as the following examples will show. Schrameier writes in the *Deutsche Warte* for September 5, 1914:

> The present war will yield a mass of new material for the future regulating of international maritime law. The German sense of law and German jurisprudence will clear up the absurdities, regretted even by many Englishmen, of the existing naval war [law ?]. However, as long as England's supremacy at sea continues, the principle 'England rules the waves' will be synonymous with 'England waives the rules'.

In the *Tag* for November 20, 1914, Ehrenberg writes on 'Die Deutschen als Vorkämpfer für die Freiheit des Weltmeeres im Seekriege' (The Germans as the Champions of the Freedom of the High Seas in Maritime War). He says that the Germans have for centuries unchangeably espoused the cause of the freedom of the high seas. The ocean must not be ruled over by any one state, but must remain the unbounded highway of international commerce for all nations. This truth is the basis of the entire international maritime law. But over against the *mare liberum* the English have set up their theory of the *mare clausum*. The accomplishment of the great advance in civilization failed solely through the opposition of the British, who out of 'commercial envy' have again and again destroyed all the results already secured through centuries of struggle for civilization. For the Germans there is only one measure against this: force of arms. Their constant struggle for the freedom of the ocean must show neutrals that they need never fear from a Germany that is powerful at sea what Great Britain has practised for centuries.

The *Frankfurter Zeitung* for September 12, 1915, on the other hand, admits that shipping on the high seas was limited before the war merely in so far as the seafaring nations had obligated themselves to observe certain international agreements, serving mainly the safety of shipping. Beyond this, with the exception of a few restrictions in coast waters, every one was free to sail on the sea as he wished. It could, therefore, not be a question of the freeing of the channels, when the German people sets for its goal the liberating of the ocean, although the most important passages and straits on the sea are in possession of foreign states; for in times of peace German ships sail all waters free and unrestrained.

That which oppressed us and made us unfree, was something else: it was the barriers with which England sought to oppose our free activity, the natural growth of our political and economic power.

An agreement on the freedom of the seas has, however, nothing to do with these political factors of power. In war the seas are not free. England has departed from the type of the great war of the past century and adopted the fundamental ideas and methods of warfare which were believed to have been the distinctive character of a bygone vanquished age and a lesser civilization. England has resorted to a more indirect war measure, to the siege of the German empire. Thus began the war of commerce.

In a struggle between two great states, taking place upon the great thoroughfares of world commerce, the sea can never be completely free, just as little as intercourse on land can be completely free in the case of a war on land. The freedom of the seas in war is a conception that depends entirely upon the aims which warfare sets up for itself and upon the least measure of the interruption of intercourse and commerce that warfare claims as unavoidable or even as a necessary means of combat. Whether this least measure transgresses against international customs and laws, whether the belligerent state scornfully disregards everything that justice and usage prescribes, does not matter here.

It is not the purpose of this article to concern itself with moral judgements and commands, but merely with what has actually taken place. The Declaration of London does not guarantee perfect freedom of the seas, but merely the minimum of freedom that one believed at that time to be able to grant and guarantee to commerce and to enemy shipping in war. The idea that constitutes the real meaning of a freedom of the seas, the inviolability of private property at sea, did not find expression in the Declaration of London. Private shipping of belligerents, their private commerce and intercourse on the high seas, must be guaranteed if one wishes to create and guarantee the 'freedom of the seas' in war times. Only the conception of contraband as well as the proclaiming of an orderly and effective blockade may limit freedom and determine the essential difference between the condition of shipping in war and in peace. What permits the enemy to restrict the freedom on the seas is the common tenet that all the private property of an enemy state is absolutely unprotected at sea. As long as this tenet prevails, the seas are not free.

Count Reventlow spoke on the 'freedom of the seas' in the Institute for Marine Science.[1] In his opinion it is only a question of the freedom of the seas in war, 'and then it can naturally not be generally guaranteed, but for us only to the extent that *we* secure the freedom of the seas for *ourselves*, by dissuading the other power from its purpose or preventing it from blocking the seas for us'. Reventlow places no value upon *bona fides* in the making of contracts, and in reflecting upon the words of the chancellor and Sir Edward Grey he observes :

> Just there lies the trouble ; to make agreements after the war has no practical sense or purpose whatever ; for such paper agreements will upon the next war again fly in tatters into the sea.

The German lack of freedom of the seas cannot be removed by treaties after the war, but only at the conclusion of the war, according to the slogan, 'Heraus aus dem nassen Dreieck' (out of the wet triangle), through gaining the freedom of the strategic line for the development of the German sea power. This does not imply the displacement of British supremacy at sea by the German ; for thus only would one arrive at a sort of balance of powers. Under no conditions may Germany withdraw from the responsibility of guaranteeing for itself at a decisive place in the North Sea the freedom of the seas *through its own power*.[2]

It is worthy of note that in the year 1916 the *Deutsche Vereinigung für internationales Recht* (The German Association for International Law) proposed as the next international or war law problem to be taken up that of the 'freedom of the seas', and in the first place the preparation for the problem from the standpoint of scientific and technical international law. Edwin

[1] Cf. with this the *Tägliche Rundschau* for January 17, 1916.

[2] The same view is, for example, also expressed in an article in the *Reichsbote* for June 14, 1916. International law paper guarantees cannot be depended upon. The goal to be attained is 'Freedom of the Seas' founded upon one's own sufficient strength.

Katz has prepared a list of queries for the above association, in which he considers especially the questions whether the right of capture of prizes and, in connexion therewith, the right of search for neutrals (and possibly also for enemy trading vessels) are to be abolished, and, if so, for what voyages ; further, whether in case capture of prizes be not abolished, the prohibition of contraband be restricted to the objects of Article 22 of the Declaration of London (absolute contraband) upon exclusion of one-sided additions to the list of articles that are contraband. Other queries relate to the putting to sea of merchant vessels belonging to belligerent states from enemy or neutral ports upon the declaration of war, as well as the return home of such vessels as find themselves out upon the open sea ; further, the right of destroying vessels carrying contraband ; also the question of the treatment of enemy merchant vessels that are armed or of transports as warships ; and lastly the fact of the existence of the blockade, namely, whether it is necessary that the entrance to the blockaded port or the blockaded coast be unconditionally prevented, or whether it suffices if the entrance is made dangerous, and whether the London definition of blockade shall be made a subject of the peace treaty.

Katz explains in detail that agreements about the freedom of the seas are necessary for peace in so far only as Germany must see to it that she has sufficient coaling stations granted her. On the other hand, the freedom of the seas in war must be placed upon a new basis through *individual* treaties ; Germany must not allow herself to be consoled by the agreements of a third Hague Conference.[1] The principles of war on land would also have to be made applicable to war at sea. Katz recommends an agreement with respect to the conception of a war territory, such as a space of water between the belligerent ships. This zone should be absolutely unfree ; there no one should ask protection of life or of property of private individuals, just as little as in the war zone on land. But outside this war zone, the space of water

[1] On the contrary, Triepel, *loc. cit.*, p. 16, rightly points out that it is clear that development can only be furthered quickly and thoroughly through a treaty codification on the part of a large number of states. Only such more general treaties would be of value for the law of war. That would be true in the first place for the rights of neutrals, since in a normal war between two states about sixty neutral states are opposed, and it would obviously be inconvenient were the relations between the belligerents and the neutrals regulated by norms with a dozen different contents.

must be free.[1] From this, however, grows the demand for the undisturbed intercourse of individuals and of property on the open sea. In particular, it must be determined whether it be to the interest of Germany to discontinue entirely the right of the capture of prizes and therewith the right of search. Katz comes to the conclusion that the right of capture is one of those measures which only cause injury, without hastening the end of the war; consequently the entire abolition of the right of capture together with that of search is justifiable. If, on the other hand, one wishes to uphold the prohibition of contraband, it is well to have a clear agreement in respect to the limits of this idea.

Of interest, too, is that which the Austrian Gellmann writes about *Meeresfreiheit und Handelsfreiheit* (Freedom of the Sea and Freedom of Trade).[2] He says the existing conception of the absence of the state idea in respect to the sea must be replaced by that of a state of freedom of the sea which will guarantee order in war as well.

The sea in its function of serving intercourse, the exchange of material goods, and the spreading of civilization among distant peoples, is only a means to these ends. The permission to use these means is an attribute of the external sovereignty of every state, embracing the whole complex of intercourse with the other states, and is consequently the individual right of every state. This right to free intercourse at sea belongs to all states in like measure. On the highway of trade equality of the sea prevails. Freedom of the sea is the authorization of all states to do anything on the high seas that will not injure the equality of the rights of the others. The neutrals would be bound to ward off any encroachment on the freedom of the sea on the part of the belligerents as an outrage against their external sovereignty.[3] The solidarity of interests on the high seas brought about by the progressive industrialization of all states would in this way be transformed into a protective solidarity against attacks not upon mere interests, the injury of which on the part of belligerents could be made

[1] Conversely, Eltzbacher, p. 70, thinks that the freedom of the seas has shown itself to be an annoying obstacle in the waging of war. 'It has fallen in this war and will not soon rise again. In spite of all the good intentions of individual states, it cannot be assumed that, within a conceivable space of time, there will be created a common will of nations, which will again restore the freedom of the seas as an international arrangement.' On the other hand, in the tenth edition of his *Völkerrecht*, Von Liszt writes: 'Even now there is approaching what is perhaps the most important goal to be striven for, namely the freedom of the seas. The struggle will ultimately revolve about it. Earlier or later it will be the most valuable prize of victory.'

[2] Cf. *Internationale Rundschau* for July 15, 1916.

[3] These views are of special interest in view of the present submarine warfare.

good by compensating the neutrals, but, on the contrary, against attacks upon the political honour injured in its sovereign right of equality on the sea, which honour cannot be an object of compensation to the neutral state.[1]

In conclusion, I should like to add what a neutral, the Norwegian Lie, writes about the freedom of the seas.[2] First of all, on the basis of an historical retrospect, Lie points out that the cry for 'freedom of the seas' raised in our day is of an entirely different purport than in the times of Hugo Grotius. From the standpoint of the law of nations, it includes the claim that private property is to be respected in maritime war just as much as in war on land and that no state is any longer to have the right to look upon vessels and cargoes belonging to the subjects of enemy states as good prize. If a vessel does not violate a blockade and carries no contraband, it is to remain unmolested, as if it were sailing under a neutral flag. The demand of the 'freedom of the sea' is, however, also understood as meaning that the laying of mines in the open sea shall be forbidden, since it is the common highway of all nations. The interest of belligerents to establish such a blockade is to yield to the right of neutrals to move about upon the high seas freely. The abolition of the laws of contraband and of blockade is also demanded upon the ground of the principle mentioned. Moreover, the same is often also understood as containing a claim of an entirely political character. Just as no single state has or should have the privilege of a supremacy on land, so no state should rule upon the sea. The regulation of the numerous common interests that are attached to intercourse upon the sea is to rest upon the free co-operation of all seafaring nations. The supremacy of a single state can easily lead to the same unhealthy conditions that have been shown in the case of every supremacy on land.

Lie then especially points out that the wish that private property at sea be treated like that on land has been expressed in many quarters. But the question is not so simple, since the purpose of conducting the war is in both cases a different one, and this fact must naturally also determine the means and methods of the war. In war on land the war aim is to break the military resistance of the enemy, and, with this aim, to conquer

[1] Cf. *supra*, p. 51.

[2] Mikael H. Lie, 'Freedom of the Seas', in the *Recueil de Rapports*, vol. ii, pp. 175 ff.

enemy territory. This purpose is in no way furthered through the seizure and destruction of private property.

In naval warfare the aims are different. First of all to bring about such confusion of the maritime intercourse and international trade of the enemy, that its government feels the same necessity of obtaining peace as by occupation of its territory. Destruction of the navy of the enemy is only one of the means leading to that goal. Such destruction is naturally of special importance where the communication with the colonies, the transportation of military forces, &c., come into consideration. But commercial warfare may proceed to the utmost degree even if no great naval battles are fought. This is plainly shown by the present war. And up to this time the means of commercial warfare has been in the first place the capture of the enemy's ships and cargoes, wherever they are found outside neutral territorial waters. And in the second place blockade of the coasts of the enemy's country. The aim is to break the *economic* power of resistance by stopping all kinds of import and by destroying the export trade of the enemy. Between these two means there is a difference. Capture is exclusively directed against the trade of the enemy, while blockade of every kind will hit the neutrals as well. The blockade, acknowledged by international law, is even principally directed against their commerce with the hostile country. In the present economic war blockade plays by far the most important part. The intense want from both sides has led to a system of arrangements—declarations of blockade without any directly debarring of certain ports or coasts, special war zones and mines in the high sea which all are outside of all actual international law. The main principles have on these points become uncertain and vague. At the coming peace negotiations it would no doubt be perfectly useless to claim that the great maritime powers should desist from commercial blockade and matters naturally connected with it. The problems—as they have appeared in this war—are too new and too uninvestigated to let us hope for the establishment of any fixed and effective international order in this regard. It is not at all impossible that the means of warfare, here in question, will be of decisive importance with regard to the time of the opening of peace negotiations. One might as well raise the question of the abolition of naval warfare altogether.

Lie thinks that in respect to the right of capture the case is, of course, different. Also that the war has taught us to see so many things with different eyes that we shall perhaps also come to an agreement about the abolition of the right of capture at sea.

Should not the terrible experience of the present war have prepared the way for a similar compromise, which might make possible the fullest recognition of the principle of the freedom of the seas in the three international spheres of action, to which the sense of justice in modern times has wished to apply it? That would mean the abolition of the right of capture at sea, of the law of contraband, and of the planting of mines in the high sea.

Also President Wilson, in his note in answer to Germany of July 21, 1915, has emphasized that 'the United States will continue to contend for the freedom of the seas, from whatever quarter violated, without compromise and at any cost '. And in his message to the senate of January 22, 1917, he declared :

So far as practicable, moreover, every great people now struggling towards a full development of its resources and of its powers should be assured a direct outlet to the great highways of the sea.[1] Where this cannot be done by the cession of territory, it can no doubt be done by the neutralization of direct rights of way under the general guarantee. . . . No nation need be shut away from free access to the open paths of the world's commerce.

And the paths of the sea must alike in law and in fact be free. The freedom of the seas is the *sine qua non* of peace, equality, and co-operation. No doubt a somewhat radical reconsideration of many of the rules of international practice hitherto thought to be established may be necessary in order to make the seas indeed free and common in practically all circumstances for the use of mankind, but the motive for such changes is convincing and compelling. There can be no trust or intimacy between the peoples of the world without them. The free, constant, unthreatened intercourse of nations is an essential part of the process of peace and of development. It need not be difficult to define or to secure the freedom of the seas if the governments of the world sincerely desire to come to an agreement concerning it.

I insert here certain further publications concerning the 'freedom of the seas'. The following was communicated by the British consul-general at Zürich.[2]

I

'Since President Wilson in the year 1916 has again proposed his old plan of the league of peace, the idea of the "freedom of the seas" has been moved into the foreground of the discussion as one of its chief aims. Not only has the ever-increasing fury of the war made pressingly urgent the necessity of a more accurate definition and regulation of the rights of the belligerents at sea and of sanctioning them, but this necessity has been placed in the foreground in the plan of the president.

'The words which he originally used in his plan were : "An universal association of the nations to maintain the inviolate security of the highway of the seas for the common and unhindered use of all the nations of the world." The modern thought

[1] Since there is propaganda in Germany in favour of the freedom of the seas, German policy, on its part, could not aim at keeping Russia shut off from the ocean.

[2] Taken from the *Neue Zürcher Zeitung*, Nos. 787, 800, 820, and 871 of May 3, May 5, May 8, and May 15, 1917, respectively.

of a general union of nations, in contrast to the mediaeval and "prenational" tendencies, dates back to the sixteenth century. It arose from the "Great Plan" of Queen Elizabeth of England and Henry IV of France, and was stated in their treaty of 1596, which the States General of Holland had also signed. With the death of these two great rulers vanished also the Great Plan, but during the two following centuries it was continually resuscitated, by political philosophy as well as by practical statesmen, until at the close of the Napoleonic wars it was realized in the form of the "Holy Alliance". As is well known, this became the curse of Europe, and had it not been for sea power it would have become the curse of the whole world. Under the influence of the powerful military nations it degenerated into an antidemocratic conspiracy, with such pernicious effects that Great Britain and the United States had to take refuge in the Monroe Doctrine, in order to prevent its evil operations from reaching across the Atlantic Ocean. The new doctrine here achieved its purpose. But in examining the ideas which are connected with the expression "freedom of the seas", it is of prime importance not to forget that the Monroe Doctrine from the very beginning could lean for support on British sea power, and that successful resistance against the degenerate descendant of the "Great Plan" was due only to this circumstance.

'If we wish to smooth the road for a sincere consideration of the question raised by President Wilson, we must first of all exclude all extraneous matter that might lead to confusion, and then define the connotation of the phrase with the greatest possible exactness. In the first place, this statement must be accepted, that it can have reference only to the *condition of war*. In peace, as is universally admitted, all seas are free. That to be sure has not always been the case. Until comparatively recent times certain states laid claim to rights of sovereignty and of property over certain seas. As far as straits were concerned these pretensions were usually acknowledged. As long as Venice was a great power it succeeded in enforcing its claims to the Adriatic Sea, against even such powers as Spain. The Baltic and the Black Seas were not completely opened to commerce until the years 1856 and 1857. But when Spain and Portugal in the sixteenth century tried to extend their rights over the high seas, they were vigorously opposed, and to these struggles is to be ascribed the birth of British sea power. This power grew to man's estate through a similar stubborn resistance to the claims of the Dutch. They for their part wished to forbid the Portuguese access to the seas of the Far East, while at the same time they contested the claims of sovereignty of the British over the straits and narrow seas. The latter confirmed their claim by the three Dutch wars; but it remained a dead letter and was kept in memory only by the salute of the flag of a British ship of war. Even this remnant of vanity was looked upon towards the end of the next century as a meaningless anachronism. Finally, at the close of the Napoleonic wars, when British naval supremacy had reached its height and was undisputed, England voluntarily renounced the salute as a relic of the Middle Ages quite irreconcilable with the great ideas for which Great Britain had fought during this epoch-making struggle.

'Although these facts might seem unimportant, it is nevertheless necessary to refer to them and to keep them clearly in mind if we wish to see the subject under discussion in its proper light. If the ruler of a great and highly esteemed state, in referring to such a subject as the freedom of the seas, and with the full seriousness and dignity of a great official act, appeals to the higher ideals of mankind, we are inclined to take two things for granted, first that the freedom of the seas does not exist, second that it is attainable. In the present case neither the one nor the other of these hypotheses is justified. In peace the freedom of the seas, as we have seen, already exists. In war it does not exist, has never existed, and has never in its complete application, by any authority to be taken seriously, been represented as the aim of international policy.

'It has at all times been the accepted opinion of the world, and held as an unchangeable and universally acknowledged principle of law, that it lies in the very nature of the case, that in war times the neutrals would have to submit to a certain limitation of their absolute freedom of commerce on the seas. Therein is a universal recognition of the fact that a complete freedom of the seas in war has in practice always been regarded as impossible. It is probably still regarded as impossible. For although the President has given no clear public expression as to what he understands by the term "freedom of the seas", it is nevertheless probable that as an experienced statesman he is conscious of the impossibility of an absolute freedom as long as naval warfare must be regarded as a part of the mechanism of international relations. Whether the complete abolition of naval warfare is an attainable ideal or not, it is at any rate out of the question, for reasons that will later be stated, to continue to permit it and at the same time also seek to maintain the absolute freedom of the seas.

'What the world is most seriously called upon to examine is therefore not the question of the absolute freedom of the seas but this problem : how far below the standard formerly demanded are the rights of belligerents at sea to be limited, without entirely abolishing the right of maritime warfare ? Asking the question in another form, taking the right of naval warfare for granted, just how much limitation of the freedom of the seas is to be recognized by neutrals ?

II

'After we have shown that the conception "freedom of the seas" has reference to war only, that this freedom already prevails uncontested in peace times, and after we have cursorily described the question as an attempt to reduce the rights of the belligerents over neutral commerce to the smallest measure compatible with the recognition of naval warfare, we wish to find out what the expression means in practice.

'According to the explanation of its more extreme advocates, it signifies the complete abolition of the custom of confiscating private property at sea, and the most extreme political writers would like to see the prohibition extended not only to neutral property, but also to that of the belligerents themselves. To them the idea appears intolerable that peaceful merchants and fishermen, it matters not whether they belong to a neutral or a belligerent nation, should not be permitted to pursue their occupations undisturbed, just because hostile fleets are engaged in mutual combat. This demand is limited to the sea only, for up to the present no one has as yet seriously asked that while the armies are engaged in warfare, peaceful merchants and peasants should be allowed to go peacefully back and forth unmolested. It is quite evident that such a curtailment of the rights of the belligerents on land would make the task of the

M 2

armies an impossibility. Even if battles could be fought they would lead to no results. There would be no fruits to reap. If non-combatants and private property were protected against all restrictions, the pressure through which one belligerent imposes its will upon another could no longer be exercised. For it is not victorious battles that lead to peace, but the fear and the knowledge of what such battles make it possible for the victor to do. It is a self-understood maxim that military successes on land put it in the victor's power to crush the national life of his opponent, so that he has no other choice than to surrender or perish.

'In the case of the less familiar naval warfare, that has never been so self-evident to people. To the great majority of land dwellers a naval war is a struggle enacted at a great distance, in which fleets fight for the defence of their respective coasts and cruisers undertake privateering expeditions. People in general are not quite clear about this point, that the fleets exist chiefly for the purpose of giving the cruisers freedom of action against hostile commerce. Nor are they clear on this other point, that if the cruisers do not succeed in carrying their operations so far as to actually crush the national life of the opponent on the sea, no booty in the world, however great, will bring peace. Only by preventing hostile commerce is it possible for fleets to exert the pressure which armies, in practice as well as in theory, seek to exert on land; and it is only by the confiscation and the possibility of confiscation of private property at sea that the prevention of commerce on the sea is to be attained. Without the right of confiscation of private property naval battles, as a means of compelling the enemy to surrender, become meaningless. Without this right a naval victory brings forth no other results than the security of the home land and the possibility of devastating the enemy's coasts—a species of pressure which to-day no one would any longer wish to justify.

'The matter reduces itself therefore to this: an unconditional prohibition against the confiscation of private property at sea would in practice be equivalent to a prohibition against the effective use of sea power. Such a prohibition may be a pious wish, but it is not the subject of the present discussion. It may, therefore, be taken for granted that in the present appeal to the judgement of the nations there is involved at the most the freedom of neutrals to pursue unhindered their trade with the belligerents. So far, however, the demand for the freedom of the seas has in reality never gone. From time immemorial two sorts of restrictions have been recognized; first, the right of belligerents to seize contraband, and second, that the trade of neutrals may not hinder military operations. As such have always been considered military blockades, under which are reckoned the blockade of a naval port, or a port against which a siege is in progress. But this right has been disputed in so far as *commercial* blockades are concerned, that is, in regard to blockades the purpose of which is merely the prevention of commerce without having any immediate reference to military operations. The legality of such blockades has repeatedly been disputed, especially in America, on the basis of the supposition that neutral trade with the belligerents is free, as long as it is not carried on through a harbour against which operations are actually in progress.

'The objection, that neutral trade with the belligerents should have its natural freedom, as long as it does not disturb the military operations, is without doubt important. But it has never destroyed the universal impression that the commercial blockade is a legitimate military measure before which neutrals must bow. This arises from the fact that the basic supposition contains a contradiction. Commerce is by its very nature mutual. Trade with a belligerent is not merely neutral trade but also belligerent. Here the rights of neutrals come into direct conflict with the right of the one belligerent to hinder the trade of its enemy if it can. A serious practical difficulty is here involved. For it is evident that if a belligerent can carry on its commerce by means of neutral ships, the enemy will scarcely be able to exert any greater pressure upon it than if the commerce of the belligerents were altogether free. Waging war at sea would become almost as powerless as if the hindering of trade were entirely forbidden. In recognition of this evident injustice to the sea powers, the neutrals have always agreed to a limitation of their freedom on the sea and conceded the right of the commercial blockade as well as the right of seizing contraband. By virtue of the first concession a superior sea power can still hinder the national life of its opponent from being nurtured with neutral help, by virtue of the second it can prevent neutrals from contributing means to continue the war.

III

'From the foregoing observations it is evident that, from the standpoint of practical international politics, freedom of the seas signifies nothing further than the freedom of the neutrals to trade with the belligerents under the traditional limitations of blockade and contraband. If we descend from idealistic conceptions to the questions which a world congress would have to decide, we find that the whole thing amounts to this: how and to what degree these two limitations upon free commerce between neutrals and belligerents shall continue to exist.

'The startling new factor, added to the old problem, is the deplorable degree to which both restrictions have been stretched in the course of this war. The strong groups of powers opposing each other both appear to have interpreted the right according to their own good pleasure and to have extended it more and more beyond the old boundaries, corresponding to the measure that the unheard of development of the art of war made necessary. The neutrals submitted reluctantly, in part because they realized the difficult situation arising from the new developments, and in part because at no time did a new step or a refusal to right committed wrongs seem to them to justify an appeal to arms. Nevertheless, this yielding was only made possible by the prospect of improving the evil conditions after the war. As President Wilson declared before the Senate and for the information of the whole world: "No doubt a somewhat radical reconsideration of many rules of international practice hitherto thought to be established may be necessary in order to make the seas indeed free and common in practically all circumstances for the use of mankind." According to this declaration there is proposed here not only a doing away with the new developments, but also a greater measure of freedom than that which before the war was considered as established.

'"It need not be difficult", he added, "either to define or to secure the freedom of the seas if the governments of the world sincerely desire to come to an agreement concerning it." In so far as these words are the high-minded exhortation to a conquering of difficulties by common exertion, every one will give them hearty applause. If, however, we wish that these exertions bear fruit we must all become clear as to what the difficulties are. Those who have stood in the midst of the struggle and have each time taken the next step with inward reluctance know that they are not small. Some of these steps, we felt, were perhaps inseparable consequences of certain developments of war conditions, the mastery of which lies beyond the power of governments.

'Let us examine first the question of contraband: here we must remember that as long as countries conducted war with comparatively small standing armies and comparatively few weapons and simple war material it was possible to limit the list of contraband to a few articles, which could readily be characterized as war material. When, however, the armies and the branches of the government that feed them are no longer to be distinguished from the nation, and when, as to-day, the enormous number of combatants and war workers demand all the resources and methods of a highly developed technique, the list of war material grows with such rapidity that it becomes almost impossible to draw a definite and permanent boundary line.

'The question is similar in regard to the blockade. As long as it was still possible for a fleet during an indefinite time to lie before the enemy's harbour, with the exception of bad weather or of being chased away by a superior force, it was not difficult to establish blockade rules. But with the appearance of sea mines, torpedoes, and submarines, conditions vanished which were favourable to a simple regulation. The result was that not only did the freedom accorded to the blockading side have to be considerably extended, but that rules, in respect to what was allowed and what was not allowed, lost much of their definiteness and opened wide the way for all sorts of indefinite demands on the part of both sides.

'But with these statements the difficulties and the confusion which have arisen out of modern developments are by no means exhausted. They seem to stand in the way of every attempt, such as weighty neutral opinion desires, to distinguish between the military and the economic blockade. For when the nation coalesces with the army and when, as the immediate consequence of the development of modern warfare through the development of technique, the whole country is placed upon a war basis, it is no longer possible to distinguish between military and commercial blockade.

'In this connexion attention must be called to another radical transformation, namely the development of means of communication within the country. Its comparative importance for the national life has, as compared with commerce on the sea, greatly increased, and has given the armies an unheard of growth in power. Not only have the armies become comparatively more mobile than the fleets, but the mass armies which to-day march against the enemy's country, form automatically a commercial blockade which, as far as rigour is concerned, place deep in the shade all that a fleet has ever accomplished. It is by no means easy, if justice is to prevail, to forbid to the forces on the sea what cannot be forbidden to the armies on land. But such an injustice would be unavoidable if the freedom of the seas should in any sense be made a definite rule of warfare.

'It is therefore clear, as soon as we seriously examine the question, that, with the best intentions in the world, the difficulties of finding redress for the present untenable conditions are by no means slight. And the chief reason is that the recent extension of the encroachments of the belligerents upon neutral commerce is not to be imputed to the whims or to the selfishness of mighty groups of peoples, but is to be viewed as an immediate consequence of the changing conceptions of international law, caused by the normal development of the means of war.

IV

'Enough has already been said to make it evident that the question which is to be laid upon the green table of a world conference is bristling with thorns, and that in it are involved the most fundamental conceptions which up to this time have determined the regulation of warfare at sea. Under these circumstances it is absolutely necessary to avoid all expressions which might stand in the way of a clearing up of the matter.

'The words which President Wilson has chosen in order to give expression to his lofty-minded aspirations are a conspicuous example of such dangerous modes of speaking. The "freedom of the seas" is one of the phrases which sound very fine, hold the ear captive and confuse the judgement. Not until we have freed ourselves from its insidious charm can we advance. It does not express what he really means. It does not denote any practical policy, and it is certainly a practical policy which he is recommending to the world. From reasons already given it is clear that there can be no freedom of the seas as long as wars at sea are permitted, since without a very considerable measure of sea mastery fleets cease to have significance.

'It is not the poet's dream of the absolute freedom of the seas which Wilson is recommending to the consideration of the nations. To such a dream, however beautiful it might be, no sea power could lend a hearing. What he really purposes is a limitation of the rights of the belligerents over against the neutrals. That is a practical policy which can be regarded by all with sympathy and even with hope. For all must deplore at least some of the latest extensions of the encroachments of the belligerents upon neutral commerce, as well as the destruction and the suffering which they have caused; and yet they did not essentially contribute to the influence of the naval operations upon the outcome of the war. There are few to whom more reasonable and more humane rules at sea would not be welcome even at the cost of a somewhat diminished influence of sea power. But however far such rules may go in this direction, they must fall far short of an absolute freedom of the seas.

'There is no doubt but that all the sea powers will take their places at the conference table in the spirit in which they have been invited. But in order that their position may not later be misunderstood, they must all stipulate that at the discussions *one* circumstance be not left out of consideration, namely this: since the influence of sea power in the world is measured by the degree to which they can exercise their mastery of the sea, every limitation in this direction, although it brings us nearer the desired freedom of the seas, has the effect of restricting the influence of the sea powers. And in inverse proportion to the degree in which it decreases the influence of the sea powers, it increases the strength of the land powers.

'Does this then correspond to the wish of President Wilson and of those who with him advocate the freedom of the seas? Do they believe that it makes for the best interests of the world, of civilization, and of mankind to seriously disturb the long preserved balance between sea power and land power? Does it serve these great interests that the influence of the sea powers be diminished in comparison with that of the land powers?

For that history has only *one* answer. With this answer the sea powers may be satisfied as long as mankind remains conscious that beneath the question of the freedom of the seas lies another, more profound, and more essential than it for the whole structure on which international relations is built.

'Before the powers come together for the proposed discussions, this highly important point may certainly be brought forward without awakening mistrust; for the practical success of a council of the nations will in the main depend upon its solution. In fact the highly promising attempt of President Wilson to revive the old plan for the maintenance of world peace would have to miscarry, as did so many of its predecessors, if this point should be overlooked or find insufficient consideration. The feasibility of the plan depends, as is generally acknowledged, not only on honesty of purpose, but also on the sanction of an international power. Should, however, the freedom of the seas be realized to any high degree, nations like the United States and Great Britain would lose their ability to contribute to this coercive force in such proportion as their position as powers of the first rank would demand. The task of carrying out the decisions of the great council of nations would fall chiefly to the lot of the leading military powers, and with the power of executing these decisions would also go the power of shaping them. For it is only too well known that in international councils the weight of the arguments of the various members corresponds exactly to the armed power which they represent.

'Thereby the same conditions would be re-established which drove the Holy Alliance towards an end lamented by few. Like that concert of nations, of which so much was expected, we also would run the danger of delivering the future of the world into the power of a tribunal which on principle takes a hostile attitude towards every democratic progressive measure for which we have fought in this war.

'Has the President observed this danger which lurks behind his high-minded appeal? This appears not to be the case. "The paths of the sea", he said in his eloquent address to the senate, "must alike in law and in fact be free. The freedom of the seas is the *sine qua non* of peace, equality, and co-operation." In this we see not the slightest intimation that the truth might present a quite different face; no suspicion that what seems to be a broad way, yes, the only way to his goal, leads directly to the inequality and away from the common task of the nations. And nevertheless we find this to be the naked truth if we inspect the mechanism by virtue of which the goal is to be attained. By seriously infringing upon the executive ability of the sea powers, he destroys the equality of nations and makes the common task an illusion. How then shall we maintain peace? Assuredly the President, keeping his gaze fixed all too steadily upon the task of his council of peace, has overlooked the nature of the effect of its first action upon its independence. He demands that the council begin its labours by lopping off half of the mechanism by which alone the task can be achieved. How could those who have built up this mechanism, whose very existence is dependent upon it, and whose only means of action it is—how could they hope to maintain an effective voice in the negotiations? Surely neither the council nor its peace task could long survive such a beginning. If it should ever give birth to the freedom of the seas, it would be by a Caesarean operation. The child might be born alive, but the mother would have to die.

'It is not in the spirit of opposition that this warning is given. A long and manifold experience in the might of the sea weapon to maintain peace leaves in British public opinion not a residue of doubt but that the proposal of the President to weaken this power from the very beginning will, if carried out, inoculate his greater plan of the league of peace with the germ of death. It is difficult enough to establish a league of peace, even when all the conditions for it are favourable. The plan has been wrecked again and again. There is much to be said in its favour, and now, when it is being urged with greater authority and lesser hope than ever before, those who sincerely wish the realization of the "great plan" can only lament that this confounding of means and end threatens to destroy all chances of a happy solution of the international discord.'

In a few words I wish here to speak also of Triepel's pamphlet, *The Freedom of the Seas and the Coming Treaty of Peace*, since it contains a *complete confirmation* of the doubts to which I gave expression above. It forms an interesting counterpart to the just quoted English conception.

Triepel proceeds from the idea that the German Government has characterized the freedom of the seas as the prize of victory which is to be wrested from England. But there has been no plain speaking as to what interpretation is to be ascribed to the phrase 'freedom of the seas', nor has it been shown in what form and in what way the goal is to be attained and secured. Therefore, in the discussion of the problem in the press and in literature, they are playing with words whose sense and import may be interpreted very differently. The 'struggle for the freedom of the seas' has in Germany gradually become a universally adopted catchword, to which one attaches this, another that meaning, and the majority no meaning at all, save that it has to do with the combating of the high-handed methods of the British on the seas. The English have justly reproached President Wilson with setting up a demand concerning the purport of which one at present is referred to empty surmises. It is therefore urgently necessary to bring the catchword out of the mist in which up to this time with more or less intention it has been veiled.

Not only because in political matters it is always a misfortune if a catch phrase becomes current, but because in this case the coming peace treaty might bring the most bitter disappointments in regard to the freedom of the seas, interpreted in this or in that fashion.

Triepel has here very justly characterized the state of affairs, and he further emphasizes, and again rightly so, the fact that it is indispensable clearly to understand that it is not a question of the freedom of the seas in *peace times*. Toilsomely attained in a struggle lasting for centuries, this is to-day no longer questioned or threatened by any one, not even by England. On this point there is no doubt :

In peace times the high seas are open to all states and their dependents for equal use and profit. In peace times no state lays claim to the right to commit violence in any form on the world seas upon ships sailing under a foreign flag. The few exceptions which, according to ancient common law or modern international treaties, grant to warships or public vessels the right to police the seas, even in respect to craft of foreign nationality—for the suppression of piracy or the slave trade or for the protection of submarine cables—are not merely exceptions which confirm the rule. They are at bottom regulations in the service of the freedom of the seas, for they protect peaceful navigation and hinder the abuse of freedom.

That is exactly what I have explained in the text above. And Triepel is, therefore, fully in the right when he continues :

He among us who fights for the freedom of the seas to-day desires to make the seas free for merchant commerce even in times of *war*. Free—at any rate freer than they now are. We need waste no words to show that they are not free to-day.

Triepel is of the opinion that, according to the universal verdict, Germany, and the neutrals no less so, suffer terribly under this lack of freedom, and that the guilt for it is to be laid at England's door. It seems a prize of battle worthy of the blood of the noble if the attempt to free the world from this serfdom should succeed. I leave it undecided whether and to what extent Triepel is correct in casting the guilt for the present situation upon *England*—I have already expressed my opinion in regard to Germany's attitude at The Hague in reference to the problems of the laws of naval warfare—and decline to enter into a discussion with Triepel as to whether there are not other prizes of battle still more worthy of the blood of the noble than the regulation of the rules of war. On this point, however, one must agree with him, that the sea in war times is not free to-day, and that he, therefore, rightly proposes the further question: *What* rules are referred to when one speaks of a guarantee for the freedom of the seas to be established at the conclusion of peace or in the treaty of peace?

There are, according to Triepel, *three* possibilities. In the *first* place, it would be possible to be 'satisfied with the assurance that the international law of naval warfare as it existed *before* the world war, and which was without doubt violated by our opponents in many acts of brutal violence,[1] should continue unchanged'. In this solution Triepel rightly sees a very modest gain:

Every one knows that according to present international law there is no real freedom, that is, the right to traverse the seas at such times and at such places as one chooses does not exist, neither for the commerce of the belligerents nor for that of neutrals.

Triepel then points to the rights of capture of prizes, of contraband, and of blockade, and also states that a universally binding system of principles of naval warfare existed before the outbreak of the war only to a very limited extent. As a *second* possibility, Triepel points out that England might be required to ratify the Declaration of London, in order to gain a freedom of the seas considerably more extended than that of the present time. That

[1] *Really* only by the opponents?

would be [he says] no freedom of the seas in the full sense, since the Declaration adheres to the rights of capture at sea, of contraband, and of blockade. But it would signify the solution of many disputed points which would not be entirely without value. The *third* possibility consists in this, according to Triepel: that a still further alteration of previously accepted rights than that of the London agreements be striven for. This is evidently what hovers most frequently before the minds of the advocates of the freedom of the seas: complete freedom for commerce on the seas. The development of this ideal would have to begin in places where the lack of freedom is most oppressive, above all with the right of capture, perhaps also with that of contraband and of blockade. As examples of these demands, Triepel cites the 'Minimum Programme' of The Hague, the article in the *Frankfurter Zeitung*, quoted on p. 153, as well as the historian Meinecke, who has demanded: 'The freedom of the seas, that is, the abolition of the right of capture at sea, and if possible the abolition of the rights of contraband and of blockade.'

In the face of the demands Triepel emphasizes first of all the undoubted fact of the present lack of confidence in paper agreements.[1] Nevertheless he declares that he will take his stand upon the ground of the defenders of the freedom of the seas in answering the question whether, so understood, it is really a goal worth fighting for. Yet he expressly wishes to consider the question solely from the standpoint of *German interests*, and moreover with the supposition that Germany and England are the two *belligerent* states. From this standpoint Triepel on his part now sets up the thesis:

> The complete doing away of the rights of contraband and of blockade is a Utopia. The abolition of the right of capture of prizes without at the same time doing away with the rights of contraband and of blockade would be not only a futile innovation, but one decidedly injurious to Germany. For the rights of capture, contraband, and blockade are three fetters of maritime trade so ingeniously welded together that as soon as one is loosened or destroyed the other lays hold so much the more firmly.

Triepel now dedicates to the proving of this thesis more detailed explanations, into the particulars of which I cannot here enter, however interesting they might be. He tries to show that in the first place there is not the least prospect that the institution

[1] I am thoroughly in accord with Triepel in regard to this *fact*. It is only concerning the *reasons* for it that I have a different opinion.

of contraband will ever disappear from the law of warfare. If the right of capture of prizes should be abolished, but that of contraband be retained, then the conception of contraband, which up to the present has referred only to neutral property, would be applied also to that of the enemy. This enemy property would then fall a prey to the opponent, not as booty but as contraband. There would then arise the danger that by the great extension of the idea of contraband sea booty might again be introduced, by means of which the maritime commerce of the enemy could be crippled just as much as by the right of capture. The abolition of the right of capturing prizes, without the abolition of the right of declaring contraband, would be advantageous to *the* sea power which could manipulate the weapon of the capture of contraband goods the more readily. As long as the geographical situation, the proportions of power, have not changed, Germany will derive more harm than benefit from such freedom of the seas. The prospects for an abolition of blockade are just as slight. If, however, the right to capture prizes should be abolished but not that to blockade, the results would likewise be ineffectual. For the blockade would then signify to the adversary nothing else than capture. Ships would fall a prey to the enemy either as prizes or as blockade runners. The blockade would destroy the enemy's commerce by its very existence. Therefore a blockading sea power could, if necessary, dispense with the right of capture; for one military measure could be substituted for another. The abolition of the right of capturing prizes would have to be followed, as a logical conclusion, by the abolition of the right of blockade. In England the deduction was made that because they could not dispense with the blockade, neither could they do so with the capture of prizes. At any rate the retention of the right of blockade would make the abolition of the right of capture an illusion. On the other hand, the abolition of the right of blockade with the retention of the right of capture would not have the least advantage for Germany. Yes, even if *both* institutions should be abolished there would be no gain; for at once sharper emphasis would be laid upon other means of warfare, upon substitutes for the blockade. The suppression of the introduction of contraband goods might very successfully replace a blockade; even the mere prohibition of the right to import contraband goods might operate as a blockade. The same effect might be attained by the extension of the conception of contraband; likewise by the obliteration of the distinction between absolute and relative contraband. At any rate the abolition of blockade could without the least difficulty be rendered ineffectual by the energetic application of the right to declare contraband. The problem would work out just as in the case of trying to abolish the capture of prizes. Capture, contraband, and blockade are like the three keyboards of an instrument, on any one of which one can at pleasure play the same melody. If necessary, contraband could be renounced if it were permitted to retain the blockade; both blockade and capture could be given up if contraband remained. A renunciation of the capture of prizes is, therefore, according to Triepel, only possible if both blockade and contraband are abolished without leaving either a trace or a substitute. And that [he says] is impossible of realization. Substitutes for the one or the other would always be present. Moreover, Triepel does not lose sight of the possibility that England in a future naval war might be more vulnerable than it has so far been. In that case the *Germans* would be the *fools* if they should rob themselves of the right of capture and of blockade. Consequently, Triepel comes to the conclusion that the abolition of the right of capture of prizes would bring Germany at least no advantage, but perhaps detriment.

The *result*, then, of Triepel's book is, upon the basis of this exposition, the following:

Shall therefore the 'freedom of the seas' cease to be our military goal? I say: certainly not, and this in spite of everything,—only in a somewhat different sense than the vulgar mind is accustomed to interpret it. A freedom of ocean commerce in war times, completely assured by principles of justice, is a dream, capable of realization just as little as the abolishment of war itself.

Triepel rightly emphasizes this point:

If war is directed against *all* the powers of the hostile state—and that is permitted—it will also direct its energies against its economic powers, and therefore against its single economic interests, as far as its purpose of forcing the enemy to submission imperatively demands. This is especially true of naval warfare, which by its very nature, through military means alone, can almost never quite attain its aims. Attacks on hostile maritime commerce will never cease until naval warfare is abolished. Von Maltzahn very pertinently remarks: 'To preserve the right of waging war to the members of the community of states is of advantage to the interests of all, and for this reason it is only consistent to concede internationally to naval warfare the sole means it possesses of compelling peace—attacking hostile commerce.'

Triepel concludes :

There is, however, another 'freedom of the seas', which consists of something besides paper agreements. And for this we shall assuredly fight to the last. That is, the freedom of the seas from the tyranny of England. For us it means to weaken British power in all its parts and all its forms—to speak with Moltke, 'even to its prestige'. Not only temporarily but permanently. Let us strive that the seas in the future become *actually* freer than to-day. But the sea is free only for the mighty, never for the weak. Let us see to it, then, that we have naval power. Then we shall have the free sea. Let us see to it that this war makes England smaller, us greater. Let us see to it that we gain naval bases beyond the seas, that we find an outlet from the 'wet triangle', that we get into our hands the coast of Flanders and the secure land route to it. Then we shall have achieved the freedom of the seas for ourselves, and also for the neutrals groaning under England's arbitrary rule, and the world will breathe a sigh of relief. We live in the cheering hope that in this we shall succeed. For Carthage *must* finally be destroyed, and *will* finally be destroyed.

I again state that this exposition of Triepel's contains a full confirmation of what I have said above (p. 149) in regard to the law of warfare. In the first place, Triepel recognizes throughout the justification for economic war, and concedes that one can abolish war against ocean commerce only by abolishing naval warfare. Moreover, he grants that for him the struggle for the freedom of the seas is not a fight for *rules of law* but for *might*. As soon as the postulate of the freedom of the seas is no longer treated as a *question of right* but as a *question of might*, it is excluded as a matter of course from the discussion of the law of nations. The 'freedom of the seas', according to Triepel—and with Triepel agree, as we have seen, most Germans—is not a problem of *international law*.

The pamphlet by Pohl on *Englisches Seekriegsrecht im Weltkriege* (English Law of Naval Warfare in the World War), which came into my hands at the eleventh hour, confirms the doubts which I have already expressed in regard to the postulate, 'freedom of the seas'. He says in conclusion :

Perhaps the peace treaty will try to formulate new principles of maritime warfare. Has not the freedom of the seas been an often emphasized German war aim ? It dare no longer be possible for England to attempt to throttle us through her disregard of neutral rights. Peace aims must be *might* aims. The new law of naval warfare, the freedom of the seas, such a freedom as we need for our national future, cannot be anchored in 'the moral feelings of all the nations', not in any 'international police authority', by no means in phrases and Utopias.

It can be securely built only upon the foundation of increased German sea power. Substantial guarantees, not statutes, are what we need. Fine phrases in the peace treaty will not ensure the world against the return of the blessings of British sea tyranny. We already possess more than one substantial guarantee. The success of arms gave the coast of Flanders into our hands. We must keep it, this 'pistol directed at England's breast'. We need numerous well-distributed naval bases for our strong battle-proved fleet. This fleet is our most substantial guarantee. . . . In the decisive struggle . . . there has been assigned to the fleet the task . . . to open the passage for the new right of naval warfare, the freedom of the seas.

No explanation is necessary to show that for Pohl also the 'freedom of the seas' is a question of *might*, not of *right*.[1]

A memoir was addressed by Schücking to the Imperial Chancellor: *Meeresfreiheit gegen Friedensgarantien. Ein Weg zur Abkürzung des Weltkrieges* (Freedom of the Seas for Peace Guarantees. A Way for the Shortening of the World War). Wherein this freedom of the seas is to consist is not definitely stated. According to the memoir it is to be attained by placing the seas, up to the present time a *res nullius*, under the control of the totality of civilized nations. The high seas must be made a *res omnium*. Then in a future naval war the neutrals could demand that no warlike acts be committed on the high seas. With this legal situation only would we have the necessary juridical conditions for actually assuring the freedom of the seas. The Hague League of Nations should organize this mastery over the seas in peace times, and create an international executive power strong enough to hold the belligerents at sea, in war times also, within legal bounds. This executive power should be built upon the basis of maritime quotas from the states. In consequence of the agreement concerning armaments, it would be superior to the fleet of any single state.

I am of the opinion that if an international executive power should ever be created, it will be its task to serve not the principle of the 'freedom of the seas', but that of observance of the law of nations. It will be an organ not only of the rights of *war*, but also of international law. Schücking's assumption that England could be compelled to give up 'its actual mastery of

[1] It is worthy of note that the present German teachers of international law, as these examples show, are almost without exception Pan-Germans. For them what I wrote in *Wissen und Leben* of July 1, 1916, concerning the right to existence of a nationalistic science of international law, is pertinent.

the seas by a forced assent to the establishment of international control' does not seem to me very likely to be realized. It must attract attention that Schücking also writes :

> If, however, war has broken out, there exists for each of the participants 'a state of necessity', and from this viewpoint each belligerent believes himself justified, without acting immorally, in overstepping the bounds of law.

Surely the standpoint of *right* can never be supported with this 'theory of a state of necessity'. It leads, consciously or unconsciously, from right to its antipode might.

I wish to refer further to the article by Persius on *Krieg, Handel und Piraterie* (War, Commerce, and Piracy).[1] According to Persius it is a sign of the diplomatic cleverness of the Imperial Chancellor that he did not make it known what direction his thoughts concerning the attainment of the freedom of the seas were taking. The German jurists [he says] are now striving to fathom these thoughts, or, presuming that they have not yet taken definite form, to guide them into the path which seems desirable to them. Persius remarks :

> Most jurists who have given public expression to their thoughts advocate the standpoint of might. They subscribe to the opinion, widely spread throughout Germany, which with the conception of the freedom of the seas unites the abolition of the mastery of them by Great Britain. They maintain that if another power should possess a dominion of the seas equal to that of England unhindered trade on the world seas for all nations would have been attained in the war.

Persius does not share this opinion. Neither does he approve the abolition of the right of capture at sea. According to his opinion paragraphs have very slight prospects of being obeyed, unless there stands behind them an organ provided with superior force, which may intervene with punitive measures directed against the violator. It is therefore almost useless to indulge in speculations as to the standards to be set up for improved maritime laws, as long as no international agreement is reached as to the method by which the violation of universally accepted laws is to be hindered. The foundation for every structure of the law of warfare must be laid by the establishment and organization of an international power, which as a police force sees to the obeying of the laws. Persius would like to build maritime law upon the basis of an

[1] Cf. *Berliner Tageblatt*, May 25, 1917.

international police-fleet, and lays stress upon the fact that with this is united the problem of disarmament according to treaty. Without that the 'freedom of the seas' would remain a Utopia.

Unless every disturber of the peace can be held in restraint, and every violator of the law can be punished by a police force to which the necessary authority is given, the freedom of the seas can be disregarded by the state finding it to its advantage. Only international power, but not the might of arms of a single state, that is, only the moral will of the nations which then deserve to be called *Kulturvölker*, will help to drive war and piracy out of the world and thus bring commerce to its rights.

[Persius expressed himself later more explicitly concerning the 'freedom of the seas'. He writes with regard to it :[1]

Up to August 1914 the 'freedom of the seas' was understood to be guaranteed in time of peace under all conditions ; the use of the commercial waterways in time of war was restricted under certain international treaties. Will the conclusion of peace bring the desired freedom of the seas without reservation in times of war as well as in time of peace ? Will an understanding be reached for times of war, will a way be found by which private property can be considered as inviolate on the sea as it is to be on land, according to international regulations ; and for times of peace will not the freedom of the sea, up to now free in times of peace, become an illusion, by rendering more difficult the conditions of commerce, by declarations of boycott, &c. ?

Dozens of ambitious writers have tried during the last three and a half years to make it clear to us in what manner Germany must guarantee the freedom of the seas in the future. The advocates of the viewpoint of might consider principally the conquest of England as the indispensable preliminary condition, the advocates of international agreements hope to attain the desired end through the extension of the rules of warfare on land to the sea, i. e. through abolition of commercial warfare. The less extreme representatives of the 'standpoint of might', who do not count on the complete subjugation of England, make propositions of every kind as to how the British Navy can be reduced in order to bring about the freedom of the seas. . . .

One can easily see the ultimate consequences of the desire for the freedom of the seas. . . .

The sceptical will neither anticipate the realization of the freedom of the seas for times of war by means of the destruction of England's supremacy of the seas, nor from an international agreement. International agreements, which are dependent upon the present public conception of culture (*Kulturstandpunkt*) by the European powers, cannot be said to be worth the paper they are written on. If the power of the British fleet, which now dictates the regulations governing the use of the ocean, could be broken, it would not mean that anything in particular had been accomplished in this direction. For, if the English fleet had to resign its first place to another fleet, the latter would, without doubt,

[1] Cf. *Berliner Tageblatt*, March 2, 1918.

exercise no politics of sentiment, but real politics, i. e. it would operate in the national interests. The interests of the power which may be supreme on the seas will not permit, from purely military reasons (sources of information, &c.), that in time of war the entire enemy and neutral sea commerce should pursue its course unhindered, that every trader be necessarily a 'touch-me-not'. . . .

An unrestricted use of the seas in time of war cannot and will not ever come about. Mankind most nearly approaches the desired goal of the 'freedom of the seas' when it tries to settle certain clashing interests other than through the power of the sword, and when it strives to maintain peace. As long as the wisdom of man has not soared into this highest realm of civilization, it is advisable not to indulge in any illusions that the 'freedom of the seas' is a conception without any foundation of reality. When an international conference, which shall deliberate upon the matter of the freedom of the seas, is once more appointed, it is to be hoped that it will render the decision that the seas in time of war are to be considered as war zones, that all war fleets be conceded the right to capture, or, if necessary, that every ship, neutral or otherwise, be sunk. The temporary proclamation of the greatest restriction of the seas is therefore consistent and just. It is at the same time in the interests of the ultimate goal—the freedom of the seas. The more rigorously war may be extended upon the sea, just so much greater it is to be hoped will be the fear of it, and precautions taken to prevent it in every possible way. So much for the freedom of the seas in *time of war*.

In time of peace the freedom of the seas was, up to the present time, considered a self-evident fact. Our traders, together with all the other seafaring peoples, pursued unhindered their course upon the seas, made use of foreign ports for loading and unloading, and were treated cordially everywhere. Will this ideal condition be reinstated after the war? Every trader is himself conscious that the domestic prosperity of his own people implies also that of his rival. This obtains particularly in the case of English merchants. . . .

At the same time we must be clear in our own minds that although our army and our fleet were in a position to win the greatest victories, we could not force the other peoples to trade with us, we could not force them to exchange their raw materials for our manufactured products. If the other peoples are not willing to enter into friendly trade competition with us again, then will our merchant marine bring us no gain, since there will be no business for it. The 'freedom of the seas', even if internationally established, would be useless for us. Our enemies in the west hold a great portion of our means of livelihood in their hands. In recognition of this condition, Dr. Michaelis, the Imperial Chancellor, expressed himself on the 19th of July 1917, in the presence of the representatives of the people: 'We must guarantee the vital interests for the German people by way of *agreement* and *compromise*, on the continent and on the sea.' We can only acquire *a freedom of the seas favourable to us by means of an amicable peace.* Any peace by force would preclude the 'freedom of the seas' for us in time of peace as well.]

[Another German teacher of International law who expressed himself concerning our subject is Wilhelm van Calker, in the publication *Das Problem der Meeresfreiheit und die deutsche Völkerrechtspolitik* (The Problem of the Freedom of the Seas and German International Law Policy). He strives, through the discussion of the 'political problem of the freedom of the seas arising in international law', to make friends 'for the idea of a revision of the laws of war on sea as pertaining to us, according to the national point of view'. This shows the standpoint of the author. He speaks of the 'struggle for the freedom of the seas to which England challenged us in the summer of 1914, in grave apprehension of losing her arbitrary supremacy of the sea'. The problem of the freedom of the seas is the central point of the war aims according to van Calker.

> Like a mighty breath of spring, to-day the longing for the freedom of the seas sweeps over the world! Among us in Germany as an open war cry against England, our enemy; among the enemy and his friends, as a hypocritical prayer against us, the stubborn despisers of the 'chosen', sons of Britain who consider themselves a blessing on humanity.

According to van Calker, the decision concerning freedom or restriction of the sea has become one of vital importance for Germany. In spite of the fact that he conceives the problem as an essentially political one, he declares further that 'the so-called Anglo-American conception of international law' is nothing but a matter of politics. Van Calker protests against the fact that people, when they represent political principles, do so 'with the innocent disguise of the protector of international law'.

> It is to be hoped that . . . in Germany in the future things will so transpire that Anglo-American doctrines, developed through the English arbitrary supremacy of the seas, will be stripped of their cloak of international law and placed in their proper light in opposition to German rights and the standpoint of German interests. We have recognized our might, and will not exchange the attributes of this power any longer for uncertain international assurances of England. For whatever concessions England may make in reference to her experiences in the world war, still the fact remains that through her inability to conquer a continental world power in land warfare, she will not relinquish of her own free will, except with the conscious intention of self-annihilation, the use of her fleet for the destruction of her opponent in the manner which seems most profitable. Also, he who does not know that England's practice for centuries has been, in international agreements, to leave a back door open; and whoever does not know England's aptitude in the framing of agreements, nor her unscrupulousness in tearing them up, will no doubt—even as will finally every nation intent upon the preservation of its life—in the case of utmost necessity, place the command of self-preservation above that of right.

These observations lead van Calker to the following conclusions :

1. Our international law policy must be entirely dictated by German interests. Cosmopolitan ideas and other ideal wishes must be subservient to the national interests.

2. No new obligations to be entered into by international agreements in connexion with the right of maritime warfare.

3. So far as we feel any necessity of subjecting our procedure towards hostile and neutral powers in war to fixed legal rules, they shall be cloaked in the form of imperial laws. German imperial law shall be in the future the foundation of our laws of warfare.]

[The best German presentation of the subject is that of Stier-Somlo in his book *Die Freiheit der Meere und das Völkerrecht* (The Freedom of the Seas and International Law). It advocates essentially making an end of this supposed international postulate.[1] Stier-Somlo proves conclusively that the question is not one of international law. Then he asks whether one can *politically* demand any assurance of the freedom of the seas in time of peace, according to which it is conclusive that one cannot possibly do so in time of war. Stier-Somlo finds—

that the freedom of the seas in time of peace is a justified demand, but it is still a demand which is to exalt the legal binding regulations which Germany, too, with all the means at its command, should aid in developing ; that on the other hand the freedom of the seas in case of war, under all circumstances and to the fullest extent, is impossible to assure, because this would mean practically abolition of maritime war. Therefore it would naturally be ill advised for Germany if she should declare any such sweeping demands necessary and aspire to them.]

It is necessary for our position, as has been said, to gather everywhere from the commonplace phrases which play a rôle in many of the above statements the *kernel of international law* contained in them. Only the *enforcement of an assured legal status* may be recognized as a justified tendency in this postulate of the freedom of the seas. Political considerations in favour or disfavour of a state, must, as I have already emphasized, be put aside. Otherwise a basis can never be obtained that is acceptable to all the parties nor will any one ever succeed in approaching the problem unbiased. If we approach the question from this standpoint, according to the import and right of the demand, aided by

[1] See in this connexion my criticism of the book in the *Schweizerische Juristenzeitung* of April 1, 1918.

the material here offered, we shall next come to the result that the problem can clearly only have reference to the period of the war. Generally speaking, the freedom of the seas already indisputably *exists* in times of peace. Germany especially was able under the conditions that have up to this time prevailed to raise its commerce and its shipping to a high degree of prosperity,[1] a prosperity that would most probably have risen higher yet but for the intervention of the war and which after this war will presumably not be attained again for decades. But in so far as barriers may still exist in times of peace we can surely agree with President Wilson that these barriers must fall.

In war times, then, the demand for the freedom of the seas is manifestly tantamount to this from the viewpoint of international law : Private property at sea is to be protected, the commerce of the belligerents and of neutrals shall no longer be disturbed by naval war, while the institutions of capture of prizes and of contraband especially are to be abolished or limited. But if one realizes that, according to its very nature, naval war is a commercial war and must be so, it is easily recognized that the German demand for the freedom of the seas in this sense would finally amount to nothing else than restricting or making innocuous, so to speak, the economic war, the naval war, to the advantage of the military war, or war on land. Aside from the fact that such a development would naturally be to the interest of one single country, namely Germany, this tendency is very clearly in opposition to all the experiences of this war, which have taught us just this : that the more modern and more humane *commercial war* is to be greatly preferred in the *future form* of war to the military war made obsolete by modern technical science.

If this is to be said about the tendency in general, something must, however, be specifically said about the German demand. At the second Hague Conference England was willing that the *law of contraband* should be abolished. The retrogressive course of the institution in the London Declaration goes back, for the most part, to German influence.[2] Consequently Germany has only herself to blame if the law of contraband to-day still continues to be

[1] See also my *Antwort an Ludwig von Sybel* in my pamphlet, *Meine offene Korrespondenz mit Philipp Zorn, Ludwig von Sybel, Prinz Alexander zu Hohenlohe.* Bern, 1918.

[2] Katz, *loc. cit.*, points out that Germany voted against the abolition and writes : 'If the demand of England had been approved by all the states, England

law. As far as the *right of capture* is concerned, England, as we have seen, was likewise ready to make concessions at the second Hague Peace Conference, if Germany would be willing to enter into a discussion of the question of armament. With the refusal of Germany to come to an agreement about the problem of armament, this advance was consequently also frustrated at that time. Is there not in this a clear indication as to *how* the 'freedom of the seas' could *actually* be achieved? But to what has been said must be added. It is apparent that the 'freedom of the seas' also means that no *mines* be laid in the high seas outside of territorial waters. As is well known, England demanded this at The Hague, but Germany was opposed to such a prohibition. It was Germany, too, that made a reservation to the provision that in a blockade no mines were to be laid before the coasts and harbours of the enemy the sole purpose of which was to tie up commercial shipping.[1] Also in respect to other questions, e. g. the question of the conversion of merchant vessels on the high seas, the destruction of neutral prizes, &c., the German standpoint at The Hague was by no means the one that would have corresponded to the principle of the freedom of the seas. And, finally, if one turns to the period of the war, it must also be said that clearly the German *submarine war* can in no wise be made to accord with the German demand of the freedom of the seas.

If one is to draw a conclusion from all these historical facts, it is clear that the German propaganda for the freedom of the seas has not received its impulse from pure considerations of *international law*—for if nothing further than progress in international law was intended it could have been secured earlier and without a war—but that political motives are in the background. This can perhaps be explained by the fact that Germany sees in English maritime supremacy a hindrance to its own development at sea—

would not have been able to say that the searching and seizure of neutral trading vessels, which paralysed all commerce, was in compliance with the legal order.' The German government declared in 1907 that the importation of wares that by nature aid the enemy in waging war must be absolutely prevented, and that, to this extent, the seizure of contraband is to be maintained. But the war has taught that Germany could not enforce its prohibition of contraband against any of its enemy states. The maintenance of the prohibition [Katz writes] had therefore no practical significance for Germany.

[1] Germany has also acted in compliance with this view in this war, by seeking in August 1914 to obstruct the entrance into English harbours by mines. The English closure of the North Sea was the *answer* to the German mine blockade. The details will be found in my larger work, *Deutschland und das Völkerrecht*, Part IV.

this German belief is incorrect, for Germany has been able to develop its commerce unhindered—and that it aims to limit or tie up the economic war in favour of the military war. These are considerations that certainly do not lie in the field of international law and with which Germany could hardly expect to make headway.[1] From the standpoint of international law it will, of course, be necessary to work in behalf of the development of the law of naval war.[2] I have already pointed out wherein such development might be most opportune. This development of the law of naval warfare, earnestly to be striven for, can surely be included under the name of the 'freedom of the seas'. But one must be aware of the fact that, for the above-mentioned reasons, this designation may easily occasion misunderstandings. In so far, however, as anything *more* far reaching should be striven for under this name than that which lies in the field of international development and which President Wilson has so well characterized, one would be right in approaching the postulate with scepticism.

It were better to substitute, in Germany also, the phrases '*the progress of international law*' and '*the enforcement of peace*' for that of '*the freedom of the seas*'. This is certainly far more important than any progress in the law of naval warfare, of whatever nature it may be! These phrases also answer to the suppression of everything that has proved to be an obstacle in the progress of international law. The progress of the law of naval warfare, like all progress in international law, is dependent upon the suppression of the antipodes of international law—the military system which points to self-help, to war. We have seen that the abolition of the right of capture could have been accomplished as early as 1907 through an agreement on armaments. Whoever *seriously* desires the 'freedom of the seas' would naturally desire an *agreement on armament* also, for it is in excessive armament more than in anything else that the military system has found its outward expression.

[1] Katz, *loc. cit.*, also observes that it seems natural to assume that, in consequence of the experiences of this war, the enemy states will not comply with the demand of Germany. The question then comes up whether Germany will have the power to enforce the abolition of the right of capture in the peace treaty. Moreover, the right of capture has also proved to be insufficient as a means of combat.

[2] [This is desired by America especially, and justly so.]

No less, however, should Germany also endeavour to oppose the inner expression of this system, her military *mentality*.[1] The consciousness of *the predominance of right over might must also be planted in the souls of the nations.* If after this war a time of lasting peace is actually to dawn, a time in which a regard for international law is not only assured, but if necessary can also be enforced—enforced above all by economic means; if this time is gradually to lead to a period when states will make use of these economic means exclusively, even in such controversial cases as exclude legal solution, so that they shall no longer wage any but *commercial* wars with each other; and if in this way, perhaps in some distant future there should come an age without war, then *one* preliminary condition must be absolutely fulfilled and that is: the abolition of the military system [2] and the *combating of the military mentality.* This *must* be the watchword of those who believe in international law. Those who refuse to accept this watchword are opponents of international law. There is no middle road.

To the extent to which *international law gradually absorbs the law of war* and the economic means of enforcement in the hands of the league of nations makes the employment of self-help either impossible or superfluous, and to the extent to which international law is thereby liberated from its antipode, the military system, to that same extent will the way be cleared for the dominance of law in the life of nations. It is to be hoped that this truth may be recognized in all lands to-day, and that all may see clearly what is at stake. Not only the future of international law, but the future of European civilization, the future of Europe depends on this knowledge. May this truth also be recognized in Germany above all, where unfortunately there are forces at work to turn the course of international law backwards to the advantage of the military system! *No* country that wishes to have a share in the cultural development of Europe and desires to help support the international legal order dares to-day to advocate the military system. We are convinced that in all countries *all the really progressive elements* will resist such a position.

[1] Fried, *loc. cit.*, p. 5, is correct in saying: 'It is no longer endurable that all the achievements of human thought should be only for the good of artillery.'

[2] It is unnecessary to note that this demand has nothing to do with *Anti-militarism.* See p. 93, *supra.*

International law, in the form in which I have presented it here as worthy of attainment, has recently been given the name of *democratic* international law. This designation is not inappropriate. The true international law, which aspires to the dominance of law and nothing else, is in its nature actually democratic. It proceeds from the idea of the equality of states, small as well as large, and has no place for imperialistic aspirations. It places right *above* might and therefore opposes militarism. Its presuppositions and aims are in the same way outgrowths of the democratic idea. And as it would be for that reason a *contradictio in adiecto* if one wished to believe in the possibility of an international law in the service of the imperialistic or militaristic idea, one might, on the other hand, rightly say that *democracy* and *international law* are two conceptions that must be complementary to each other and to a certain degree also conditioned upon each other ; for the international idea can only prosper *fully* in the soil of democracy.

If one takes a survey of the forces and tendencies which seek to influence human development to-day, one readily sees that on the one hand there are democratic, and on the other hand military-imperialistic forces which we see at work.[1] After what has been said, there can be no doubt from which of these tendencies international law has more to expect. Its hopes rest upon the victory of the democratic idea, and it is therefore only to be hoped that in *all* countries this idea will increase in power after this war, for the good of international law. If this be the result of the present war, then it will have brought something great to maturity and it will not have been fought in vain.

The entire cultural world of Europe is to-day interested in the victory of the democratic idea and with it of international law. It is a solidaric interest that unites them and that prompts them also to watch over this interest mutually and protect the European world of states against a further incursion into the channels of imperialism and of militarism. One need only cast a glance into the larger world about him in order to recognize this. A dozen years ago I once pointed out that we, indeed, still live to-day in the period of preponderating European influence, that, it is true, the *East* would first have to create for itself its political and

[1] I wish to note *expressly* that the above was written *before* America entered the war and *before* the revolutionary outbreak in Russia.

economic position, but that we shall have to reckon absolutely with the realization of the event at some early or later date, and that then the question of political and economic preponderance might also perhaps become a question of the hour.[1] Through this war we have to-day been brought quite considerably nearer to this problem. Less than ever should we therefore to-day lose sight of these and other viewpoints that remind the nations of their solidarity, and on this account we should seek to bestow upon the new Europe and with it upon the remaining community of states a sounder basis after this war than they had before. But let us at the same time also constantly say that the final victory will some time fall to that system which has *morality* and *law* on its side. Upon the progress of *law* and not of force must the future of Europe and of the world be established.

[1] Cf. with this my pamphlet, *Ein Blick in das europafreie Japan*, 1905.

APPENDIX

APPENDIX

I

OTHER PROPOSALS

It may perhaps be of interest if, in addition to my own ideas, I give space here to a few proposals that have been made by other parties. I shall select a number of publications which appear especially significant to me. At the same time, however, I shall also add a few expressions of opinion, concerning whose value or worthlessness I should not like to express myself further and with which I wish in no way to be identified ; but it seemed interesting to me to reprint them here, because they reflect the opinions and the wishes which stir humanity to-day and because they may therefore be regarded as being symptomatic, even if they should prove to be useless from a juristic standpoint. It is, however, not my purpose to criticize all these proposals, since it is not the purpose of this book to enter upon individual problems.

(A)

At the head of the proposals that have been made for the formulation of the new international law I should like to place the declaration which the *American Institute of International Law* published in December 1915 concerning the rights and duties of nations :

DECLARATION OF THE RIGHTS AND DUTIES OF NATIONS

I. Every nation has the right to exist, and to protect and to conserve its existence ; but this right neither implies the right nor justifies the act of the state to protect itself or to conserve its existence by the commission of unlawful acts against innocent and unoffending states.

II. Every nation has the right to independence in the sense that it has a right to the pursuit of happiness and is free to develop itself without interference or control from other states, provided that in so doing it does not interfere with or violate the rights of other states.

III. Every nation is in law and before law the equal of every other nation belonging to the society of nations, and all nations have the right to claim and, according to the Declaration of Independence of the United States, 'to assume, among the Powers of the earth, the separate and equal station to which the laws of nature and of nature's God entitle them.'

IV. Every nation has the right to territory within defined boundaries and to exercise exclusive jurisdiction over its territory, and all persons whether native or foreign found therein.

V. Every nation entitled to a right by the law of nations is entitled to have that right respected and protected by all other nations, for right and duty are correlative, and the right of one is the duty of all to observe.

VI. International law is at one and the same time both national and international: national in the sense that it is the law of the land and applicable as such to the decision of all questions involving its principles; international in the sense that it is the law of the society of nations and applicable as such to all questions between and among the members of the society of nations involving its principles.

The principles here expressed may without further ado be declared as pointing out the way for us.[1] The spirit, to which they bear testimony, will, let us hope, be the prevailing one among all nations after this war.

(B)

If the tenets of the American Institute seek once and for all to determine the theoretical side, another American institution has endeavoured to attack the actual problems from the practical side. I refer to the *League to Enforce Peace.* This League has made the following proposals :

We believe it to be desirable for the United States to join a league of nations binding the signatories to the following :

First. All justiciable questions arising between the signatory powers, not settled by negotiation, shall, subject to the limitations of treaties, be submitted to a Judicial Tribunal for hearing and judgement, both upon the merits and upon any issue as to its jurisdiction of the question.

Second. All other questions arising between the signatories and not settled by negotiation, shall be submitted to a Council of Conciliation for hearing, consideration, and recommendation.

Third. The signatory powers shall jointly use forthwith both their economic and military forces against any one of their number that goes to war, or commits acts of hostility, against another of the signatories before any question arising shall be submitted as provided in the foregoing.

Fourth. Conferences between the signatory powers shall be held from time to time to formulate and codify rules of international law, which, unless some

[1] Cf. with this the speech given before the *American Society of International Law* by Root on April 27, 1916.

signatory shall signify its dissent within a stated period, shall thereafter govern in the decisions of the Judicial Tribunal mentioned in Article I.

In view of the importance of the subject, I shall also attach here the commentary which has been given on these four articles: [1]

We believe it to be desirable for the United States to join a League of Nations binding the signatories to the following:

The league of nations here proposed would be brought into existence after the close of the present European War and would have as its object the establishment of a permanent condition of law and order among the nations. The League does not concern itself in any way with the war now in progress. It seeks instead to unite the great mass of sentiment against war which will exist in this and other lands after the unparalleled slaughter now going on, in a practical plan to prevent the repetition of such a disaster.

The maintenance of law and order in its own territory is an imperative duty which every nation owes to its citizens. A farther duty is to join with other nations in maintaining law and order in the society of nations. Neglect of the former duty results in anarchy at home; neglect of the latter, in anarchy among the nations.

For the establishment of law and order in their own territory, the thirteen American States found it necessary to create a federal government. For the establishment of law and order among the nations of the world, it has manifestly become necessary to create a federation, or league, of the nations, with definite but limited powers.

As America has in the past borne her part in working out and establishing the principles of justice and democracy between individual men within the nation, it is now her duty to share the burden of the nations in making the world, their common heritage, a place where peacefully inclined states can be secure in their rights and liberties. Oceans which formerly required months to traverse have shrunk almost to rivers with the advent of modern means of communication. The day has passed for maintaining America's traditional policy of isolation, as it passed a half century ago for the maintenance by Japan of her peculiar policy of isolation.

Article I

All justiciable questions arising between the signatory powers, not settled by negotiation, shall, subject to the limitations of treaties, be submitted to a Judicial Tribunal for hearing and judgement, both upon the merits and upon any issue as to its jurisdiction of the question.

Comment

A justiciable question is one which can be settled according to the principles of law and equity. Our claims against England arising from the ravages of the

[1] Cf. further, the publication issued by the League at its session in Philadelphia on July 17, 1915. See further the commentary by A. Lawrence Lowell, the remarks of Wilson, Taft, Grey, Briand, Bethmann, Bryce, Straus, Lodge, Houston, and others.

Confederate cruiser *Alabama* were justiciable. So were the Alaska Boundary and the North Atlantic Fisheries disputes. Many of the quarrels between nations are of this character.

Just as individuals settle between themselves many controversies which might be carried before the courts, so nations settle by negotiation, through diplomacy, most of the disputes which arise between them. The habit is a good one and ought to be continued. But when diplomacy fails to settle a quarrel between nations, it is no more logical and right for them to resort at once to war than it would be for two men who had failed to settle a private difference to draw their pistols and begin to shoot.

Against the time when citizens fail to agree, the state has provided the courts as agencies to mete out justice and to promote peaceable relations between them. Against the day when two or more states of the American Union fail to settle their controversy, the federal constitution has provided the Supreme Court as an agency for administering justice and maintaining peace between those states.

The problem of securing justice among the civilized nations and of maintaining peaceful relations among them is, in its essence, the same as we have successfully solved in the national and municipal realms and can with equal propriety and success be entrusted to a Judicial Tribunal or Court. The best thought in all the civilized nations is, indeed, already agreed that such an international court ought to be constituted and to have jurisdiction over all justiciable questions, save those which may be reserved by treaty agreement for settlement in some other way.

Article II

All other questions arising between the signatories and not settled by negotiation, shall be submitted to a Council of Conciliation for hearing, consideration, and recommendation.

Comment

Disputes arise between nations which they are unable or unwilling to settle according to rules of international law. Political questions and questions of national policy often belong to this class. A controversy concerning the Monroe Doctrine would probably present a non-justiciable issue, as might also the arbitrary exercise of our undoubted right to admit or to exclude such immigrants as we might think to be helpful or harmful to our national life.

But if one's neighbour believes that he will be injured by a proposed course of action, a just and peace-loving man is ready to talk it over, even though his legal right to do what he proposes is perfectly clear. So a nation which desires justice and peace will be ready to listen to the advice of a Council of Conciliation concerning a policy or course of conduct which aggrieves a sister nation, before persisting in it.

While America would not readily consent to have the Monroe Doctrine go before a court for judicial review and decision, there is no reason why we should not listen to what a board of distinguished and honourable men, intent on securing justice and preventing war, have to say concerning the broad international aspects and results of a *proposed application* of this doctrine. On the contrary, there is every reason why we should listen to such impartial advice on this or any other question, given, as it would be, under a deep sense of responsibility. The more certain we were of the justice of our cause, the more desirous we were to maintain just and peaceful relations with the world, the more ready we should be to listen.

It hardly needs to be pointed out to Americans to-day that the interests of humanity and of neutral nations are more sacred than is the right of any one state to insist on taking her own course without waiting to see what other nations think about its justice, or what the results to the world may be. Valuable as the principle of arbitration and conciliation is in keeping peace between individuals, it is still more vital for the solution of the grave questions on which the welfare and the peace of the whole world depend. No nation has a right to claim exemption from the obligation to give a hearing to friendly nations in disputes to which she is a party.

Article III

The signatory powers shall jointly use forthwith both their economic and military forces against any one of their number that goes to war, or commits acts of hostility, against another of the signatories before any question arising shall be submitted as provided in the foregoing.

Comment

The chief instrument by which peaceful relations are promoted between individuals is law, interpreted by the courts and enforced, when necessary, by police and military power. No better way exists for promoting peaceful relations between the nations than the extension of this method to the international sphere. In frontier towns without a police, citizens had to arm to protect themselves, and assaults and assassinations abounded. In the absence of an agreement among the nations to establish at need a posse comitatus for the protection of any state which may be wrongfully threatened by another, each nation, no matter how devoted to peace, is compelled to arm for its own defence. It is a sort of *frontier* condition which exists among the nations and its results are disastrous as we now see plainly. The only way to bring national preparation for war within reasonable limits is by a better and stronger international proparation to keep the peace.

The kernel of the proposals of the League to Enforce Peace is found in the provision for using the joint forces of the nations, economic and military, against any state which breaks the peace before resorting to arbitration or conciliation, and doing it forthwith without stopping for consultations and parleyings which often result in doing nothing.

The difficulty of ascertaining which nation begins a war will not impair the effectiveness of the proposal that the League shall combine against the aggressor, any more than the effectiveness of the police as peace officers is impaired by the fact that it is often impossible to tell which of two men began a fight on the street. In doubtful cases the policeman does not attempt to decide who was the aggressor, but subdues the man who resists arrest and takes both parties to the quarrel before the magistrate, whose duty it is to decide the responsibility for the assault. So the League would not have to decide who committed the original offence, but would use its forces against the nation that persisted in making war before submitting the dispute to the court or the Council of Conciliation.

The League does not propose that decisions of the Court and recommendations of the Council of Conciliation shall be enforced. Experience teaches that if a conflict is postponed until the cause of controversy has been publicly examined, war will generally be prevented. In those rare cases in which differences are so profound that people will fight over them at any cost, it is still worth while to postpone the conflict, to have a public discussion of the question at issue before a tribunal, and thus to give to the people of the countries involved a chance to consider, before hostilities begin, whether the risk and suffering of war is really worth while.

Article IV

Conferences between the signatory powers shall be held from time to time to formulate and codify rules of international law, which, unless some signatory shall signify its dissent within a stated period, shall thereafter govern in the decisions of the Judicial Tribunal mentioned in Article I.

Comment

An international assembly which should meet periodically to formulate and codify rules of international law, is an essential part of the plan for securing international peace. It would provide a means for anticipating controversies before they arise and settling them in a spirit of friendly co-operation in time of peace. It would afford an opportunity for raising the standards of international law and laying down fundamental principles which, without such conference, are liable to remain indefinite. If it were provided by international agreement that the acts of such a body should have the force of law unless some nation within the League interposed a veto within a specified period, such a conference would steadily grow in moral power and might well prove to be, in the end, the most valuable feature of the proposed League.

Conclusion

These proposals are put forward as pointing out the road along which the nations must sooner or later travel in their efforts to establish a just and stable peace, and not as a complete and final plan. It is realized that they are not free from objections. The representatives of the nations assembled to draw up a treaty which should establish a League to Enforce Peace would no doubt modify them. They might not be willing to go so far as is here proposed; they might wish to go much farther and to provide for a more complete form of world government than is now suggested.

Full confidence in the general wisdom of the plan existed, however, among the three hundred distinguished men who composed the Independence Hall Conference and the much larger number who had examined and approved the resolutions but were unable to attend. It was felt to be of vital importance to begin now the unification of opinion around a plan so simple as to be practical and attainable, so that a great body of supporters in many lands will be prepared to present and urge it upon the attention of their governments when the reorganization of Europe and of the world is under consideration at the close of the war.

The Executive Committee has given the following additional interpretation to Article 3 :

The signatory powers shall jointly employ diplomatic and economic pressure against any one of their number that threatens war against a fellow signatory without having first submitted its dispute for international inquiry, conciliation, arbitration or judicial hearing, and awaiting a conclusion, or without having in good faith offered so to submit it. They shall follow this forthwith by the joint use of their military forces against that national if it actually goes to war, or commits acts of hostility, against another of the signatories before any question arising shall be dealt with as provided in the foregoing.

It is at once evident that when the preceding plan of the League to Enforce Peace comes to a realization and an actual League of Nations is brought about, which will seek to enforce international law in the sense of that League, that international law will then, at least within the boundaries of the states belonging to this League of Nations, take on the form which I have indicated in my preceding discussions as being desirable. The plan of the League coincides in every way with the programme that I have proposed above, and if, as its authors say, this plan is still far from being perfect, from the standpoint of the relations of to-day it is nevertheless the most practical proposal which has hitherto been made ; in fact, I am inclined to see an advantage in its very imperfection, for it is this very imperfection that warrants its realizability. The more perfect the projects which are on every side being produced with such alacrity, so much the further are they as a rule removed from practicability. The plan of the League to Enforce Peace, however, guarantees both progress *and* practicability. It aims at a genuine progress, but only upon the basis of the attainable. However, the attainable signifies more to-day than it did yesterday. And since we may assume that after the lessons of this war much will be attainable to-day that previously had to be looked upon as unattainable, the possibility of an actual bringing about of a future league of nations for the enforcement of peace need at the outset by no means be doubted.

An advantage of the American plan is its very brevity. Contrary to the numberless projects which have been hatched out during this war and in which the constitution of the future world federation of states has already been worked out in all its details, so that in the future there really remains nothing at all for the statesmen to do, the League to Enforce Peace is satisfied with four short articles in which, however, everything that is necessary to say to-day is actually said. I have on previous occasions opposed the big projects which assume that the world can be reconstructed with one stroke. It is comparatively easy to forge such projects, to proclaim federal constitutions and decrees which will after all never be translated into reality. The really *difficult* thing is to indicate the ways by which the desirable progress can actually be *attained*. To be sure this seems a less pretentious task. But fortunately the world is not being ruled by great words but by *deeds*. With a modest but realizable programme one accomplishes more than with plans for revolutionizing the world. This must also apply to the present in spite of all the changed conditions. And for this reason it is to be welcomed that the League to Enforce Peace has obviously been influenced by this knowledge in constructing its programme.

Apart from this, I should like only to add the following to the programme of the League, since my position to the problem can readily be seen from the discussions in this book. While the first article is occupied with those state controversies that can be submitted to arbitral decision, the second has to do with those which seem to evade arbitral decision and for which, according to accepted international law, either mediation or a commission of inquiry would be the advisable way for adjustment. Instead of this, Article 2 provides for a Council of Conciliation. This Council would consequently have to unite the tasks of the mediator with those of an investigating commission. At the same time it must be remembered that the character of the investigating commission has not at all times and places been the same historically, as has already been shown above. The Council of Conciliation, just as many of the proposed commissions of investigation, might also have a more or less permanent character. Naturally, it is in itself of secondary importance whether in a concrete case a mediation or a commission of investigation takes action, as long as the purpose, the adjustment of the difference, is accomplished. It may therefore be quite useful if, in place of these two complementary possibilities, a single one be allowed to take its place and in consequence be developed so much the more effectively. If in comparison with the institutions of existing international law the Council of Conciliation proves to be the more perfect institution, it will be gladly accepted.[1] Moreover, it will always remain possible to fall back upon the forms of mediation or of the investigating commission and comply with the spirit of Article 2 too, since only the name would be different. In other respects the state of affairs is quite the same as characterized above: the arbitral decision *settles* the difference, the Council of Conciliation *endeavours* to settle it. With this proposal, the League manifestly remains on the grounds of the attainable.

The third article is entirely in accord with the postulate that we have set forth above for the creation of a system of international economic and military means of enforcement.[2] Consequently it needs no further comment.

The fourth article finally follows as a necessary consequence from the actual formation of a league of states. The states united in such a league must of course hold conferences from time to time, and if they then occupy themselves with the problems of the development of international law, we can only welcome this tendency. In so doing they would take over the task which the Hague Conferences have hitherto sought to accomplish. But in view of the opposition shown at The Hague, it must be assumed that the field for the progress of international law within such a league would from the outset be an essentially more favourable one than has been the case at The Hague. The League to Enforce Peace consequently wishes to pave the way not only for judicial decisions, but also for legislation in international law. Moreover, it seems to me to be proof of a wise self-restraint that it has

[1] The new form of the Council of Conciliation has recently been recommended by various parties. Thus Lange, in *Die amerikanischen Friedensverträge*, 1916, p. 86, writes that perhaps after this war an organization will be welcomed which would in no way endanger the complete independence of the states, which would not even hinder the recourse to weapons, but which would only desire to offer an opportunity for council and consideration. If there existed an international council of investigation, that were completely organized and prepared to act upon the request of the powers, the powers would surely not only appeal to it, but, on the contrary, would in given cases also remind the controversial parties of its existence. Lange then points to the problems which would be connected with the establishing of such an institution, problems of organization (number of delegates in the Council, manner of election, representation of the states), of competence, &c. Cf. further van Houten, in *Wissen und Leben* for October 1, 1916, who desires a council of nations that merely renders decisions and opposes a world confederation of states. He proposes the organization of a common council of nations which would render decisions upon international affairs and upon points of controversy.

[2] For military means of enforcement, cf. Général Perein, 'L'armée internationale', in *La paix par le droit*, 1917, p. 65.

refrained from further details about the character and the organization of these conferences, as it would thereby only have made more difficult the realization of a league of states on the basis proposed. The main thing is that the states seriously desiring peace come together on the basis of the principles set up by the League to Enforce Peace. The rest will take care of itself.[1]

It remains to be observed that the alliance of American Chambers of Commerce have, for example, resolved to recommend that the United States shall form an alliance with other powers with the purpose of applying the means of economic enforcement against any state that resorts to war, without having made use of the international procedure.[2] Military means should only be resorted to as the extreme recourse, when the economic fail.

(C)

I should like here to call further attention to the *Central Organization for a Lasting Peace* at The Hague. It has first of all set up the following *minimum programme* :

1. There shall take place neither annexation nor transference of territory against the interests and wishes of the population. The consent of the latter shall, wherever possible, be obtained by plebiscite or in other ways.

2. The states are to guarantee to the nationalities of their territory legal equality, religious freedom, and the free use of their language.

3. The states shall agree to bring about free trade or at least the equalization of all nations, in their colonies, protectorates, and spheres of interest.

4. The work of the Hague Conferences in reference to the peaceful organization of the community of states shall be carried on.

The Peace Conference shall be furnished with a permanent organization and hold periodical sittings.

5. The states shall agree to submit all their disputes to a peaceful procedure. To this end, besides the existing court of arbitration at The Hague there shall be established : (*a*) a really permanent International Tribunal ; and (*b*) a similar permanent International Council of Investigation and Mediation.

[1] Cf. also with the programme of the League to enforce Peace my articles in the *Neue Zürcher Zeitung* for November 18 and 25, 1916 ; further, Lammasch, in the *Neue Freie Presse* for November 30, 1916, and von Liszt in the *Zeit* for November 26, 1916.

[2] Lammasch, in the *Zeit* for November 12, 1916, writes that it might be doubted whether all the powers would be ready to renounce the advantage which their real or supposed lead in armament might secure for them in war, and to obligate themselves to enter into procedure before the council of mediation in every case before they resort to arms. But a power that refused would simply place itself outside the pale of the peace community. It could not be a member of a league of peace and would isolate itself. It is the very aim of the peace federation to combat such militaristic conceptions.

6. The states are to bind themselves to carry out a united action—diplomatic, economic, or military—in case a state resorts to military measures instead of submitting the disputed point to a judicial decision or obtaining the verdict of the Council of Investigation and Mediation.

7. The states are to agree to a reduction of armaments.

8. In order to facilitate the reduction of armaments at sea, the right of capture is to be abolished and the freedom of the seas secured.

9. The foreign policy of nations is to be subjected to an effective control of parliaments.

Secret treaties are to be null and void.

At this place we are interested only in those parts of the programme which have reference to the *law of nations*, since the problem of the conclusion of peace and of the treaty of peace does not come within the scope of this work.[1] There are therefore to be considered here Articles 4 to 8 of the programme. The postulates therein advanced can without doubt be accepted. The enlargement of the work of the Hague Peace Conference assuredly appears as desirable as the organization and stabilization of these conferences. It still remains to be seen whether such a progressive step may be hoped for in the immediate future and whether, even if the work of The Hague be continued, the centre of gravity of the progress of international law, in spite of that step, will not come to repose temporarily in a league of peace. At any rate the essential thing is this, that the progress demanded by the whole world be made, it matters not whether at The Hague or elsewhere.

The statements concerning international proceedings can also be approved. In this plan there has been recommended, in addition to the decision of the Court of Arbitration, the establishment of a Council of Inquiry and Conciliation, the latter of which is to be a permanent institution. This Council corresponds approximately to the Council of Conciliation of the League to Enforce Peace. It is to unite in itself the functions of the Commissions of Conciliation and Investigation.[2] Under certain circumstances, it may turn out to be very useful that the

[1] The name ' minimum programme ' is not as pertinent as it might be. One might just as well speak of a ' maximum programme '. The points of the programme embrace in part postulates which fall within the domain of *domestic* policy, and which can therefore scarcely be made the subject of a peace treaty. The programme has doubtless on that account become unacceptable to many who would be inclined to regard the realization of the postulates singly as *per se* highly desirable.

[2] Cf. on this also A. Bugge Wicksell, ' Einige Bemerkungen über den ständigen internationalen Untersuchungs- und Vermittlungsrat ', in the *Recueil de rapports*, vol. i, p. 350.

institution is considered as permanent. It is of course difficult to predict whether this would correspond to an existing need. The future only can reveal that. A permanent International Court of Justice has been planned in addition to the Hague Tribunal of Arbitration. This demand has already been made by the Second Peace Conference at The Hague. The point has been emphasized above that the realization of this wish is greatly to be desired. One cannot avoid asking himself if the Hague Tribunal of Arbitration could not under certain circumstances be so enlarged as to incorporate in itself a permanent court of justice. There is no need of two international courts of justice for each and every case.

Sanctions have also been provided for in the programme. These are conceived in the same spirit as our proposals cited above and in that of the proposal of the League to Enforce Peace.

In the seventh article of the programme an agreement concerning armaments is demanded. In the eighth, the abolition of the right of capture and the assurance of the freedom of the seas. I have already expressed my sentiments in regard to armaments, and in the discussion of military law above the latter demands have likewise been debated.[1]

The international central organization has already had published, in addition to the above-mentioned articles of the programme, some more detailed treatises.[2] Among them there is worthy of special mention a plan which is to take the place of the Hague Convention for the Pacific Settlement of International Disputes. I give here the text of this plan.[3]

ADVANCE PROJECT OF A GENERAL TREATY, RELATIVE TO THE PEACEFUL ADJUSTMENT OF INTERNATIONAL CONFLICTS

Introductory Provisions

Article 1. There is an International Court of Arbitration and an International Council of Conciliation. They have their seat at The Hague.

Article 2. In order to assure the maintenance of peace, the contracting states agree to submit all their differences to the decision of the International Court of Arbitration or of the International Council of Conciliation.

[1] Cf. also with the programme *Une paix durable, Commentaire officiel du programme-minimum,* The Hague, 1915.

[2] *Recueil de rapports sur les différents points du programme-minimum,* 3 vols., The Hague, 1916–17. With this Recueil compare Lammasch in the *Zeit* of November 12 and in the *Neue Freie Presse* of November 30, 1916.

[3] I have given a symposium of plans from the time *preceding* the outbreak of the war in 'Das Problem der obligatorischen Schiedsgerichtsbarkeit', in the *Jahrbuch des öffentlichen Rechts,* 1913.

Article 3. The contracting states agree to respect and to execute conscientiously the decisions and the decrees which shall be obligatory for them by virtue of Articles 51 and 106.

CHAPTER *1*

CONCERNING THE INTERNATIONAL COURT OF ARBITRATION

Part 1

Composition of the International Court of Arbitration

Article 4. The Court is composed of judges and deputy judges appointed by the contracting states.

Each contracting state designates at least two and at most four judges and as many deputy judges.

They are appointed for a term of twelve years.

The appointment goes into effect on the day fixed by the state which has made it, but never before the day on which the notice of the appointment has been sent to the recording office of the Court.

The appointments are made for the first time within the six months following the ratification of this treaty.

Article 5. Provisions concerning the qualifications, complementary appointments in case of decease, &c., inviolability, rank, incompatibility, &c.

Article 6. The Court designates its President and its two Vice-Presidents.

They are appointed for a term of four years.

The appointment is made by a majority vote.

If the second ballot fails to give an absolute majority, the appointment is made by a plurality vote.

If the votes are equally divided, a decision is reached by drawing lots.

Germany, the United States of America, Austria-Hungary, Great Britain, France, Italy, Japan, and Russia have each three votes. The other states have only one vote each.

Article 7. The Presidential Bureau is composed of the President and the Vice-Presidents. They have their residence at The Hague. They render decisions by a majority vote.

Article 8. The President, the Vice-Presidents, and the members receive annual compensations respectively of 24,000 fl., 16,000 fl., and 2,000 fl., the current money of the Netherlands, payable at the expiration of six months, and for the first time six months after the first session of the Court.

During the duration of a session of the Court or of one of its commissions, the judges and the deputy judges who are in office, as also the members of a commission, receive a salary of 400 fl. per day.

These disbursements are a part of the general expenses and are paid by the recorder.

Article 9. In addition to the above-mentioned payments, no further compensation is allowed, either to the judges or to the deputy judges, except:

1. Travelling expenses, which are to be refunded to the judges and deputy judges by their respective states, according to the provisions of their national laws.

2. The expenses incident to the maintenance of the dignity and of the residence of the President and of the Vice-Presidents, which will be defrayed by their respective states.

Article 10. Excepting in all cases of *force majeure*, the sessions of the Court, as well as those of the commissions, shall be held at The Hague unless, in the interest of the investigation and with the assent of the parties concerned, some other place is designated for the holding of the sessions.

The Court and the commissions are permitted to convene upon the territory of a third party only by its consent.

Article 11. The Court draws up its rules of order for itself and for its commissions.

The vote takes place conformably to the provisions of Article 6, paragraph 6.

Article 12. The International Bureau mentioned in Article 111 shall serve as a recorder's office for the Court and its commissions.

Its General Secretary or one of his substitutes shall perform the functions of keeper of the records.

Article 13. The Presidential Bureau draws up an annual report. The recorder's office sends it to the contracting states, to the judges, and to the deputy judges.

Article 14. The functions of a judge or deputy judge are compatible with those of judge or deputy judge in the International Prize Court.

Article 15. Upon the request of the government of the Netherlands, the Court shall hold its first session. At the earliest this shall be six months after the ratification of this treaty.

The President and the Vice-Presidents being appointed, the Court will meet whenever convoked by the Presidential Bureau.

Part 2

Concerning the Competence of the International Court of Arbitration

Article 16. The Court takes cognizance of the conflicts of a legal nature arising between the contracting states.

The following are so considered:

All conflicts concerning the interpretation of treaties and those relating to the rules or principles of the law of nations, including the fixing of damages incurred by a violation of treaties, or of the rules or principles of the law of nations.

The Court likewise takes cognizance of the differences arising between the contracting states, which by some special treaty are submitted to arbitration. These differences are considered to be of a legal nature, even if they do not fall within the definition of the preceding paragraph of this article.

Article 17. If the states in litigation have signed a *compromis*, the Court will accept the *compromis* deposited at the recorder's office.

If these states have not succeeded in coming to an agreement concerning the terms of a *compromis*, they may conjointly ask the Court to draw up a *quasi-compromis*, which will take the place of the *compromis*.

The Court draws up the *quasi-compromis* as soon as the conjoint demand has been deposited at the recorder's office.

Even if the request is made by only one of the parties, the Court will draw up a *quasi-compromis,* provided that it has the legal right to take cognizance of the dispute.

Article 18. The Court is empowered to draw up a *quasi-compromis* at the request of one of the parties when it is a question of :

1. A conflict submitted to arbitration by virtue of the provisions of a treaty, concluded or renewed subsequently to the entrance into effect of the present treaty :

(*a*) Provided that the competency of the Court is not excluded, or,

(*b*) Provided that the opposing party does not declare that the conflict is not to be submitted to arbitration and provided that, as far as the preceding question is concerned, the competency of the Court be not excluded by the treaty of arbitration.

2. A conflict concerning contractual debts, due to subjects of a state which exacts their payment from another state, if it is agreed that this difference be settled by arbitration.

This clause, however, is not applicable if arbitration was accepted upon condition that the *quasi-compromis* should be agreed upon in some other manner.

Article 19. The Court takes cognizance of a request to draw up a *quasi-compromis* just the same as of a request for a *compromis.*

The provisions of Part 3 (the procedures) will be applicable.

Article 20. The Court itself determines the extent of the competency attributed to it by :

1. A *compromis* or a *quasi-compromis* ;

2. The joint demand of the parties to draw up a *quasi-compromis* ;

3. The provisions of Article 18 and the treaty-clauses mentioned in this article providing for the drawing up of a *quasi-compromis* on the demand of one of the parties.

Article 21. A commission of the Court takes cognizance of litigations submitted to the judgement of the Court by a *compromis* or a demand to draw up a *quasi-compromis.*

This commission is composed of :

1. The two sole, or of the two senior judges in respect to service, or in default of judges, of the two senior deputy judges in point of service, designated by each litigating state.

2. A president designated by the states in litigation not later than a month after the deposit of the *compromis,* or of the afore-mentioned request, at the recorder's office of the Court.

If the request emanates from only one party, the recorder sends a copy of it as soon as possible to the opposing party.

If the appointment has not been made before the expiration of the term agreed upon, the president will be appointed by the Presidential Bureau of the Court.

The president of the commission should be chosen from among the judges or the deputy judges of the Court. He may not be chosen from among the judges and the deputy judges appointed by the parties.

Article 22. If the Presidential Bureau is called upon to designate the president of a commission, those of its members who have been appointed judges of the Court by the parties in litigation will withdraw from the candidacy.

Every member of the Presidential Bureau obliged to absent himself will be replaced by the senior judge, according to the order of appointment, appointed a member of the Court by a third state.

The deputies are called according to the order of a list of states drawn up by the Court.

The vote relative to the list shall take place in conformity with the provisions of Article 6, paragraph 6.

In the event of a deputy being prevented from performing his official duties, his place will be taken by the senior member, according to the order of appointment, of the next state designated in the list.

Article 23. If a member of a commission, the president included, ceases to be a member of the Court, he shall nevertheless continue to perform his official duties as a member of the commission up to the moment when the verdict is rendered.

Article 24. If a member of a commission, the president included, is prevented from performing his official duties, he will be replaced by another member. Article 21, paragraphs 2–4, and Article 22 are applicable by analogy in respect to replacement.

Part 3

Concerning the Procedure

Article 25. If a *compromis* is deposited at the recorder's office, the President of the Commission commences the preliminary proceedings as soon as possible after his appointment.

If a request to draw up a *quasi-compromis* is deposited at the recorder's office, the preceding paragraph of this article will be applicable.

Article 26. The Commission which has drawn up a *quasi-compromis* takes cognizance of the dispute therein defined.

The preliminary proceedings commence as soon as one of the parties has deposited a petition to that effect at the recorder's office.

The keeper of the records at once sends a copy of the petition to the opposing party and to the President of the Commission.

Article 27. If the *compromis* has not determined the languages to be employed, this is decided by the Commission.

Article 28. The parties have the right to appoint, in the presence of the Commission, special agents charged with the mission of serving as intermediaries between themselves and the Commission.

They are, moreover, authorized to employ for the defence of their rights and interests before the Commission advisers or lawyers appointed by themselves for this purpose.

The members of the Court may not exercise the functions of agents, advisers, or lawyers, except in favour of the power which has appointed them members of the Court.

Article 29. The arbitral procedure includes as a general rule two distinct phases: the written preliminary proceedings and the discussions.

The written preliminary proceedings consist of the communications made by the respective agents to the members of the Commission and to the opposing party, of the memoirs, the counter-memoirs, and, if necessary, of the replies; the parties add to this all papers and documents appealed to in the case. This communication will be made, directly or through the mediation of the recorder, in the order and in the periods of time specified in the *compromis.*

The periods of time fixed by the *compromis* may be prolonged by the common consent of the parties, or by the Commission when it deems this necessary in order to reach a just decision.

The discussions consist of the oral exposition of the arguments of the parties before the Commission.

Article 30. Every paper produced by one of the parties ought to be communicated, in the form of a certified copy, to the other party.

Article 31. Barring the case of special circumstances, the Commission does not meet until after the termination of the preliminary proceedings.

Article 32. The discussions are conducted by the President.

They are not public except in pursuance of a decision of the Commission, taken with the consent of the parties.

They are recorded in the minutes drawn up by secretaries appointed by the President. The minutes are signed by the President and by one of the secretaries; they alone have authentic character.

Article 33. The preliminary proceedings over, the Commission has the right to exclude from discussion all new papers or documents which one of the parties might wish to submit to it without the consent of the other.

Article 34. The Commission reserves to itself the right to take into consideration the new papers or documents to which the agents or advocates of the parties might call its attention.

In this case the Commission has the right to demand the production of these papers or documents, with the proviso that it inform the opposing party thereof.

Article 35. The Commission may, moreover, require from the agents of the parties the production of all papers and demand all necessary explanations. In case of a refusal the Commission takes notice of it.

Article 36. The agents and advisers of the parties are authorized to present orally to the Commission all the means which they judge useful to the defence of their cause.

Article 37. They have the right to take exceptions and to raise objections. The decisions of the Commission on these points are final and preclude further discussion.

Article 38. The members of the Commission have the right to put questions to the agents and to the advisers of the parties, and to request from them explanations of doubtful points.

Neither the questions put nor the observations made by the members of the Commission during the course of the discussions shall be regarded as an expression of the opinions of the Commission in general or of its members in particular.

Article 39. The Commission has the right to fix the rules of procedure for the conduct of the case, to determine the forms, the order, and the time limits within which each party must reach a definite settlement, and to proceed with all the formalities which the furnishing of the proofs requires.

Article 40. The parties agree to furnish the Commission, in the largest measure that they may deem possible, with all the necessary means for the decision of the case in litigation.

Article 41. For all the notifications which the Commission may have to make in the territory of a contracting power the Commission will address itself directly to the government of this power. This will be the case even if it is necessary to establish all the grounds of proof on the spot.

The summonses issued for this purpose will be executed in conformity with the internal legislation of the power within which they are issued. They may not be disobeyed unless this power judges them to be of such a nature as to infringe upon its sovereignty or security.

The Commission also has the right to have recourse to the mediation of the power in whose territory it holds its sessions.

Article 42. The agents and the advisers of the parties having presented all the illuminating information and proofs in support of their case, the President announces the close of the discussions.

Article 43. The deliberations of the Commission take place behind closed doors and are not published.

Every decision is made by a majority vote of the members.

Article 44. Reasons are given for the arbitral decision. The names of the arbitrators are mentioned, and it is signed by the President and by the recorder.

Article 45. The arbitral decision is read in open session, the agents and the advisers of the parties being present or duly summoned.

Article 46. Notice having been sent to the agents of the parties, the decision duly pronounced decides the litigation definitely and without appeal, except as provided for in Article 48.

Article 47. Every difference which may arise between the parties concerning the interpretation and the execution of the decision will be submitted, unless otherwise stipulated, to the judgement of the Commission which has rendered it.

Article 48. The parties may reserve to themselves, in the *compromis*, the right of lodging an appeal. Moreover, an appeal will always be permitted, in as far as it refers to questions of competency.

The time limit for an appeal shall be one month, providing that the *compromis* does not fix any other time limit.

The appeal is lodged by the sending of a memoir, furnished with reasons, addressed to the recorder.

Article 48 [*sic*]. The recorder sends a copy immediately to the opposing party.

The appeal will be decided on by a Commission composed, according to the prescriptions of Article 21, in such a fashion that three members shall sit for each party and that those who have rendered judgement in the first instance shall not hold places in the Commission of Appeal.

For every case each party may appoint as many deputy judges as may be necessary for the formation of the Commission.

If it has not appointed the necessary deputies within a month after the lodging of an appeal, the Presidential Bureau will designate from among the members of the Court the lacking members for the Commission of Appeal.

The provisions of Articles 25–45 are applicable by analogy to the procedure in an appeal.

Article 49. The parties may reserve to themselves in the *compromis* the right of demanding the revision of the verdict rendered, either with or without appeal.

Revision is requested by the sending of a memoir furnished with reasons, addressed to the recorder. The recorder at once sends a copy to the opposing party.

The Commission which has rendered the disputed verdict takes cognizance of the demand for revision. If there are vacancies, they will be filled. Article 24 is applicable by analogy.

Article 50. The request for a revision ought to be based upon a new fact which was unknown at the moment of the closing of the discussion, both to the Commission and to the party petitioning for the revision, providing that this fact might have had a decisive influence upon the decision.

The preliminary proceedings for a revision do not begin until after the express decision of the Commission confirming the existence of the new fact. This decision attributes to it the character indicated in the preceding article, and for these reasons declares the petition allowed.

Article 51. The decision is binding only on the parties concerned.

If the dispute relates to the interpretation of a treaty which is binding also on parties other than those in litigation, these latter take part in the proceedings at such a time as is convenient to all these other powers.

Each one of these powers has the right to intervene in the proceedings.

The decision which the verdict contains upon the interpretation of the treaty is equally binding upon the intervening parties.

Article 52. The parties defray only their own expenses.

Part 4

Concerning the Summary Procedure for Arbitration

Article 53. With a view to facilitating the working of arbitral justice, when it is a question of litigations of such a nature as demand summary proceedings, the contracting powers agree on the following rules. These will be observed in the absence of different stipulations, with the reservation, if the case should occur, of the application of the provisions of the preceding part which would not be contrary to them.

Article 54. If the parties stipulate the application of summary proceedings, the Commission will be constituted as indicated in Article 21, except that the number of members who sit for each party shall be reduced to one.

Article 55. In default of a previous agreement, the Commission fixes, as soon as it is constituted, the time limit within which the two parties must submit their respective memoirs.

Article 56. Each party is represented before the Commission by an agent who serves as an intermediary between the commission and the government which has appointed him.

Article 57. The proceedings are carried on exclusively in writing. Nevertheless, each party has the right to demand the appearance of witnesses and experts. The Commission has, on its part, the privilege of demanding oral explanations of the agents of the two parties as well as of the experts and of the witnesses whose appearance it judges to be serviceable.

Part 5

Concerning International Commissions of Inquiry

Article 58. In litigations of an international nature involving neither honour nor essential interests, and proceeding from a divergence of opinion concerning points of fact, the contracting powers may deem it useful and desirable that the parties which have not been able to come to an agreement through diplomatic channels institute, as far as the circumstances permit, an International Commission of Inquiry charged with the duty of facilitating these litigations by clearing up the points of fact through an impartial and conscientious examination.

Article 59. The International Commissions of Inquiry are constituted by a special convention between the litigating parties.

The convention of inquiry specifies the facts to be examined; it determines the method and the time limit for the formation of the Commission and the extent of the powers of the commissioners.

It also determines, if the occasion demands it, the meeting place of the Commission and its right of removal to another place, the language which the Commission shall employ and those languages which may be authorized to be used before it, as also the date on which each party shall depose its statement of the facts, and in general all the conditions which are binding on the parties.

If the parties judge it necessary to appoint assessors, the convention of inquiry determines the method of their choice and the extent of their powers.

Article 60. If the convention of inquiry has not designated the meeting place of the commission, it will convene at The Hague.

The meeting place once fixed, it cannot be changed save by the consent of the parties.

If the convention of inquiry has not determined the languages to be employed, the question is decided by the Commission.

Article 61. Barring a stipulation to the contrary, the Commissions of inquiry are formed in the manner specified in Articles 21 and 22 of this present convention.

Article 62. In the event of the death, dismissal, or resignation, for any cause whatsoever, of one of the commissioners, or of one of the assessors, he is replaced in the same manner as originally appointed.

Article 63. The parties have the right to appoint, in addition to the commission of inquiry, special agents charged with the mission of representing them and of serving as intermediaries between them and the Commission.

They (the parties) are moreover authorized to charge the advisers or advocates appointed by them to state and to sustain their interests before the Commission.

Article 64. The International Bureau referred to in Article 111 serves as a recorder's office for the commissions which sit at The Hague, and it shall place its quarters and its organization at the disposal of the contracting powers for the work of the Commission of Inquiry.

Article 65. If the Commission sits elsewhere than at the Hague it appoints a general secretary, whose office serves as a recorder's office.

The recorder's office is charged, under the authority of the President, with the material organization of the sessions of the Commission, with the drawing up of the minutes and, during the time of the investigation, with the care of the archives which shall later be entrusted to the International Bureau of The Hague.

Article 66. With a view to facilitating the institution and the working of the Commissions of Inquiry, the contracting powers recommend the following rules. These shall be applicable to the procedure of investigation, in so far as the parties do not adopt other rules.

Article 67. The Commission will regulate the details of the proceedings not provided for in the special convention of inquiry or in the present convention and will proceed with all the formalities which the production of the proofs demands.

Article 68. The investigation takes place after both parties have been heard.

On the dates fixed each party communicates to the Commission and to the other party the statements of the facts, if there is occasion, and, in every case, the papers and documents which it judges useful for the discovery of the truth, as also the list of witnesses and experts which it desires to have heard.

Article 69. The Commission has the privilege, with the assent of the parties, to remove temporarily to whatever place it may deem desirable in order to have recourse to additional information, or to delegate one or more of its members to repair to this place. The authorization of the state, on whose territory proceedings are to be conducted for the obtaining of this information, should be obtained.

Article 70. All material statements and all visits to places should be made in the presence of agents and advisers of the parties.

Article 71. The Commission has the right to solicit from either party such explanations or information as it may deem desirable.

Article 72. The parties pledge themselves to furnish the commission of inquiry in the largest measure possible with all the means and all the necessary facilities for the attaining of complete knowledge and exact appraisement of the facts in question.

They agree to use the means placed at their disposal by their internal legislation, to secure the appearance of the witnesses or of the experts located in their territory who have been summoned to appear before the Commission.

If they are not able to appear before the Commission, the parties may proceed to have them heard before their own competent authorities.

Article 73. For all the notifications which the Commission may have to make upon the territory of a third contracting power, the commission will address itself directly to the government of this power. This rule will also hold if it is a question of proceeding to the spot for the purpose of establishing all the grounds of proof.

The demands made with this purpose in view will be executed in conformity with the means over which the power called upon disposes according to its internal legislation. They may not be refused, unless this power judges them to be of such a nature as to infringe upon its sovereignty or its security.

The Commission will also always have the right to have recourse to the intervention of the power on whose territory it holds its sessions.

Article 74. The witnesses and the experts are summoned at the request of the parties, or *ex-officio* by the commission. In all cases the summons is served by the government of the state in whose territory they are located.

The witnesses are heard, successively and separately, in the presence of the agents and advisers, and in an order to be determined by the Commission.

Article 75. The interrogation of the witnesses is conducted by the President.

The members of the Commission may nevertheless ask each witness such questions as they believe advisable for the clearing up or completing of his testimony, in order to inform themselves, within the limits necessary to the making known of the truth, in regard to everything which relates to the witness.

The agents and the advisers of the parties may not interrupt the witness in his deposition, nor ask him any direct question, but they may request the President to ask the witness such complementary questions as they may deem desirable.

Article 76. The witness ought to testify without being permitted to read any written draft. Nevertheless, he may be authorized by the President to make use of notes or documents if the nature of the facts reported necessitates their employment.

Article 77. The minutes of the testimony of the witness are drawn up forthwith and they are read to the witness. The witness may make such changes and additions as seem good to him. These shall be entered below his testimony.

The whole of his testimony having been read to the witness, he is required to sign it.

Article 78. The agents are authorized, either in the course or at the end of the investigation, to present in writing to the Commission and to the other party such statements, applications, or *résumés* of the facts which they deem useful for the disclosure of the truth.

Article 79. The deliberations of the Commission takes place behind closed doors and are not published.

Every decision is reached by a majority vote of the members of the Commission.

The refusal of a member to take part in the voting ought to be mentioned in the minutes.

Article 80. The meetings of the Commission are not open to the public, and the minutes and documents of the investigation are not made public, except by virtue of a decision of the Commission adopted with the consent of the parties.

Article 81. The parties having presented all the illuminating facts and proofs, all the witnesses having been heard, the President announces the closing of the investigation and the Commission adjourns to draw up its report.

Article 82. The report is signed by all the members of the Commission.

If one of the members refuses to sign, mention is made of that fact. The validity of the report is, nevertheless, not impaired thereby.

The report of the Commission is read in open session, the agents and the advisers of the parties being present or duly summoned.

A copy of the report is placed in the hands of each party.

Article 84. The report of the Commission, limited to the statement of the facts, does not in the least have the character of an arbitral decree. It leaves the parties complete liberty of action in regard to this statement.

Article 85. Each party defrays its own expenses and an equal share of the expenses of the Commission.

Chapter II

Concerning the International Council of Conciliation

Part 1

Concerning the Composition of the International Council of Conciliation

Article 86. The Council is composed of members and of deputy members, appointed by the contracting states.

Each contracting state appoints at least two and at most four members and as many deputy members.

They are appointed for a term of six years. The appointment goes into effect on the day fixed by the state which has made it, but never before the day on which the recorder of the council has been informed of the appointment.

The appointments are made for the first time within the six months following the ratification of this treaty.

Article 87. The following may not be appointed:

1. Diplomats in active service.

2. Members of the International Court of Arbitration or members of the International Prize Court.

The appointment is made in each contracting state by the chief executive, from a list presented by the legislative body.

Article 88. Provisions concerning substitutions in the event of death, &c., concerning inviolability, rank, incompatibility, &c.

Article 89. The Council appoints its President and two Vice-Presidents.

The appointment is made for four years.

Article 6, paragraphs 3, 4, 5, and 6, are applicable.

Article 90. The Presidential Bureau is composed of the President and of the Vice-Presidents.

They have their residence at The Hague.

The decisions are reached by a majority vote.

Article 91. The President and the Vice-Presidents receive annual compensations of respectively 24,000 fl. and of 16,000 fl., the current money of the Netherlands, payable at the expiration of each period of six months and for the first time after the first meeting of the Council.

These disbursements are a part of the general expenses and are paid by the recorder.

Article 92. Beyond the above-mentioned payments no other compensation is granted to the members and deputy members, except:

1. Travelling expenses, for which the members and deputy members will be reimbursed according to the provisions of their national laws.

2. Expenses incident to the maintenance of dignity of station and of residence, which will be charged to their respective states.

Article 93. Except in every case of *force majeure* the meetings of the Council, as also of its commissions, will take place at The Hague, provided that for the best interests of the investigation, and with the consent of the parties, the commissions do not designate some other place.

Article 94. The Council draws up rules of order for itself and its commissions.

The vote will be taken conformably to the provisions of Article 6, paragraph 6.

Article 95. The International Bureau designated in Article 111 serves as a recorder's office for the Council and its commissions.

The Secretary General of the bureau or one of his substitutes performs the recorder's duties.

Article 96. Every year the Presidential Bureau draws up a report. The recorder sends it to the contracting states, to the members, and to the deputy members.

Article 97. On the demand of the government of the Netherlands, the Council will hold its first meeting, but not earlier than six months after the ratification of this treaty.

The President and the Vice-Presidents being appointed, the Council will meet whenever it is convened by the Presidential Bureau.

Part 2

Concerning the Competence of the International Council of Conciliation and of the Rules Governing its Proceedings

Article 98. The Council is competent to take cognizance of conflicts between states.

1. On the demand of all the parties concerned.
2. On the demand of one of the parties, if the International Court of Arbitration has declared itself incompetent; if, according to the opinion of the parties, the dispute is not to be submitted to arbitration, or if there is no doubt as to the non-competence of the Court.

The recorder sends without delay a copy of the demand to the opposing party.

Article 99. The demands designated in the preceding article are submitted to the judgement of a commission of the Council.

The Commission is composed of:

1. The two sole or of the two senior members, following the order of appointment, or in default of members, of deputy members, following the order of appointment, designated by each litigating state.

During the period of a month after the deposit of the demand at the recorder's office, the states have the right to designate a larger number of members (either other members or deputy-members of the Council) as members of the Commission, provided that the number of those designated is the same for all the states.

2. A President, having the right of discussion, but not that of voting, designated by the states within a month at the latest after the deposit of the demand at the recorder's office. If the choice has not been made within this period the President of the Commission is appointed by the Presidential Bureau of the Council.

The President of the Commission ought to be elected from among the members or deputy members of the Council.

The members or deputy members who have been appointed by each of the parties are not eligible.

Article 100. If the Presidential Committee is called upon to choose the President of a Commission, the members of the Presidential Committee whom the litigating parties have appointed members of the International Council of Conciliation will refrain from voting.

Each member of the Presidential Committee who is to refrain from voting or who is prevented from doing so will be replaced by the member longest in office, from among those whom a third state has appointed members of the Council.

These substitutes will be appointed according to the order of the states designated in a list adopted by the Council. The vote relative to the list is held in conformity with the provisions of Article 6, paragraph 6.

If a substitute is prevented from voting, the senior member of the Council appointed by the state, following the order of nomination, will be appointed.

Article 101. If a member of a Commission, the President included, ceases to be a member of the Council after the beginning of the investigation of the case, he continues to perform his duties as a member of the Commission up to the moment of the decision.

Article 102. If a member of a Commission, the President included, is prevented from fulfilling his duties, he will be replaced by another member.

As to this replacement, Articles 99 and 100 are applicable by analogy.

Article 103. When the President has been designated the investigation is announced as soon as possible.

The Commission will interrogate the representatives of the parties in the presence of each other.

The parties and the third powers—if they consent to it—will furnish all the information which they are able to produce.

The investigation is made pursuant to the rules of order. It is public, if the Commission, with the assent of the parties, so prescribes.

Article 104. The deliberations are always secret.

The Commission decides by decree.

Each member has only one vote.

Article 105. The decisions are reached by a majority vote.

The majority ought to include the votes of at least one member of each party.

If the votes are equally divided the vote of the President decides, provided that all the parties have not made a request to the contrary, or provided that a joint demand has not reserved the decision to the members of the Commission.

Members of one party are the members of a Commission appointed by a party as members or deputy members of the Council.

Article 106. The decisions agreed upon conformably to Articles 104 and 105 are obligatory for the parties.

The decisions are communicated to the parties and are made public.

If no decision is reached, the reasons therefore alleged by both sides may be made public, if this proceeding is agreed upon by a majority vote and with the consent of the parties.

Article 107. The Council is competent to give an *ex-officio* opinion:

1. If a request referred to in Article 98 is not settled by a decision of the Commission.

2. If a dispute of a judicial or non-judicial nature, which has arisen among contracting states is not submitted either to the Court or to the Council.

3. If it is to be feared that a conflict of a judicial or non-judicial nature may arise between the contracting states.

Article 108. The President convenes the Council within a month on the joint demand of the members of at least five states.

Article 109. The Council deliberates and decides in plenary session upon the verdict to be rendered, provided that it does not refer the decision to a commission.

The deliberations are secret unless the Council or the Commission decides otherwise.

In the plenary session each contracting state has one vote. Nevertheless Germany, the United States of America, Austria-Hungary, Great Britain, France, Italy, Japan, and Russia have each three votes.

In the sessions of the Commission the vote is taken according to the rules fixed by the Council.

The Council and the Commissions deliberate and decide according to the regulations fixed by the rules of order.

Article 110. The decision agreed upon by a majority vote is made known to the contracting states concerned.

Final and Transitory Provisions

Article 111. There is established at The Hague an International Bureau, serving as a recorder's office to the International Court of Arbitration and to the International Council of Conciliation. It is the intermediary of the communications relative to the meetings of these two bodies. To it are entrusted the archives and the direction of all the administrative affairs.

The contracting powers agree to communicate to the bureau as soon as possible an accurate certified copy of every stipulation of arbitration pronounced by special tribunals that concerns them.

They agree likewise to communicate to the Bureau the laws, rules, and documents confirming the execution of the verdicts pronounced by the Court.

Article 112. The permanent Administrative Council, composed of the diplomatic representatives of the contracting powers accredited to the Hague and of the Minister of Foreign Affairs of the Netherlands who performs the duties of the President, has charge of the direction and the control of the International Bureau.

The Council adopts its rules of order as well as all other necessary regulations.

It decides all the administrative questions which might arise concerning the functions of the Court of Arbitration and of the Council of Conciliation.

It has absolute power over the appointment, the suspension, or the removal from office of the functionaries and employés of the bureau.

It fixes the emoluments and salaries, and controls the general expenses.

The presence of nine members at the meetings duly convoked suffices to permit the Council to deliberate legally. The decisions are reached by a majority vote.

The Council communicates without delay to the contracting powers the rules adopted by it. It sends them an annual report of the labours of the Court of Arbitration and of the Council of Conciliation, on the functioning of the administrative service and of the expenses. The report likewise contains a résumé of the essential contents of the documents communicated to the Bureau by the powers in conformity with Article 111, paragraphs 2 and 3.

Article 113. The expenses of the Bureau will be borne by the contracting powers in the proportion established for the International Bureau of the Universal Postal Union.

The expenses charged against the adhering powers will be reckoned from the day when their adhesion goes into effect.

Article 114. The present convention duly ratified will replace in the relations between the contracting powers the convention for the peaceful settlement of international conflicts of the 18th of October, 1907.

The powers which have concluded with each other, before the entrance into force of the present convention, a special treaty of arbitration, or which before this date have agreed upon a clause of arbitration, are expected to revoke all the provisions contrary to the present convention, which may be found in such a treaty or such a clause. In all disputes they shall confer competency on the International Court of Arbitration, referred to by such treaty or such clause, barring the application of Articles 17 and 18.

The presumption of the preceding paragraph will not apply if the parties or if one of the parties declares it contrary to his intentions, within three months after the deposition of the ratifications of the present convention.

Lammasch has worked out a counter plan to this preliminary plan, which I also quote verbatim.[1]

Plan of a Universal Agreement for the Peaceful Settlement of International Differences

(The figures in parentheses have reference to the plan of the Commission.)

Introductory Provisions

Article 1 (2). For the purpose of the maintenance of universal peace the treaty-making powers bind themselves to submit all their differences without any exception either to a Court of Arbitration for *decision* or to the International Council of Conciliation for an *opinion.*

Article 2 (3). The treaty-making powers bind themselves to execute without reservation the verdict rendered, in the manner and within the time prescribed by the Court of Arbitration.

The treaty-making powers bind themselves likewise, in the event of an appeal to the International Council of Conciliation, not to declare war on the opposing party nor to commit any hostile acts against him, before thirty days have elapsed after the decision of the Council has been made known to them.

Article 3 (1). The treaty-making powers shall establish in common a Court of Arbitration and a Council of Conciliation at The Hague.

I. *The International Court of Arbitration*

Article 1 (4). The Court of Arbitration consists of the judges appointed by the treaty-making powers.

Each of the treaty-making powers appoints at least two and at most four

[1] Cf., with this, Lammasch's *Apologetische und kritische Bemerkungen zu dem von dem niederländischen Komitee ausgearbeiteten Entwurf eines allgemeinen Vertrags über die friedliche Regelung internationaler Konflikte,* 1917.

judges for the term of six years. Two months before the expiration of this time new appointments are made.

Reappointment of the former members is permissible.

Article 2 (6). The Court of Arbitration elects by a majority vote a President and two Vice-Presidents for a term of six years.

In this election each state has only one vote. The member entitled to vote is designated by his government.

At least a third of the votes cast are necessary for an election.

In the case of a tie vote a decision is reached by drawing lots.

Article 3 (—). The Court of Arbitration elects (12) members as a Standing Committee for a term of six years.

The President and the Vice-Presidents are by virtue of their office members of this Committee, and they enjoy diplomatic privileges.

All the members of the Standing Committee must be citizens of different states and be appointed by different states to the Court of Arbitration.

The election is decided by a majority vote.

The three last paragraphs of Article 2 are applicable.

Article 4 (—). Special elections to fill a vacancy arising in the Standing Committee take place within a month, the votes being cast by letter or by telegram, if the voters are unable to appear personally.

The written or the telegraphic vote is communicated through the medium of the Dutch or the Swiss Legation (Consul General) located nearest to the residence of the voter.

The three last paragraphs of Article 2 are applicable.

Article 5 (—). The members of the Standing Committee have their residence at The Hague.

They take a solemn oath on the occasion of their induction into office.

Articles 6–13 (8–15). Provisions concerning salaries and allowances, concerning the place of meeting (on principle at The Hague ; the Court of Arbitration may never hold its sessions in the territory of one of the disputants), concerning the order of business, presidential reports, first meeting of a plenary session, the compatibility of a judgeship in the Court of Arbitration with a membership in the Supreme Prize Court.

Article 14 (—). The United States of America, the Netherlands, Norway, Spain, and Switzerland, provided that these states accept the treaty, appoint for life by unanimous choice a general secretary and two secretaries.

These are appointed to record the minutes of the proceedings.

On entering upon their office they take a solemn oath.

They have their residence at The Hague.

In any individual case those who belong to either of the litigating parties are excluded from secretarial duties.

To provide for a case of need the powers mentioned in paragraph 1 appoint in advance five substitute secretaries for a term of six years. These are called upon in case of need and take a solemn oath on entering upon their office.

Article 15 (—). Provisions concerning salaries of the secretaries and allowances of the substitute secretaries.

Article 16 (—). One month at the latest after the expiration of the six-year term of office, the members of the Court of Arbitration meet in plenary session at The Hague in order to proceed to the election of the presiding officers and of the Standing Committee.

Article 17 (16). The Court of Arbitration decides in all disputes of a judicial nature between the treaty-making powers.

It decides by a commission whose members enjoy diplomatic privileges (Article 22).

The following are considered disputes of a judicial nature :

1. All those which have reference to the interpretation and application of principles of international law as accepted by the parties concerned, and in particular to the political treaties concluded between them.

2. All those which have reference to the amount and extent of indemnities to be paid on account of the violation of stipulated treaty obligations or of the non-stipulated obligations of international law existing between two or more of the treaty-making powers.

3. All those which by a special treaty between the parties are referred to a Court of Arbitration.

Article 18 (17). If the litigating states have effected a *compromis*, this is binding upon the Court of Arbitration.

If the litigating states by joint action petition the Court of Arbitration to effect the *compromis* for them, it is formulated by the Standing Committee.

Article 19 (18). Even if only one of the two litigants is willing to consent to a trial before the Court of Arbitration the Standing Committee can compel the other litigant to accede to the trial:

1. If the disputed point by its nature falls, according to Article 17, under the jurisdiction of the Court of Arbitration, and if, moreover, it is to be settled by arbitration, according to a treaty concluded or renewed in conformity with the legal powers of this convention. Exception is made, provided that one party denies that the case belongs to the category of disputes to be settled by arbitration, and provided that the decision in regard to this preliminary objection is expressly forbidden by treaty to the Court of Arbitration.

2. If the disputed point has reference to claims for contracted debts, which one of the treaty-making powers presents in behalf of its citizens, and if it is agreed that the dispute is to be settled by arbitration and the decision concerning competency was not expressly ordered otherwise.

Article 20 (—). A commission of three members of the Standing Committee decides in regard to competency. This commission is formed by each of the two parties rejecting an equal number of members until only three remain.

If one of the parties should not completely carry out its privilege of rejection, the remaining exclusions are decided by lot.

In like manner one member is excluded by lot if the number of members of the Standing Committee should happen to be even.

Article 21 (98, 2). If the commission mentioned in Article 20 denies its competency in the case, it passes automatically into the jurisdiction of the Council of Conciliation.

Article 22 (21). A commission of five members of the Court of Arbitration decides in regard to the disputed point itself.

One such member is chosen by each disputant from among the members of the Court of Arbitration appointed by it.

An additional member is chosen by each of the two disputants from among the members appointed by other powers, nevertheless in such a manner, that it is always permitted to the opposing party to exclude the representatives of —— states.

The fifth member, who occupies the chair, is appointed by the litigants by a unanimous election.

Article 23 (—). If one of the litigants does not exercise the right accorded him by Article 22, paragraphs 2 and 3, within a month, this right is transferred to a commission of three members, which is formed by lot from the Standing Committee, after the exclusion of the representatives of the litigants. If the litigants do not agree within a month on the choice of the chairman, the right to appoint him is tranferred to a commission of three members, which is formed from the Standing Committee according to the provisions of Article 20. On assuming the duties of their office, the members of the commission take a solemn oath.

Article 24 (19). The commission of the Standing Committee itself decides concerning its competency, in accordance with Article 19.

The commission (Article 22) which is called on to decide concerning the main point at issue itself decides concerning the extent of its competency.

Article 25 (23). If a member of the Standing Committee or of a commission is recalled by his state, he still possesses the right to take part in the discussions and in judging of the affair already under consideration, unless the withdrawal from the commission be approved by a majority vote of the commission and by a two-thirds vote of the Standing Committee.

Article 26 (25). The replacing of members who have withdrawn from commissions of the Court of Arbitration takes place within fourteen days and in the same manner in which the member to be replaced was appointed.

In case this period elapses without action being taken, the appointment is made by the Committee.

Article 27 (—). The Standing Committee is accorded the right to submit on its own initiative its opinions and plans concerning the development of international law to the governments of the treaty-making powers.

The provisions concerning arbitral proceedings follow in general outlines those of the Hague Acts of 1907, Articles 60–82, 84 and 85, and Articles 25–47, 51 and 52, which latter coincide in the main with the proposals of the Dutch committee.

Perhaps it would be desirable to insert the following article at the close of the section :

' The treaty-making powers bind themselves, until the complete carrying out of the arbitral verdict (or at any rate during the first month after it has been rendered, which is the most critical time), not to permit criticisms thereof either in pamphlets or in public meetings.

Criticisms in parliamentary bodies are excluded from publication.

The treaty-making powers bind themselves to punish violators of the abovementioned prohibition and to suppress domestic and foreign publications appearing contrary thereto.'

A regulation such as this would render it easy for the governments to execute the verdict, as it would diminish opposition to it. It would be of especial importance for cases that affect economic interests of influential circles of society, which set all available forces at work to stir up public opinion against the execution of a decision affecting them unfavourably. The history of the *Alabama* and *Alaska* decisions shows that this regulation might be useful for other cases also.

II. *The International Council of Conciliation*

Article 1 (87). The Council of Conciliation consists of the members appointed by the treaty-making powers.

Each state appoints at least four and at most six members for a term of six years. Two months before the expiration of this time new appointments are made. Reappointment is permissible.

Diplomats in active service, members of the Court of Arbitration and of the Supreme Prize Court cannot be appointed members of the Council of Conciliation nor remain members of it.

Article 2 (90). The Council of Conciliation chooses by a majority vote its President and two Vice-Presidents, each for a term of three years.

In this election each state has one vote only. The member entitled to a vote is designated by his government.

At least a third of the votes cast is necessary to elect.

If a tie vote is cast a decision is reached by drawing lots.

Article 3 (—). The Council of Conciliation chooses further for a term of six years a Standing Committee of — members who enjoy diplomatic privileges.

The President and the two Vice-Presidents are *ex-officio* members of this Committee.

All the members of this Committee must be citizens of different states and be appointed by different states.

The three last paragraphs of Article 2 are applicable.

Article 4 (—). Special elections for the filling of vacancies in the Standing Committee take place within a month after the creation of such vacancies, the votes being cast by letter or by telegram.

The provisions of Articles 2–5 are applicable. The transmission of the votes is made through the nearest Dutch or Swiss Embassy (Consul General, if the duly accredited voter does not appear personally to cast his vote).

Article 5 (—). The members of the Standing Committee have their residence at The Hague.

Articles 6–10. Provisions concerning salaries, allowances, order of business, chancellery, president's reports.

Article 11 (93). As a matter of principle all proceedings take place at The Hague; exceptions may be made.

Article 12 (—). After the expiration of the three-year term of office of the presiding officers, the members appointed to cast the votes convene at The Hague for a new election of the officers.

Article 13 (—). The United States of America, the Netherlands, Norway,

Spain and Switzerland, provided that these states accept the treaty, appoint for life by a unanimous election a general secretary and two secretaries.

These are appointed to record the minutes of the proceedings.

On assuming the duties of their office, they take a solemn oath.

They have their residence at The Hague.

In the individual case those who belong to either of the parties are excluded from secretarial duties.

To provide for a case of need the powers mentioned in paragraph 1 appoint in advance five substitute secretaries for a term of six years. These are called upon in case of need, and on assuming the duties of their office they take a solemn oath.

Article 14. Provisions concerning the salaries of the secretaries and the allowances of the substitute secretaries.

Article 15. One month at most after the expiration of the six-year election period, all the members of the Council of Conciliation convene in plenary session at The Hague, in order to proceed to the election of the Chairman and of the Standing Committee.

Article 16 (98). The treaty-making powers are bound to submit all disputes among themselves, for the settlement of which a Court of Arbitration is not yet in operation, to the International Council of Conciliation, in order that it may give its opinion and impart its advice.

Article 17 (99). The duty of giving opinion and imparting advice to secure the peaceful settlement of differences is assigned to a commission of five members of the Council of Conciliation, who enjoy diplomatic privileges.

One such member is chosen by each party from among the members of the Council of Conciliation appointed by that party.

An additional member is chosen by each of the two parties from among the members of the Council of Conciliation appointed by another party.

The fifth member, who occupies the chair, is appointed by the parties by a unanimous vote.

If this election does not take place within a month, the Chairman is elected by the Standing Committee by a majority vote.

Each of the two parties has the right to exclude the members of —— states from the election of the Chairman.

Article 18 (—). If one of the treaty-making powers should refuse to appear either before the Court of Arbitration or the Council of Conciliation on the request of another of the treaty-making powers, on account of a difference between them, or should it neglect to appoint its representatives for the commission of the Council of Conciliation within a month, the members for the party concerned will be appointed by the Standing Committee.

The election of these members by the Standing Committee is by a majority vote.

At least one-third of the votes cast are necessary to elect.

The election of the Chairman takes place in this case in accordance with Article 17, paragraphs 5 and 6.

Article 19. The duration of the proceedings before the Council of Conciliation is limited to six months, providing that the parties do not prolong this period by mutual consent.

The proceedings begin without delay as soon as the President of the Commission is appointed.

Article 20. The parties are represented in the Commission by special envoys and advocates.

The members of the Court of Arbitration and of the Supreme Prize Court may not be appointed for this purpose.

The special envoys and advocates are to represent the interests of their state by oral testimony and by submission of documents.

Article 21. The President conducts the proceedings.

Article 22. The representatives of the one party have the right to put questions to those of the other and to request explanations of them. The President has the same right.

The party questioned or requested is under no obligations to answer or to accede to the requests. The refusal will be noted in the minutes.

Article 23. Each document submitted by the party must be submitted to the opposing party in an authenticated copy.

Article 24. The proceedings take place in the presence of the representatives of both parties, in closed session, unless both parties agree to an open session.

Article 25. The Standing Committee is privileged to send one of its members as peace advocate to take part in its proceedings, but he does not have the right to vote. The peace advocate enjoys diplomatic privileges.

The peace advocate has the right to put questions and to request explanations. The party questioned or requested is not obligated to answer or to accede to the request. The refusal will be noted in the minutes.

At least two-thirds of all the votes cast are necessary for the election of the peace advocate.

Article 26. The minutes of the proceedings will be written out at length, and they will be authenticated by the members of the Commission, by the general secretary (unless he belongs to one of the parties), and by the acting secretaries or their substitutes.

Article 27. After each session the Commission draws up an abstract from these minutes and it is authenticated by the persons designated in Article 26.

The parties have free choice as to the publication or non-publication of this abstract. The treaty-making powers bind themselves not to permit the publication of other communications concerning the proceedings, outside of the minutes or this abstract, earlier than thirty days after the pronouncing of the opinion.

Criticisms of this report, either in print or in public meetings, are forbidden, until after the expiration of thirty days from the giving of the opinion.

Criticisms in parliamentary bodies are forbidden to be published within this period.

Violations are to be punished.

Domestic and foreign publications which disregard these prohibitions are to be suppressed.

Article 28. Vacancies caused by the recall of members of the Commission by the party appointing them may at once be filled by the appointment of a substitute from among the members of the Council of Conciliation. The substitution of recalled members of the Commission takes place within a week, in the same manner in which the member whose place is to be filled was appointed. In case this period elapses without action being taken, the Standing Committee appoints the substitute.

Recall of the Chairman is not permissible.

Article 29. A unanimous vote of the Commission is necessary for the adoption of opinion and advice, if they are to be considered as those of the Council of Conciliation.

The opinion and advice are imparted by the Standing Committee to the parties and are published twenty-four hours later. If the attempt to secure a unanimous vote does not succeed, the opinions and advice of the individual members of the Commission are made known by the Standing Committee and published.

The governments of the states concerned may not publish the submitted opinions and advice separately, but only in their entirety. They are bound to fine and suppress even the private publications of separate opinions and advice.

Article 30. Within the first thirty days after the making known of the opinion or opinions, criticism thereof in publications and public meetings is forbidden. Article 27, paragraphs 2–6, are applicable.

Article 31. The opinions and advice are not binding upon the parties. Thirty days after either the opinion of the Council of Conciliation or the opinions and advice of the single members of the Commission have been published by the Standing Committee the parties receive full freedom of action.

III. *Sanction*

Article 1. The treaty-making powers bind themselves, if one treaty-making state should violate, in regard to another, the duty incumbent upon it according to Article 3 and should refuse to appear before either the Court of Arbitration or the Council of Conciliation :

1. To regard all treaties of alliance that may have been concluded with it as annulled.

2. To forbid their subjects to lend any assistance to that state during the war.

3. To permit their subjects to lend any sort of assistance to the adversaries of that state during the war.

4. After the termination of the war to demand full reparation from the state violating its treaty obligations for the loss incurred by them or their allies by the war.

Article 2. In case a power which has not ratified this treaty opens hostilities against another (it matters not whether this power has ratified the treaty or not), without having previously submitted the difference to the mediation of other powers or to a body analogous to the International Council of Conciliation, the treaty-making powers are ready jointly to consider the question whether or not they shall adopt the proceedings described in Article 1 against this state.

In case no unanimous decision in regard to this question is reached, each of the treaty-making powers reserves to itself the right to proceed against that warring state, either alone or in conjunction with other treaty-making states, in the manner indicated in Article 1.

I do not wish to enter at this point upon a detailed criticism of these plans, since I have here merely set myself the task of presenting a general survey of the problems, but not of discussing the problems themselves. From my preceding expositions one can readily see in what particulars my conception differs from the two plans, which unfortunately did not come into my hands until after my book had gone to press. At any rate I should like to reserve the criticism of these plans for another place.

Then, too, more detailed expositions of the remaining points of the programme have appeared. Particularly is this the case in respect to the development and the organization of the work of The Hague.[1] The question might readily arise whether, at the present time, it is not a little *premature* to consider some of these problems. First of all one would have to know whether the work of The Hague will continue and, if so, in what form. Then there arises the further question: will a League of Nations closely bound together eventually take its place alongside of the Hague League of Nations or will it supplant it? All this will remain undetermined until *after* the war, and not until then, in my opinion, can these questions of organization be solved. In the meantime it seems that the best thing to do is to confine oneself to a few guiding principles, as the League to Enforce Peace has done, and to postpone the details of the organization to the time when we shall know exactly on just what foundation the whole new structure is to be erected.

[1] Lange and Schücking are engaged in the study of these problems, Lange in *La conférence de la paix et son organisation permanente*, and Schücking in the 'Ausbau des Haager Werkes', which appears in the *Recueil de rapports*, vol. i, p. 181. Lange draws up a plan for the organization and periodicity of the Hague Conferences and for a 'Comité préparatoire permanent'. Schücking demands a basic treaty for the Hague League of Nations, and, in addition, an order of business and a number of provisions for the various methods of procedure, among them an international enactment providing for the execution of decisions. Cf. also Hull, *The Development of the Hague Conference and its Work*, vol. ii, p. 287. There had not yet come into my hands, on the completion of the proof-reading, the *Développement de l'œuvre de La Haye. Organisation de la conférence de la paix. Rapport présenté par une Commission*, La Haye, 1917. On this subject see *Friedenswarte*, April 1917. Cf. further van Houten, 'The Way Out', in *Recueil*, vol. iii, p. 45.

II

MY PUBLIC CORRESPONDENCE WITH PHILIPP ZORN CONCERNING GERMANY AND THE HAGUE PEACE CONFERENCES

Germany and the Two Peace Conferences at the Hague [1]

An Answer to Baron d'Estournelles de Constant, by Philipp Zorn

There have come into my hands, unfortunately very late, two numbers of the *Neue Zürcher Zeitung* (of April 16 and May 7, 1916), in which the well-known French senator, Baron d'Estournelles de Constant, expresses his opinions with great bitterness concerning the motives actuating Germany and France in the present world war. Hermann Kesser in the *Neue Zürcher Zeitung* of April 18 has published an excellent reply to the first of the two articles of d'Estournelles. If I now beg the *Neue Zürcher Zeitung* to be allowed a brief word of reply to d'Estournelles, I do not do so with the intention of entering into a detailed discussion with him. At the close of his article Hermann Kesser has already stated that 'what d'Estournelles de Constant erects as a goal, after almost two years of war has erected as a goal, ought forever—one should think, in France also—to be rejected as the sad result of a psychopathic "turning away from the truth"'. And the editor of the *Neue Zürcher Zeitung* has in his comment 'been obliged to give expression to his painful astonishment, that the distinguished pacifist couches his expressions in a manner and in language so very little calculated to bring about reconciliation, and which therefore do not readily offer to friends of peace a possibility for a point of contact'. I thoroughly agree with these two statements, and it seems to me love's labour lost to enter into a detailed discussion with d'Estournelles—at the present time. I can also only express my painful astonishment at the fact that a man of such intellectual distinction as d'Estournelles, that indeed to all appearances present-day Frenchmen have been unable to gain any conception of what it must mean to a great industrious people to have finally gained a centralized national government, and the political and economic power which this union has brought with it. For a thousand years the German people was politically divided into wretched fragments, with all the unspeakably sad results, political and economic, which this division entailed as a necessary consequence. The French have possessed this highest goal of political developments ever since the time of Louis XI, the English in the main since that of Queen Elizabeth, or at any rate since that of William of Orange; for both nations the attaining of this goal lies historically so far in the background, and the attained goal is for them so absolutely a matter of course, that they utterly fail to comprehend what the attaining of this goal in the years 1866 to 1870 has meant to us Germans. This and this alone lies at the bottom of the present world war. But the French and the English will recognize—so firm is our confidence in the immanent forces of world history—that they must also grant us Germans that which they regard for themselves as an obvious and unconditional matter of course. Then the ground will be prepared for recon-

[1] Cf. *Neue Zürcher Zeitung*, No. 1134, July 15, 1916.

ciliation, and the three great civilized nations of central Europe will again be able to take up their common task of the service of mankind in mutual confidence. But on viewing the 'manner' and the 'language' of d'Estournelles, we see, as the editor of the *Neue Zürcher Zeitung* pertinently and justly emphasizes, no possibility of friendly contact.

For this reason I decline to enter into a discussion with d'Estournelles. My conscience bids me protest most strongly against *one* sentence only of the French Senator. D'Estournelles justifies the alliance of the progressive western democracies, in which he sees the ideal of political development, with the autocracy of Russia, because Russia took the initiative in the summoning of the First Peace Conference at The Hague. That can be understood, even if one has a different opinion in regard to the motives back of this alliance. Then, however, d'Estournelles continues: 'with my own eyes I saw, how, on the other hand, the representatives of the German government, with the exception of Professor Zorn, *bent all their energies toward causing this first conference, as well as the following one, to miscarry.*'

Against this sentence I must, for conscience sake, raise the sharpest protest, and most positively decline the meed of praise therein accorded me. Do not think that I wish to claim for myself also the glory of having 'bent all my energies' toward 'causing the conferences to miscarry'. But the reproach, in regard to the other German representatives, is not only a bitter injustice, but an untruth. And d'Estournelles knows just as well as I what really happened. That in spite of this he has not the least scruples against making this reproach, shows to what height the disorder of minds, the 'sad result of a psychopathic turning away from the truth', has risen in this war.

At the first conference the real task for Germany lay in the hands of Colonel Gross von Schwarzhoff, of Sea Captain Siegel, and of the author of this article. The minutes of the conference show with what untiring zeal, with what intimate knowledge, and with what penetration of mind, the two first-named noble men, who have in the meantime passed away, co-operated in the tasks set them. On that point there was, this I may say with all confidence, only one opinion at the First Conference. D'Estournelles knows this, as I have already said, as well as I do. I owe it to the memory of my two departed friends to testify publicly that they also bent 'all their efforts', the fullness of their knowledge, not 'to cause the conference to miscarry', but to bring to the conference a contribution corresponding as far as possible to the necessities of the realities of political life. D'Estournelles is perhaps making a thrust at von Schwarzhoff, because this intellectually highly-gifted German officer was in a way the spokesman in the opposition to the Russian proposals for disarmament. One must, however, not forget to stress the fact that *all* the military members of the commission, with the exception of the Russian representative, agreed with the German representative, and that *the French General Mounier showed himself in the discussion entirely of the opinion of von Schwarzhoff.* The rejection of the Russian proposals, —'unanimement à l'exception de M. Gilinsky', as the minutes say—was directed primarily against the form which the idea of disarmament took in the Russian plans, and which in this form was universally recognized as impracticable. And as to Prince Münster, the first German representative, and that too is well known to d'Estournelles, in the great crisis of the first conference known to all the world, he expended all his strength and labour, not in 'causing the conference to miscarry', but in helping it to overcome the crisis and thereby make it possible for the conference to produce great results. I owe it to the memory of Prince Münster, who in the meantime has also died, to testify solemnly before all the world that, after Prince Bülow, we have primarily Prince Münster to thank that the conference did not miscarry, but that it produced results. In so far as officials are concerned, the decision was not made by officials but by the Emperor. Compare with this statement the book of the pacifist leader Alfred Fried on the *Friedenskaiser* (Peace Emperor).

So much on the first conference. I repeat: the reproach of d'Estournelles is not only a bitter injustice but, what is sadder, an untruth.

And the same is true of the Second Peace Conference. The German representatives at the Second Conference were, in addition to the ambassador Baron von Marschall, General von Gündell, Admiral Siegel, and Privy Councillor Kriege. They all, to the fullest extent of their powers—and they were often compelled to strain every nerve—worked for the success of the Conference according to their best knowledge and conscience.

It is, of course, well known that Germany at the Second Conference prevented the adoption of a world arbitration treaty on the basis of obligatory arbitration. It is of that alone that d'Estournelles is thinking, and he therefore believes himself justified in the judgement given above. I have always regarded the attitude that Germany took in regard to this question as a grave political mistake for which it would one day pay a heavy penalty. I have at all times openly given expression to this opinion, and at the present day still maintain it unchanged. But in spite of that the verdict of d'Estournelles is unjust and untrue. In the first place, Germany co-operated with great zeal in the reforms of another nature—and these were in part very important—which the convention of arbitration underwent at the Second Conference. In the second place, German opposition was directed only against the manner of the carrying out of the principle. *The principle of obligatory arbitration itself was thoroughly approved of*, and formal expression was given to this approval. Finally however—and this above all—this question was only *one*, to be sure an important one, of the questions before the conference. At least as important, from the practical standpoint much more important, were the questions of *laws of naval warfare and of the freedom of the seas for neutrals.* But in these matters *Germany performed a downright enormous task for the conference and at the conference.* Germany was the only state which appeared at the conference thoroughly equipped as a consequence of a preparation carefully worked out through the years, and with completely finished, most thoroughly considered plans for these great problems of the human race. Is this whole enormous work then a mere nothing? I repeat: The opposition of Germany to obligatory arbitration was, according to my firm conviction, a grave political mistake; but one should nevertheless not forget the fact that the doubts of Germany were to some extent shared, not only by Austria-Hungary, but by other states, such as Rumania, Belgium, Switzerland, and Greece.

At any rate, the reproach of d'Estournelles, that the German representatives, at the First Conference as well as at the second, bent all their energies toward causing the conference to miscarry, is an enormous injustice. Nay more, since d'Estournelles knows the true state of affairs just as well as I, it is an untruth for which there is not the shadow of an excuse. Every honourable and unbiased man who knows the history of the two conferences will be compelled to acknowledge this.

Germany and the Peace Conferences at the Hague [1]

An Answer to Professor Philipp Zorn, by Otfried Nippold

I regret exceedingly that I must come forward in opposition to my friend Professor Zorn, for whom I have the highest personal esteem ; but what he wrote last Saturday to the *Neue Zürcher Zeitung* dare not pass by uncontested. Zorn himself complains in his article that the disorder of minds, the sad result of a psychopathic turning away from the truth, has in this war risen to such a height. Unfortunately his own article is only too evident a proof of this turning away from the truth. Zorn censures the 'language' of Baron d'Estournelles and quite overlooks the fact that his own language is far more bitter. He upbraids d'Estournelles for his enormous injustice and his untruthfulness without the shadow of an excuse, in spite of the fact that the sentence of d'Estournelles, which Zorn attacks, accords completely with the truth.

Baron d'Estournelles in his article has called attention to the fact that the Czar convoked the First Peace Conference, 'while with my own eyes I saw how, on the other hand, the representatives of the German Government, with the exception of Professor Zorn, bent all their energies toward causing this Conference, as well as the following one, to miscarry.' This sentence, he says, is not only a bitter injustice, but also an untruth. To this I must unfortunately reply that Professor Zorn, politically speaking, would have shown himself much wiser if he had not made such an assertion. There is not the slightest doubt, and it is a fact historically confirmed, that the opposition to international progress manifested at The Hague proceeded chiefly from Germany. Without this opposition the conferences would have yielded materially greater results, results that might even have made the present world war impossible. If at The Hague an understanding concerning armaments could have been reached, and if, moreover, obligatory arbitration could have been introduced, the political situation would never have come to such a crisis. The opponent of these two progressive measures, as Zorn himself must grant, was Germany. Why then does Zorn, since he must agree with d'Estournelles *on the whole*, represent him as a liar ?

One has merely to read the minutes of the Hague Conference to recognize clearly that it was the 'irreconcilable opposition' of the German representatives which caused the miscarriage of the chief progressive measures ; and one would recognize that, even if one did not know the attitude of the German Government, and did not know what was going on behind the scenes. And if one wishes to learn what was the attitude of German public opinion in regard to the progressive measures, so important for the advancement of civilization, one has only to take in hand German newspapers of the Conference years. There one will everywhere find confirmation of the truth of Baron d'Estournelles' statement.

Zorn considers it his duty to defend his German co-workers at The Hague against the 'reproach' of d'Estournelles. He had better left it undone. The utterances of Baron Münster, for example, in regard to the Conference must certainly be known to Zorn also. It may surely be taken for granted that, for instance, he has also read the memoirs of Andrew White concerning the

[1] Cf. *Neue Zürcher Zeitung*, No. 1171 of July 22, 1916.

Conference. The very choice of representatives for the Hague Conferences which the German Government hit upon cannot well be interpreted otherwise than that it proceeded from the desire to cause their miscarriage. Zorn himself was at that time well known as a theoretical disclaimer of the existence of the law of nations. His colleague von Stengel had published a vicious pamphlet against the First Conference, and since then has opposed in every possible way its chief ideals. And at the second Conference Zorn, who was still considered as being too friendly towards progress, was replaced by a one-sided bureaucrat, Herr Kriege, who had not the least conception of the far-reaching political significance of the proposed measures of progress. All that Zorn knows as well as I, and therefore I cannot understand how he can accuse d'Estournelles of untruth in the sentence quoted above.

That Germany at The Hague in other fields co-operated in positive fashion cannot be denied. That was especially the case in regard to the law of war. But all that amounted to merely this : after the main bed of the stream had been completely dammed, Germany turned the work of the Conference into a side channel. This is therefore simply a confirmation of the fact that Germany would have preferred to thwart completely the purposes of the Conferences which it looked upon with disfavour.

In my book *Die zweite Haager Friedenskonferenz* I referred to the fact that the German Government had committed a terrible political mistake in opposing the Hague Peace Conferences, and said that this attitude could not but entail political disaster. Alfred H. Fried, for instance, has expressed himself also to the same effect. It may be that this truth is to-day recognized in Germany. But what has happened cannot be undone. Historical facts cannot be blotted out of the history of the world. So much the less, as the whole world is acquainted with them.

Consequently, as I have already emphasized, it would have been politically a wiser stroke if Zorn had left his dirty linen in the closet. He merely calls the attention of the world anew to the sins of the German Government committed years ago. All this Zorn might have known, since he is thoroughly conversant with the true state of affairs. His protest can therefore only be excused as the 'psychopathic turning away from the truth' of which Zorn has spoken, and which is a distinguishing mark of this war—in Germany not by one jot or one tittle less than elsewhere. Let us hope that after the war the minds of men will again be cleared of their disorder ! As for myself, I esteem the merits of both d'Estournelles and Zorn so highly that nothing would give me greater pleasure than to find them after the war again working together at the common task. And just because this is my wish I regret Zorn's step, and it is only with the greatest reluctance that I have come forward against a man such as he is.

Once more: Germany and the Hague Peace Conferences[1]

By Philipp Zorn

Otfried Nippold, in No. 1171 of the *Neue Zürcher Zeitung*, has felt himself called upon to answer my protest against Baron d'Estournelles' scathing attacks on the 'representatives of the German Government', which appeared in No. 1134

[1] Cf. *Neue Zürcher Zeitung* No. 1278 of August 12, 1916.

of the same paper. I hope that the non-partisanship of the editorial staff will assure the publication of the following reply to Nippold's 'answer'.

First of all a brief clearing up of two misunderstandings. The sharp expression 'a psychopathic turning away from reality', which I have employed, was coined by a distinguished contributor to the *Neue Zürcher Zeitung*. It was applied in the issue of April 18, 1916, to d'Estournelles' article directed against Förster. Nippold, on his part, adopts this sharp expression in order to show that this 'psychopathic turning from reality' is present in my case also, and that it is to be found in all Germany 'by not one jot or one tittle less than elsewhere'. If Nippold thereby means to say that this circumstance, that is, this universality of a 'psychopathic turning away from reality', renders my protest excusable, I decidedly wish to reject this 'excuse'. With me the protest was a matter of conscience, a memorial erected to my deceased friends and co-workers at the First Peace Conference. I stated this to be my motive in my first article, and it is to-day still the case.

In regard to my mention of Fried's book on the *Friedenskaiser*, the editor very justly corrects me by stating that the title of the book reads: *Kaiser Wilhelm und der Weltfriede.* My remark, however, did not have reference to the title but to the *contents* of the book, the epitomized characterization of which by that word can scarcely be deemed inapplicable.

In respect to the subject matter itself Nippold reproaches me with employing 'language much worse' than that of d'Estournelles, for I upbraid him with 'untruthfulness' and it would have been 'politically wiser' if I had not done this. Likewise the remark about the 'language' employed does not come from me, but from contributors and the editorial staff of the *Neue Zürcher Zeitung*. That I have accused d'Estournelles of 'untruthfulness' is of course true; and it is just about that point that the whole discussion turns. I feel neither occasion nor need to discuss 'political wisdom' with Nippold. In this grievous time of the greatest world catastrophe every one must act in all that he does and omits according to his own conscience, and seek what justification he can bring to his conscience, Herr Nippold to his and I to mine. Therefore I pass over the reproaches directed against me personally in complete silence. This, however, surprised me, that Nippold again dragged forth the charge against me that I was a 'disclaimer of the law of nations'. As an authority on international law, Nippold knows well enough that it is a question alone of certain theoretical judicial interpretations, but in no wise a rejection of the international legal material itself.

Finally, in regard to the main point, d'Estournelles has upbraided the '*representatives* of the German Government' and maintained that they 'bent all their energies on causing this first Conference, as well as the following one, to miscarry'. That I have characterized as an 'untruth', and this I still assert. All the 'representatives' of Germany taking part in the real work at the two Conferences placed their best knowledge and ability during months of hardest labour in the service of the great task to which they were appointed. And they were appointed not in order to cause the conferences to miscarry, but to effect a result of the greatest possible value and practical utility. Only those who directly participated in the labours can know with what strength, with what intense exertion, the work was carried on at both Conferences. To this number Herr Nippold did not belong. Often enough have I spoken with d'Estournelles concerning the progress of the work, especially at the first Conference, and never shall I forget these pleasant hours. Never at that time did d'Estournelles make the reproach which he has now made. On the contrary, he expressed his highest appreciation of the work of the German representatives in behalf of the common interests of the Conference. The late Herr Beernaert, certainly an unimpeachable witness, repeatedly discussed in my presence, and in the most flattering manner, the work of Schwarzhoff at the first Conference. And I should like to know what Louis Renault, who may be characterized, for the second Conference at any rate, as the intellectual centre of all the labours undertaken, would have to say as an honest man and a most acute observer of the whole work of the Conference, to the criticism of his colleague d'Estournelles on the work of the German 'representatives' at both Peace Conferences.

I willingly concede that the aged Prince Münster did not know how to accommodate himself to the new development in international affairs, and sometimes made light of it. That, however, does not alter the 'fact, historically confirmed', that Prince Münster in the most difficult hour of the first Conference chose the right way without the slightest hesitation, and thereby prevented the complete shipwreck of the Conference.

The fact remains, therefore, that the reproach made by d'Estournelles that 'the *representatives* of the German Government bent all their energies on causing this first conference, as well as the following one, to miscarry' is an untruth without the shadow of a justification.

Nippold, however, shifts the disputed point by transferring what d'Estournelles says against the *representatives* of the German Government to the *German Government* itself, and maintains: 'there is not the slightest doubt, and it is a fact historically confirmed, that the opposition to international progress manifested at The Hague proceeded chiefly from Germany. Without this opposition the Conferences would have yielded materially greater results—results that might even have made the present world war impossible.' I of course recognize the intimate connexion of the two points; but this distinction must nevertheless be made: The attack of d'Estournelles was directed against the German *representatives*, and my defence therefore was confined primarily to the vindication of the reputation of the German *representatives* at the Peace Conferences.

Nippold's attack on the German *Government* must likewise be taken sharply to task. From his, as it now appears, purely pacifist standpoint, Nippold characterizes the question of 'disarmament' or that of a 'truce in the manufacture of arms', as also that of arbitration, as the chief points of the Conference labours, and he regards all the rest as side issues. In these side issues Germany also 'co-operated in positive fashion'; but in his opinion, 'all that amounted to merely this: after the main bed of the stream had been completely dammed, Germany turned the work of the Conference into a side channel.' And this was 'simply a confirmation of the fact, that Germany would have preferred to thwart completely the purposes of the Conferences which it looked upon with disfavour'.

To measure the significance of the various tasks of the two Conferences is in its essentials a matter for the subjective judgement and the personal standpoint of the critic. Surely no one will demand that this standpoint be unconditionally the pacifist one. The two great tasks of the first Conference were: the *question of arbitration* and the *codification of the most humane laws possible for a war on land.* Which of the two tasks was the greater must virtually be decided by the subjective judgement. However, the question need not be asked at all, for Germany did her utmost and co-operated successfully in *both* tasks, and contributed to the great success of the first Conference just as much as any other of the great states. It is not at all a question of an attempt to prevent the adoption of the 'chief progressive measures' and of 'diverting' the labours of the Conference into an insignificant 'side channel'. Even Herr Nippold will neither be able nor wish to deny this 'fact, historically confirmed'.

The great tasks of the Second Conference were once more the *question of arbitration,* and then the final codification of humane *laws for a maritime war,* upon the basis of the principle of the *freedom of the seas for neutrals* in times of war. Here also there is no justification for speaking of a 'chief progressive measure' in reference to one of these tasks, and of a 'side issue' in regard to the other. Surely many authorities on international law can be found who will regard the second-named task as greater and more important for mankind than the first. And again Herr Nippold will not be able to deny that Germany at the Second Peace Conference, and again at the London Conference, has expended an enormous amount of pains, labour, and strength on the solution of this great problem of mankind. After all the terrible experiences of the present world war, which especially neutrals have had to undergo, to hear this enormously great human problem characterized as a 'side issue' by a distinguished authority on international law, is almost amusing. I have often enough expressed my opinion of Germany's treatment of the question of arbitration at the Second Conference. But Germany has at one time done meritorious service at the Second Conference also in important points for the cause of arbitration, it has in addition presented to the Conference a court of arbitration, perhaps universally typical of those of later times, in its plan for a prize court. And it has declared its allegiance to the principle of obligatory arbitration. Therefore, in regard to this question also the judgement passed by Nippold does not tally with the truth, at any rate not in the universal and unconditional form in which he pronounces it.

I did not address a question to Herr Nippold. But I hope that with the above explanation I have satisfactorily replied, for unprejudiced readers, to the 'answer' that he has felt himself obliged to make to me. The reproaches, which d'Estournelles has made against the 'representatives' of the German Government at the two Peace Conferences, are an untruth. The reproaches which d'Estournelles, and still more sharply Nippold, have made against Germany, that is to say the German Government, are in this universal and unconditional form wide of the mark. The work of the Germans at the two Peace Conferences and at the London Conference becomes evident, with a certainty exclusive of every doubt, by an examination of the 'facts, historically confirmed'. By no one at either Conference, competent to form an opinion, was the problem of a 'truce in the manufacture of arms' regarded as soluble. And the debates of the Inter-parliamentary Union at Geneva in 1912 have shown clearly that in regard to the solution of this problem not even the preliminary questions have been settled. Even if one grants that Germany, at the Second Conference, did not adopt the proper attitude with respect to the problem of arbitration, it did nevertheless render much worthy positive co-operation at both Conferences. And it is unjust, in view of this 'fact, historically confirmed', to make charges against Germany of so grievous and sweeping a nature, as d'Estournelles and still more Nippold have done.

I herewith close the debate as far as I am concerned. The opposing principles involved lie too deep for solution by discussions at the present time. World history will finally pronounce its just verdict.

Germany and the Hague Peace Conferences[1]

By Otfried Nippold

To the reply of Philipp Zorn in No. 1278 of the *Neue Zürcher Zeitung* I have but little to say. Zorn must certainly be thoroughly conscious of the fact that he has not and cannot disprove what I have written. If he particularly thinks that I have shifted the disputed point from the *representatives* of the German Government to the German *Government* itself (I had spoken briefly of Germany), I must reject the implied distinction as unpermissible. The representatives are commissioned by and act under the instructions of their government. The government, therefore, which they represent must be made responsible for what they do and say.

Zorn then makes his chief objections to the fact that I have characterized the questions of armaments and of arbitration as the main problems before the Hague Conferences and that I have considered the problem of the codification of the laws of warfare brought by the Germans to the foreground, as a mere 'side issue'. He is of the opinion that only the subjective judgement can decide which of the two tasks was the greater. Many would find the codification of the laws of warfare, and especially that of maritime law, built upon the basis of the principle of the freedom of the sea for neutrals in war times, as the more important. It is almost amusing, he says, if any one, after the experiences of this war, can characterize these latter tasks as a mere 'side issue'.

To all this I should like to make the following reply. The experiences of this war have taught one thing above all others, namely, that the regulation of the law of war has been a complete failure. The nations after this war will certainly not be satisfied with a mere doctoring of the manner of conducting war, which by the way is an object but little adapted to doctoring. They will demand *more*. They will desire not a regulation of the laws of warfare, but a *strengthening of the law of nations*. If *before* the war people were not yet conscious of the fact that the regulation of 'the law of war' is a 'side issue', surely they are so to-day. The task for the future therefore can only pass through such a channel as would have been the main one at the Hague Conferences, can only be in the field of international law, and above all in that of international procedure for the settlement of disputes between states. What we need is therefore an international system of justice which affords protection and security already in peace times, and not merely an adjustment of the regulations for warfare. That this is the '*main* issue'

[1] Cf. *Neue Zürcher Zeitung* No. 1313, August 19, 1916.

is not merely a question of subjective judgement, but it has become to-day the solemn conviction of the whole thinking world.

We can therefore only hope that Germany in her future labours for the progress of the law of nations will not again isolate herself, as she once did at The Hague. For in that case, at the future Conferences she would surely have the whole world arrayed against her, and the progress of civilized mankind would be accomplished *in spite of* her opposition. If we ask what basic motive lay at the bottom of Germany's antagonistic attitude at the Hague Conferences, a reply can be given in two words. She wished to hold *might* in her hand, and not subject might to right, as would have been necessary if various proposals at The Hague had been realized. If to-day we read the comments of the German press on the 'aims of the war', we can readily see that the views of wide circles of German society are to all appearances essentially the same as those that were so evident at The Hague. There is much talk of the *strengthening of might*—the simple-minded can see this in annexations—and little talk of the *strengthening of right*. The Hague Conferences, however, purposed a strengthening of right. They wished in all sincerity to gradually subject, at least in part, might to right. And it was just this that Germany in many respects could not pardon. That is the explanation of the German opposition at The Hague. Whether this opposition proceeded chiefly from the German representatives or from the German Government is a matter of but little importance, since unfortunately it was based mainly on the present German mentality. After the experiences of the present war mankind will demand more energetically than ever a strengthening and a guaranteeing of international justice. May Germany then not again stand behind the other states!

In his discussion of the regulation of maritime law, Zorn mentions also the 'freedom of the seas'. If thereby is meant the abolition of the right of capture Zorn knows very well that this could have been obtained at the Second Hague Conference. If Germany had shown a conciliatory spirit on the question of disarmament, England would have been ready to make reciprocal concessions on that of capture. The abolition of the right of declaring contraband had just then been proposed by England.

Speaking from the standpoint of *international law*, the present war would not have been necessary in order to obtain the 'freedom of the seas', but merely a yielding of Germany on the question of armaments. But the 'freedom of the seas' has to-day become in Germany in many respects a *political* postulate (What do the neutrals have to do with the question? We believe in no such altruism), which has very little to do with the strengthening of *right* by so much the more, however, with that of *might*. In this political sense the postulate has nothing in common with the Hague Conferences; for these will and shall serve only the idea of *right*.

From what has been said it is easy to see what significance would have been accorded to the discussion of the problem of armaments, which discussion, as is well known, was blocked by Germany. But Zorn speaks of my 'as it now appears purely pacifist standpoint', evidently because I have characterized this problem along with that of arbitration as one of the chief points of the Hague Conferences. To that I merely wish to reply that what I have said has nothing to do with pacifism. The contrast reads simply 'might' or 'right', and as an exponent of the law of nations, I take my stand upon the latter. Zorn thinks further that no one has a right to demand that the standpoint of him who judges be unconditionally that of the pacifist. I for my part have never demanded this. But I believe that if, after the experiences of this war, the world should ever have to choose between 'pacifism' and 'militarism', almost the whole world would to-day elect the former, and presumably also the overwhelming majority of the German people.

It is fundamentally this which I have to reply to Zorn. If he is surprised that I have intervened in the discussion, I can only answer that it appeared to me to be my duty to take precautionary measures against the growth of a legend on our neutral soil. If Zorn had expressed his opinions in the *Kölnische Zeitung*, I should perhaps have been silent. Moreover, how Zorn writes there in regard to the Hague Conferences may be seen in the *Kölnische Zeitung* of June 15, 1915, where he gives voice to the following sentiments:

> I have deeply regretted that the noble common task of the first and the second Peace Conferences ended with a jarring note. I acknowledge openly and honestly that I have considered and still consider this to be the fault of the German representatives—all my entreaties to my honoured friend, the Ambassador Marschall von Bieberstein, were without avail.

In this statement Zorn evidently concedes just what d'Estournelles and I have maintained. Why then should he accuse others of untruthfulness? Zorn is also very much surprised that I have reminded him of his being a 'disclaimer of the law of nations'. He says that he does not in the least reject the international legal matter. I have, however, expressly characterized him only as a *theoretical* disclaimer. I have always recognized and to-day likewise give full and free recognition to Zorn's highly meritorious *practical* co-operation at The Hague. Yes, I will go a step further, and hope that Zorn in the future also will contribute much towards paving the way for the ideas of international justice in Germany, in spite of all intervening obstacles. The labour involved in the attainment of this high goal demands to-day more than ever before that one confess himself without reservation a convert to the basic thought by which the work of the Hague Conferences was governed: that right shall triumph over might.

POSTSCRIPT

Since the appearance of the above articles Zorn has on different occasions expressed his opinion in similar vein on this subject. I cite only his following articles: 'Friede auf Erden' (Peace on Earth) in the *Neue Freie Presse* of November 26, 1916; 'Völkerfriede' (The Peace of Nations) in the *Germania* of December 24, 1916, in the *Reichsbote* of December 20, 1916, and in the *Belgischer Courier* of December 21, 1916; 'Deutschland und die Abrüstungsfrage auf der ersten Haager Friedenskonferenz' (Germany and the Question of Disarmament at the First Peace Conference at The Hague) in the *Tag* of January 24, 1917.

The memoirs which Nossig has addressed to the German

plenipotentiary at The Hague, Baron Marschall von Bieberstein, now offer an interesting supplement to the previously known material. Of these Elsner speaks in the *Neues Wiener Tagblatt* of January 3, 1917. Among other things he says :

It was no easy task to make the 'peace' delegates at The Hague dance to the music of its pipes, for this pacifist conference for the salvation of mankind was, as seen in the light, nothing but a masked preliminary conference to consider the methods of future war. Marschall's activities at The Hague were therefore scarcely distinguished from the trade that he was called upon to exercise at Constantinople. Here as well as there he had to defend Germany against a coalition of opponents, who amidst a thousand feints made use of every opportunity to put Germany in a disadvantageous position. He was charged with the extraordinarily difficult mission of preserving a free hand for Germany, so that she might not become the sacrifice of a perfidious convention, which had as its aim the weakening of Germany. On the other hand, on account of Germany's genuine love of peace, he had to take all possible pains not to appear as the adversary of the peace endeavours. In spite of that he did not hesitate to pronounce a categorical no in the name of Germany, when by the introduction of an 'obligatory' world court of arbitration, without any compulsion, a comedy of pacifism was about to be performed.

What does Zorn say to this description ? And what does he say to what Lammasch writes in the *Neue Freie Presse* of November 30, 1916 :

Kriege tore to threads every concrete proposition, which was made with this end in view, with the biting dialectics of judicial subtlety, until he and also Marschall could finally represent it as wholly unacceptable ?

One more article by Zorn on 'The Future of the World', which appeared in the *Tag* of November 8, 1916, might be of interest. In it he takes issue with the Russian historian Walischewski, who characterizes the alternatives of the future of the world as : *Berlin* or *The Hague*. By Berlin he means the militarization of the world. By The Hague he signifies the ideal which the peace palace there erected typifies. The world will go either to Berlin or to The Hague. In contrast with the danger of militarism for mankind Walischewski presents the ideal of a pilgrimage to The Hague. He rightly sees in the restoration of downtrodden justice and ethical ideals the only salvation of the world, the only compensation at all commensurate with the gigantic sacrifices of the world war.

Zorn opposes this conception and writes in conclusion :

But the time has come for the Germans also openly to avow that the peaceful settlement of international disputes, especially that by arbitration in so far as this is possible, corresponds throughout to the principles of German policy. This avowal has been repeatedly and formally made by Germans. And if formerly in the working out of this principle, especially in the year 1907, mistakes have been made, we sincerely trust that they will not be repeated. The German empire, far removed from all thoughts of world dominion, and every intention of imposing its tutelage upon other states, is striving only to preserve its unity, its security, its political and economic independence. It has not the least reason for opposing stringent regulations compelling the peaceful settlement of international disputes, provided that these regulations rest upon the principles of equal rights for all states and fall within the province and within the limits of justice. We denounce therefore the contrast which the Russian scholar sets up with his question: Berlin or The Hague? on the contrary, we are fully ready to go with him the pilgrim's road to The Hague, if this road leads to an honourable, assured, international reign of peace within the realm of political possibilities and is built upon the firm foundation of equal rights for all nations.

It is certainly very gratifying that Zorn declares himself ready to go the road to *The Hague.* Only he ought to be quite clear about this point: As long as he finds the idea 'almost amusing' that one should regard the assurance of peace as more important than the regulation of war,[1] *he himself* is by no means on the road that leads to The Hague.

As to the *German Government,* it is certain the words of the German Chancellor of November 9, 1916, will scarcely suffice to convince the rest of the world that the German Government now suddenly finds itself also on the road leading to The Hague. After all that has preceded, *confidence* in the honest intentions of the German government is still to be *won,* and that not through *words* but through *deeds.* There are, it is true, isolated symptoms to be observed in the *German people* that justify us in the hope that German mentality will one day free itself from the chains of militarism. Such gratifying symptoms are, for example, the statements in the section on International Law, which I have already quoted. But it must not be overlooked that these are

[1] Burckhardt says in the *Politisches Jahrbuch der schweizerischen Eidgenossenschaft,* 1916, p. 117, that it will perhaps be easier to procure guarantees against the repetition of wars than to regulate the laws of warfare and to harmonize the rights of warring nations and neutrals. That I also believe, for this if for no other reason, because in the solution of the first-named task the opinions will not be as divergent as in that of the problems involved in martial law, for the securing of peace depends virtually upon *good will.* Justly, therefore, does Kurt Neumann in the *Grenzbote* of February 24, 1915, emphasize the fact that a fundamental error was committed when at the beginning of the century The Hague delegates turned their chief attention from their labours on the international law of the future to the law of war. This basic error was committed, as is well known, by the Germans, and Zorn to-day is still caught in it.

only single voices which represent an insignificant minority of the population. *Popular* sentiment in Germany unfortunately points to-day much more towards 'Berlin' than towards 'The Hague', and it is greatly to be feared that the German people will need to go to the school of bitter suffering before it awakens to freedom and frees itself from the ban of the military conception of the universe.

There is not the least doubt on this point: Two *conceptions of the world* stand opposed to each other, two conceptions of the world that are mutually exclusive. They cannot even exist side by side. The one, arrayed under the banner of militarism and imperialism, purposes *might*, the other purposes *right*. One of these two conceptions must yield, since a compromise between them, as the present world war has shown, would lead to nowhere. Either militarism or the law of nations must give way. I stand upon the platform that the first must go. Yes, I believe that in this war it has dug its own grave. This war has itself paved the way for the progress of international law. If the law of nations is to make genuine progress, there dare exist after this war only such a military system as will enter the *service of the ideals of justice*, and recognize that right goes *before* might. A military system on the other hand that would exalt itself *above* right (one has only to think of Zabern) must be abolished, let it cost what it may. The world therefore will no longer put up with half measures such as Zorn conceives. Without a *genuine* progress of the right this war will indeed have been fought in vain.[1]

[1] The military view of the world is very well described in the little pamphlet by Jefferson, *The Causes of War*, of which I prepared a German edition in 1915. Compare with this especially Munroe Smith's pamphlet, *Military Strategy versus Diplomacy in Bismarck's Time and Afterwards*, 1915, and the book of the same author on *Militarism and Statecraft*, 1918.